ANGEL™

Villains & Demons

TITAN

WWW.TITAN-COMICS.COM

Angel
Villains & Demons
ISBN: 9781782763697

Published by Titan
A division of Titan Publishing Group Ltd.,
144 Southwark Street,
London
SE1 0UP.

Collecting material previously published in the
Official Buffy the Vampire Slayer Magazine and
the Official Angel Magazine, 1997-2007.

A CIP catalogue record for this title is
available from the British Library.

First Edition May 2016
10 9 8 7 6 5 4 3 2 1

Printed in China.
Titan.

Editor Natalie Clubb
Senior Art Editor Rob Farmer
Additional Design Andrew Leung
Senior Executive Editor Divinia Fleary

Art Director Oz Browne
Studio Manager Emma Smith
Publishing Manager Darryl Tothill
Publishing Director Chris Teather
Operations Director Leigh Baulch
Executive Director Vivian Cheung
Publisher Nick Landau

Acknowledgments
Titan Would Like to Thank…
The cast and crew of *Angel* for giving up their
time to be interviewed, and Josh Izzo and Nicole
Spiegel at Fox for all their help in putting this
volume together.

ANGEL

HELLBOUND...

"Once upon a time, there was a vampire. And he was the meanest vampire in all the land. I mean, other vampires were afraid of him..." - Doyle

With his alter-ego of Angelus having the dubious accolade of being the most feared vampire to ever walk the planet, Angel could consider himself pretty well-placed to be an authority on all things monstrous – and during his time in LA, he certainly ran the gauntlet of terrifying adversaries. From narcissistic vampires to demon hunters, ancient body-snatching evils to rogue Slayers, and worse – a demonic firm of lawyers (yes, they really are the ultimate evil), Angel and his team's mettle was tested time and time again.

Packed with star interviews, exclusive behind-the-scenes set visits, rare make-up features and lots more, this collection celebrates some of the most memorable monsters and villains from the hit TV show. Revisit the dark and dangerous world of *Angel* with the best of the *Official Angel Magazine,* and prepare to be terrified once again.

ANGEL
™

Interviews

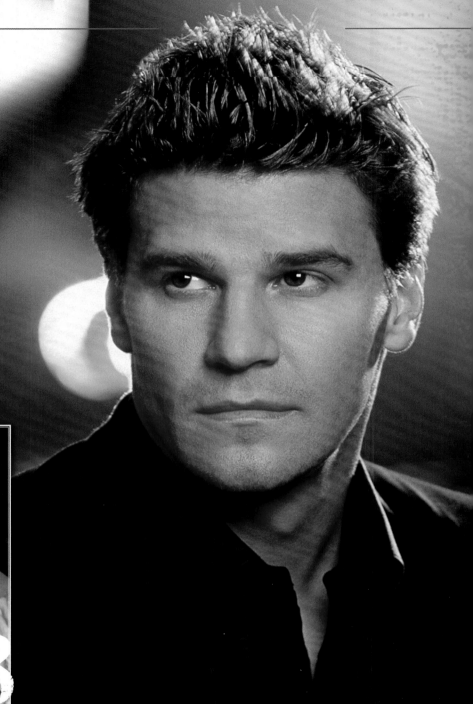

18

CONTENTS

Features

THE BIGGEST BADS

By K. Stoddard Hayes

EVIL CAN TAKE MANY FORMS — VIOLENCE, NASTINESS, INTRICATELY-PLOTTED MACHINATIONS THAT STEW OVER CENTURIES, AND — WORST OF ALL — SNIPPY COMMENTS. ANGEL HAS FACED MANY FOES, BUT JUST WHO IS THE BADDEST OF THOSE BIG BADS? WE EXAMINED THE EVIDENCE AND PRESENT OUR TOP 20!

20. GAVIN PARK

What Makes Him So Bad: A lawyer's lawyer, who thinks the best way to fight Angel is to bury him in legal paperwork, he starts with zoning and title issues, and works up to commandos and vivisecting babies, not to mention back-stabbing Lilah at every opportunity.

Nastiest Moment: Gavin sends 'exterminators' to the Hyperion Hotel. But these guys aren't killing bugs, they're installing them: a high-tech surveillance system that allows Wolfram & Hart to see Team Angel's every move.

Redeeming Quality: He wears nice suits.

Comeuppance: Along with all of Wolfram & Hart's Los Angeles employees, he's slaughtered by The Beast and turned into a zombie. Presumably he's still around somewhere, thanks to his W&H contract.

19. SAHJHAN

What Makes Him So Bad: He'll do anything to stop the prophecy that Angel's son will kill him. He falsifies prophetic texts, manipulates time and makes tools of Holtz, Lilah and Wesley. He even taints Angel's blood supply with Connor's blood, to make Wesley believe the prophecy that "the father will kill the son."

Nastiest Moment: As Angel, Holtz and Lilah face off over possession of Connor, SahJhan opens a portal to a Hell Dimension, threatening to swallow the world unless Connor dies.

Redeeming Quality: He fits so snugly in a special mystic urn.

Comeuppance: After all his efforts to get rid of Connor, another old enemy, Cyvus Vail, sets Connor on him deliberately. And when old Connor comes back, SahJhan finally loses his head, quite literally!

18. JUSTINE

What Makes Her So Bad: Justine's blind loyalty to Holtz leads her to help him betray Wesley, lie to Connor about his foster father's death, and help Connor sink Angel to the bottom of the sea.

Nastiest Moment: Justine convinces Wesley that Holtz has brutally beaten her. When he takes pity and tries to help, she cuts his throat, takes Connor and leaves him for dead.

Redeeming Quality: She helps Wesley find Angel's deep sea coffin. But only because Wes won't let her out of the closet unless she does.

Comeuppance: Months chained up in a closet, listening to Wesley and Lilah having sex.

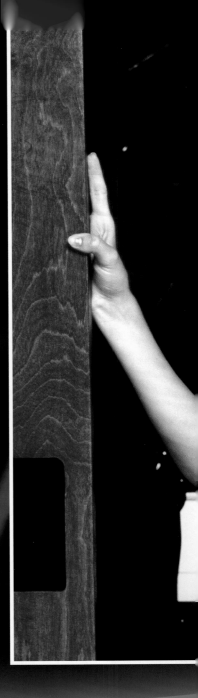

JUST CURIOUS?

Evil or just confused?

ILLYRIA
The Bad: Caused Fred's death. Killed everyone on Team Angel in "Time Bomb". Tried to conquer the world.
The Good: Developed actual feelings for Wesley and Gunn. Comforted the dying Wesley and killed the badass wizard who killed Wesley.

CONNOR
The Bad: Slept with Cordelia, helped her murder an innocent, sided with Jasmine against Team Angel, sank Angelus to the bottom of the ocean then pretended not to know where he was. And that's just the shortlist.

The Good: Killed Jasmine and SahJhan, accepted his good memories rather than his bad ones, saved Angel from Hamilton.

KATE LOCKLEY
The Bad: Blamed Angel for her father's death; locked him in a

17. EVE

What Makes Her So Bad: As the Senior Partners' liaison, she's annoyingly superior and secretive. Plus she's not only spying on Team Angel for the Senior Partners, she's also betraying the Senior Partners to her lover, Lindsey.
Nastiest Moment: Eve sets up Angel and Spike to fight each other by telling them the world can only hold one vampire champion with a soul.
Redeeming Quality: She's not a very Big Bad. Even Harmony can quite easily slap her into submission.
Comeuppance: With Lindsey dead, Eve has no protector. When the Senior Partners come looking for her, she's not just toast, she's crispy. (And that's if she got out of the W&H building alive.)

16. SKIP

What Makes Him So Bad: When he was guarding super-powered misogynist Billy Blim, and guiding Cordelia to higher planes of existence, he seemed like a decent fellow. Too bad he was only setting up Cordy to become the doomed vessel of Jasmine's incarnation.
Nastiest Moment: When Skip is luring Cordelia to the higher plane, he refuses to let her have her moment with Angel, to tell him she loves him.
Redeeming Quality: He loves *The Matrix*.
Comeuppance: A tiny hole in his exoskeleton, where a horn broke off, makes a soft spot for Wesley's dead-on aim with a handgun.

cell where he couldn't escape the sunlight.
The Good: Tried to be a good cop, despite being freaked by all the monsters Angel introduced her to.

FAITH

The Bad: Went on a vicious spree as soon as she set foot in Los Angeles. Was hired by Wolfram & Hart to kill Angel, but decided to beat Wesley senseless instead.
The Good: Turns out she was only causing havoc as a kind of self-hate mechanism. She eventually turned herself in to the authorities for her major misdeeds and ultimately broke out of prison so that she could help in the fight against Angelus.

HARMONY

The Bad: Tried to bite Cordelia and sell out Team Angel to Doug Sanders, motivational vampire. Sold out Angel to evil Marcus Hamilton.
The Good: Slapped Eve silly when some solid slapping was needed. Staked her treacherous office rival and saved the day. Plus, Angel gave her a job recommendation, so who are we to argue with that?

DARK WESLEY

The Bad: Went a bit mad for a small period, kidnapped baby Connor, assaulted Lorne and – worst of all – slept with Lilah!
The Good: It seems like it was just a phase, and good ol' Wes returned to normal eventually. Still, a far cry from the relatively harmless, bumbling buffoon that appeared in *Buffy*, however.

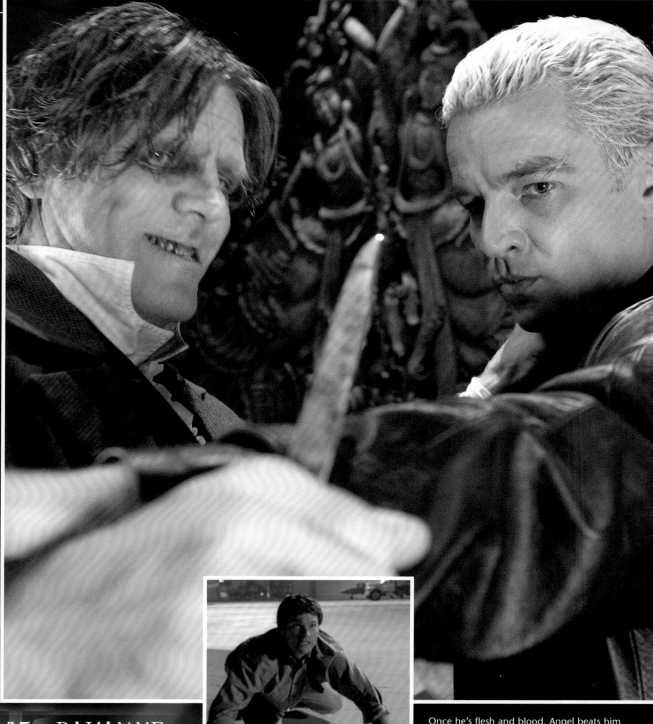

15. PAVAYNE

What Makes Him So Bad: To keep himself out of the Hell he so richly deserves, he's spent centuries capturing other souls and sending them to Hell in his place.

Nastiest Moment: After tormenting Spike with mutilated ghosts and horrific visions of torture, Pavayne shows him a gaping Hellmouth, and tells him that the soul that blesses him damns him to suffer forever.

Redeeming Quality: With all the nasty ghosts and visions he creates, he'd make a terrific horror film director.

Comeuppance: When he tries to hold Fred hostage, Spike throws him into a mystic device that makes him corporeal again. Once he's flesh and blood, Angel beats him up and shuts him in permanent stasis, where he'll stay conscious and helpless. Forever. Hopefully.

14. BILLY BLIM

What Makes Him So Bad: He spreads his violent hatred of women to every man he comes near, leaving a ruinous trail of beatings and terror and murder, that includes Gavin, Wesley and Gunn. He never

Nastiest Moment: Presiding over a psychic sweep of his underlings, Holland oversees the summary execution of Lee Mercer.
Redeeming Quality: His wine-tasting parties are a good way to get rid of evil lawyers.
Comeuppance: When Darla and Drusilla arrive at his wine-tasting party to commit a massacre, Holland begs Angel for help. And Angel locks the wine cellar doors on him, his guests and the hungry vamps.

11. DRUSILLA

What Makes Her So Bad: A crazed, psychotic sex kitten who gets off on torture and misery, she still has one foot in the 19th Century, and one in her own wacko world of pain.
Nastiest Moment: As Darla, finally at peace with herself, prepares to die, Drusilla shows up with another kind of death in mind, and sires her 'grandmom' back to vampire status.
Redeeming Quality: Her psychic abilities have their uses.
Comeuppance: She's still on the loose, last seen recovering from a good singeing at Angel's hands.

10. KNOX

What Makes Him So Bad: He's so cute, and so friendly, and such a nice guy – who knew that all the time he was scheming to sacrifice Fred to awaken a goddess of the ancient world?
Baddest moment: He explains that he chose Fred as Illyria's vessel, because he loved Fred so much.
Redeeming Quality: He seems to be a cute and friendly nice guy, and a science whiz as well.
Comeuppance: He wasn't around when Wesley shot and wounded a W&H employee who was annoying him while he was trying to save Fred – so Knox never thought about what Wes might do to the guy actually responsible for killing Fred. Ka-blam!

raises a hand himself; he just likes to watch.
Nastiest Moment: When Cordy and Angel arrive to capture him, Billy deliberately infects Angel, because he thinks it might amuse him to infect a vampire.
Redeeming Quality: He's rich.
Comeuppance: He brings his woman-bashing power to the attention of the woman most likely to bash back: Lilah Morgan. After being savagely beaten by Gavin Park under Billy's influence, she catches up with Billy and shoots him dead.

Angel for the next two years.
Nastiest Moment: When Angel knocks his mask off, his face is a writhing mass of maggots.
Redeeming Quality: He treats the minions of Wolfram & Hart with the contempt they truly deserve.
Comeuppance: Angel skewers him on a very sharp scythe. Ouch.

13. VOCAH

What Makes Him So Bad: His influence extends far beyond his one-episode appearance. He blows up Angel's apartment, and Wesley with it; drives Cordelia mad with horrible visions; and conjures Darla back from wherever dead vampires go, to be the bane of Team

12. HOLLAND MANNERS

What Makes Him So Bad: Holland is interested only in power; and his major assignment is bringing down Angel. He masterminds Darla's return and her seduction of Angel, and grooms Lindsey to be as brilliant and amoral as he is himself.

9. THE BEAST

What Makes Him So Bad: He wipes the floor with Team Angel, terrorizes Los Angeles with a Rain of Fire, and mystically blacks out the sun. Plus, he's got the hide of a dinosaur, and a voice like rocks grinding together. And he's only a minion.

Nastiest Moment: We were going to say his nastiest moment is blacking out the sun – until we remembered him snogging the Evil Cordelia. Ewww!

Redeeming Quality: He cleans out Wolfram & Hart's Los Angeles den of iniquity, all by himself.

Comeuppance: He makes the mistake of telling Angelus to take orders from him. Angelus pays him back by stabbing him with the only knife that can kill him.

8. DARLA

What Makes Her So Bad: Nearly four centuries of vampire mayhem, in the service of the Master. She sires Angelus and teaches him to be a monster; and when he regains his soul, she tries to turn him back into Angelus any way she can.

Nastiest Moment: As a human partner with Wolfram & Hart, she crawls into Angel's dreams.

Redeeming Quality: As a human, Darla is courageous and loving, and even comes back from the dead to try to save Connor's soul. Plus, she looks stunning in period gowns.

Comeuppance: She sleeps with Angel, only to discover that she hasn't got what it takes to give him that moment of perfect happiness. Instead, she gets pregnant with a human child, whose soul allows her to love again. Vamp Darla would have hated that!

LARGER THAN LIFE
One-time villains who stay in our memories.

Dr. Ronald Meltzer, "I Fall To Pieces" A psycho stalker who can send his hands or his eyes or any other body part, to any place he wants.

Ghost Maude, "Rm w/a Vu" Mom murdered her own son, then drove two innocent

women to suicide, before she met her match in Cordelia. The bitch is back!

Ryan Anderson, "I've Got You Under My Skin" A kid so evil he terrorized even the demon that tried to possess him. He'd incinerate his whole

family over a few marshmallow bits.

Dr. Fetvanovich, "Quickening" The bird-footed doctor is way too enthusiastic about his plans to dissect Darla and her unborn baby.

7. MARCUS HAMILTON

What Makes Him So Bad: He's a businessman. No compassion, just getting the deal done for the Senior Partners. To do his job, he'll terrorize Eve, try to buy Gunn's soul, seduce Harmony to betray Angel, and try to stake Angel himself.

Baddest Moment: Hamilton beats poor Illyria practically to a new incarnation. Who knew the guy in the dress-for-success suit had that much whomping ability?

Redeeming Quality: He's funny and good looking, and Harmony seems to like him. Plus, he can kick nearly everyone's butt.

Comeuppance: Never tell a vampire that the power of the Senior Partners flows in your blood! With one good chomp, Angel has the power, and Hamilton has a broken neck.

And she did shoot Billy Blim. Besides, Wesley loved her. Sort of. That's good enough for us.

Comeuppance: Hunted by Angelus through the corridors of the Hyperion, she hides with Cordelia – who stabs her in the neck. Worse, her contract with Wolfram & Hart extends after death.

6. LILAH MORGAN

What Makes Her So Bad: Amorality, thy name is Lilah. She'll do anything to advance in the company. Anything includes back-stabbing her colleagues, Lindsey and Gavin Park, working with SahJhan against company orders to finish Angel, and planning to vivisect baby Connor to find out why he's alive.

Nastiest Moment: Lilah hires a psychic demon to torture Cordelia with horrific visions that tear up Cordy's body – all to make Angel break a client from a Hell prison.

Redeeming Quality: She's witty, and vulnerable.

Marcus Roscoe, "Carpe Noctem"
An old man who steals the bodies of young men, and burns them out with high living – until he makes the mistake of swiping Angel's body.

Hamburger Guy Loa, "Loyalty" Who knew a cartoon statue of a hamburger could thunder and pronounce doom?

The Repo Man, "Double or Nothing" He's just doing his job, repossessing souls for his boss. Too bad one of them is Gunn's.

Magnus Hainsley, "Just Rewards"
A necromancer who can control the dead, is not a nice playmate for a couple of dead-guy vampire champions.

Spike, "In the Dark" Yes, you heard correctly: Spike! He may be a good guy now, but he was a nasty piece of work in Season One, as he hunted for the Gem of Amarra.

Dana, "Damage" As a child, she was horrifically abused; as a Slayer, she escaped from a mental hospital and cut off Spikes hands. We can pity her madness, but, as Spike says, she's a monster.

Roger Wyndam-Pryce, "Lineage" He was only a robot, but he sure had Wesley fooled, with his constant fault-finding, just like dear old dad. As for trying to enslave Angel and kill Fred – bad dad!

5. EVIL CORDELIA

What Makes Her So Bad: Possessed by Jasmine's will, she snogs The Beast and goes to bed with Connor, who's practically her son. Then she frees Angelus, and cuts Lilah's throat. And every time she says to Connor, "We're special" in that smarmy voice, we want to barf!

Nastiest Moment: Cutting the throat of a terrified and innocent young girl, so that her blood will bring Jasmine into the world.

Redeeming Quality: Even though Jasmine's driving, our Cordy is still in there somewhere.

Comeuppance: Evil Cordelia has to die for Jasmine to be born, leaving the real Cordy in a coma.

4. LINDSEY MCDONALD

What Makes Him So Bad: Lindsey had all kinds of scruples, but he turned his back on them at Wolfram & Hart to go for evil power. Later, he uses Spike to take on Angel and the Senior Partners together. Plus, he sleeps with Eve!

Nastiest Moment: Bringing Drusilla to sire Darla as a vampire, instead of letting her die in peace. The consequences – Angel's fall to the dark side, Connor, Jasmine – are apocalyptic.

Redeeming Qualities: He's good-looking and a terrific singer, and he seems to have

genuinely loved Darla.

Comeuppance: Lindsey thinks he deserves to die at Angel's hands. Instead, he is shot by Lorne; a "flunky".

3. JASMINE

What Makes Her So Bad: She used Angel, Darla, Connor and especially Cordelia to bring herself into the world; she snacks on a few dozen worshippers every day; and all she offers in return is mindless peace and joy – plus Angel and Connor singing Barry Manilow duets.

Nastiest Moment: The Body Jasmine, taking over the minds of her worshippers, sends them to hunt Team Angel, and as her people close in, she *laughs*.

Redeeming Quality: She's radiantly beautiful – except when she's in maggot face mode.

Comeuppance: Rejecting Angel's plea to help him make the world a better place, she promises to kill every soul on the planet. And she turns to her faithful Connor, asking if he still loves her. "Yes," he says, and smashes her skull with a single blow.

2. DANIEL HOLTZ

What Makes Him So Bad: Relentless in his hatred for vampires and demons, Holtz crosses two centuries, kidnaps Angel's son, and raises him to hate his father, all to take revenge on Angel for his family's murder.

Nastiest Moment: Holtz convinces Angel that he's forgiven him, then makes Connor think Angel murdered him, by committing suicide with an ice pick.

Redeeming Quality: He single-handedly wipes out Wolfram & Hart's best commando team.

Comeuppance: Killing himself to frame Angel ensures that he won't even be around to enjoy his revenge.

EVIL STRENGTH IN NUMBERS

Nasties that hang around in groups

The Scourge, "Hero" Ethnic cleansing acquires a new meaning with this army of pureblood demons, whose one goal is to exterminate all mixed blood demons.

The Zombie Cops, "The Thin Dead Line" Everyone's nightmare of law enforcement gone too far, these cops even beat up good guys, and put a bullet in Wesley.

The Puppets, "Smile Time" They carve their maker into a flesh and blood puppet, put dozens of kids in a coma, and turn Angel into a walking, talking felt puppet. Which is almost enough to make us forgive them for the rest.

The Priests of Pylea, Season Two They may pretend to revere their "princess", but it's really they who hold the power, which includes making Lorne lose his head.

The Circle of the Black Thorn, Season Five The Senior Partners' evil club has all the biggest baddies among its members, and forces Angel to sign away his claims on the Shanshu prophecy.

The Senior Partners The Wolf, the Ram and the Hart are the true powers of darkness in every dimension they can reach. Their Los Angeles of ice is only one modest tentacle in their empire of evil power.

1. ANGELUS

What Makes Him So Bad: He's got all of Angel's champion abilities, and a lust for pain that more than matches Angel's compassion. The way he treated Buffy, Drusilla, and Holtz shows why he's the most vicious vampire in history.

Nastiest Moment: Killing Jenny Calendar wasn't evil enough; he had to leave her body for Giles in an unspeakably cruel way.

Redeeming Qualities: He takes orders from no one, including the Master and The Beast.

Comeuppance: Willow's magic keeps re-ensouling him, and through the mystical drug Orpheus, he finds himself reliving Angel's good deeds: "I'm in Hell!"

ANGEL™
MAGAZINE

WE ARE GATHERED HERE TODAY TO MOURN THE LOSS OF DARLA, ANGEL'S TROUBLESOME EX-GIRLFRIEND, FROM OUR SCREENS. AND WHAT A WAY TO GO! JULIE BENZ TALKS US THROUGH HER HIGHLY MEMORABLE TIME ON *BUFFY* AND *ANGEL*.

"If you had told me back in 1996 that Darla would have carried on into something like how she's developed, I would have said you were nuts," Julie Benz maintains firmly. Chatting on the phone from her home in Los Angeles, the actress still evidently enjoys talking about playing the very first vampire that we ever saw on *Buffy the Vampire Slayer*. Although her appearances on both *Buffy* and *Angel* have allowed her to take on other roles, it is as Angel's one true love (at least in Darla's eyes) that audiences have come to know Julie.

"I never thought Darla would even have a name," Julie admits, casting her mind back to the original pilot for *Buffy*, a 20-minute piece that featured a number of different cast-members that was then reshot and incorporated into the series premiere, "Welcome to the Hellmouth". "[Darla] started out just as 'Vampire Girl' in the pilot, and [she] was supposed to die. Then the producers decided not to kill

BY PAUL SIMPSON
ADDITIONAL MATERIAL BY ABBIE BERNSTEIN

me, and they gave me a name, and eventually the whole story. Even getting beyond the pilot was a surprise! I never imagined it would be like this. Something like that doesn't happen to someone like me!"

There have been many highlights both for the character of Darla and for the actress herself, but of them all, Julie singles out Darla's pregnancy and eventual delivery of Connor as her favorite. "The pregnancy was probably the most exciting development," she says. "Finding out about that was the most 'wow!'

moment I had with her. We'd always joked around that maybe she would get pregnant, but it was always a joke. We never took it seriously. Then when they sent me the script and I saw that she was pregnant, I just went, 'Wow!' That had to be the most surprising moment of all."

Darla's death was equally memorable. "The last moments of playing Darla, especially the scene where I staked myself. The emotion and the intensity – to redeem Darla in the last minutes [of her existence] was amazing. I felt like I'd been given a gift."

Julie also has one funny/scary memory of working on *Angel* – when a fire stunt almost went horribly wrong during filming of "Lullaby". "We almost died!", she reveals. "We were doing fake *Entertainment Tonight* reports – 'The cast of *Angel* died in a fire, but the show will be back next week with

a new cast!' We recast ourselves – Jenny Garth would be me, Todd Bridges would be J. [August Richards], Yasmine Bleeth would be Charisma [Carpenter]."

Unusually, Julie was aware of Darla's third season character developments from quite an early stage of filming. Talking about previous years, Julie points out that she generally never really knew what was going to happen from one moment to the next. For example, series creator Joss Whedon only told her part-way through the second season that they were thinking of making Darla human – even though she had already shot some of her 'return' scenes. On this occasion, however, there were practical reasons for arcing the pregnancy storyline out carefully. "For the five episodes that I did, we did know how it was going to end," she explains. "A lot of it had to do with my schedule. I was working on another project, *Taken* [which was filming in Vancouver], so we had to know in advance what that season was going to hold for Darla." She laughs as she recollects some of the earlier situations. "I would say that Season Two of *Angel* was kind of an exploration on everybody's part! But in Season Three, we did know, and I knew in advance that it was going to be her end."

Julie was delighted with the scripts she was given. "I didn't expect them to write such a beautiful ending," she says. "I really think it was one of the most beautiful gifts I've ever received as an actor. The last three episodes of her life are so wonderful. They were such a gift to play. It was really amazing."

Julie remembers sitting in her trailer on the set of *Taken* reading the script for her final episode. "They sent me the script and I was on lunch," she recalls. "I was in my trailer crying. Everybody was asking me if I was okay, and what was wrong, and I had to say it was nothing, and that I was fine. You don't want to tell anyone anything – and, of course, we're not allowed to tell anybody anything."

Although there had been occasions in the past when Julie thought that her time on *Angel* had come to an end, she really believed that

"[DARLA] STARTED OUT JUST AS 'VAMPIRE GIRL' IN THE PILOT, AND [SHE] WAS SUPPOSED TO DIE. THEN THE PRODUCERS DECIDED NOT TO KILL [HER], AND THEY GAVE [HER] A NAME, AND EVENTUALLY THE WHOLE STORY. EVEN GETTING BEYOND THE PILOT WAS A SURPRISE!"

"Lullaby" gave closure to the relationship between Darla and Angel – although, of course, there was always the possibility of returning for a flashback. "I think we all felt in a way that the Darla and Angel storyline had run its course," she expands. "The show was looking to go in a different direction and grow, so I never really expected to return. It just didn't seem as if she would fit into the story any more. So much had been played out between her and Angel that it didn't seem like there was any way. But as you know, I did return."

Julie has returned twice now – first, for Season Four's "Inside Out" and then for Season Five's "The Girl in Question". Regarding the former, Julie only knew that there was a possibility of a return a couple of weeks before "Inside Out" was filmed. "They phoned to see if I was available, but they didn't say in what manner," she says. "Of course, I said yes! Then it wasn't until a couple of days before we shot it that they sent the script. I was actually expecting it to be for a flashback, and I had no idea what it was going to be. I was very excited to find out that it was actually Darla's spirit, and I got to work with Vincent Kartheiser, who is a really wonderful actor."

The actress thought that the interplay between Connor and his mother, as she tried to persuade him not to go along with 'Cordelia's' plan, was "great – and it was a challenge. I have to say that they always throw major challenges at me on *Angel*, and in that episode especially. The dialogue alone was... well, it was pretty much a four-page monologue. That was another 'wow!' moment. But it was so wonderful to be able to sink my teeth – literally – into something that was so good. I loved the dynamic between the two of them. Darla really is the mother who

gave up everything for her son and he doesn't appreciate it."

Julie agrees that the "Inside Out" scenes were extremely powerful, with a very theatrical feel. "Joss has always been a big supporter of people actually reading the classics and reading Shakespeare," she says. "He has people over to his house to sit around and read Shakespeare! There definitely is a theatrical influence in the words and the dialogue. Joss has such an appreciation of language and its power. There are differences in the way those characters talk and the way they use language. You can definitely see his appreciation of great literature through the scripts and writing. All the writers involved are reading Shakespeare, so you see that influence in the work. It's just so wonderful as an actor to be able to perform that for television."

Conflict between mother and son has always been a fertile ground for drama. "It's what people have written about for generations – even before television came about!" Julie says. "It really is the stuff of classic literature."

By this stage in Darla's existence, she has achieved redemption at last; to

On *Taken*, Julie Benz had the opportunity to work with two very different directors – veteran film director Tobe Hooper, and up and coming new director, Breck Eisner. "Tobe has created some of the most memorable science fiction horror films out there," Julie notes. "His films have helped to create a genre. Look at *The Texas Chain Saw Massacre* or *Poltergeist*. It was wonderful to be able to work with somebody like him. He's a creative genius, and you don't know where that genius arises from. He's a very unique individual, and extraordinary in his uniqueness. I always say he speaks a different language to a great deal. If you watch the first episode of *Taken*, it definitely has his imprint – you can see his ability to create a creepiness in a film: the moment that leads up to that scary situation. He is brilliant – it's a masterpiece in the creation of the atmosphere. He was perfect for drawing you in and introducing you to the aliens.

"Breck is this young kid who works a little differently but is brilliant in his own way. My character, Kate, is in such a different place in the second episode, and I really felt that we were able to create the feel and the strains, and the things that just weren't said between husband and wife in that time period. That second episode had an Americana feel, and Breck was brilliant in creating that. Both of our favorite moments occurs when my second husband comes in and says he's calling off the search for my son. I'm making the bed, and I'm having a breakdown. We only filmed that as a master [without any close-ups]: Breck and I were connecting on some cerebral wavelength, and just looked at each other and said, 'That's it.' There was so much going on in that scene that was being told just by our physicality. There was nothing more to reveal."

emphasize this, there were certain adjustments to the way Julie played the role. "They were very simple things," she explains. "The wardrobe was very soft, and she was wearing a dress that I don't think looks very much like a dress Darla would wear. But we decided on that dress because it gave a virginal quality to her. Everything was very soft and warm, from the lighting to the colors that were chosen for her dress – a flesh tone. It was there in everything – the way she was lit, the candlelight in the room. It was all very warm, and it emphasized that she was a good soul that had received redemption. As an actor, I tried to really find the pure love that exists in a relationship between mother and son. It's an unconditional love, and it's probably the most simple relationship Darla has ever had. With Angel, the relationship was dark and twisted and forbidden – there was a mother/son/lover twist to it, but there were so many things rolled into it. With her son, it's just a really simple line."

However, Darla fails in her attempt to stop Connor. "I think they just like seeing me covered in blood!" Julie laughs. "I'm always covered in blood on that show!"

The simplicity that Julie enjoyed about Darla's final appearance is also a feature of her character, Kate, on the recent Steven Spielberg epic mini-series, *Taken*. "I was very excited to finally be playing a woman. That's all she is," Julie says, rather surprisingly, and hastens to add, "For so long I've made a career out of playing either vampires or undercover F.B.I. agents or somebody who's got a hidden agenda. They always had something else going on that wasn't really what you saw on the surface. For me, it was

wonderful to be able to explore a woman. I was supposed to be an ordinary woman from the 1940s and 1950s in Middle America. It was very refreshing."

However, Darla had cast a vampiric shadow over *Taken*. "I got cast because of *Angel*," Julie explains. "Stephen Spielberg had seen me in an episode of *Angel*, and then they had offered me the part. I was really trying to find the link between Darla and Kate, and there really is none. It was really wonderful to have my work appreciated in that manner, and to be given such a great part to play. *Taken* is really so much more than about the aliens, and it's so much more than just science fiction. It's about humanity, and the extraordinary circumstances that happen to an ordinary man."

Following *Taken*, Julie Benz headed to the far side of the world to shoot her role

as Ursula in the just-released *George of the Jungle 2*. "We shot that in Australia, with *Buffy/Angel* director David Grossman in charge. I really did want to stretch some different acting muscles," she says. "She was really different from what I had been doing for many years. It was really great to play a character who's so innocent – it was very hard for me! But to find that innocence and that naivety, and to exercise those slapstick muscles was really a challenge. It was a lot of fun, and I really appreciated the opportunity to be able to do it. Although David Grossman knew me from *Buffy* and *Angel*, the producers didn't, so they didn't see me as the evil Darla. David was a big supporter of my work, and told them I was a hard worker

and a good actress, but a lot of it came down to me just going into the room with the producers and being really funny, handling the material well. It's great to be able to do a family movie that my whole family can watch, understand and be proud of. They don't always understand some of the darker stuff – they're asking who I'm killing this time!"

With *Angel* – and therefore – Darla's days over, at least for the time being, Julie reflects on her alter ego. "I've been in love with Darla since day one. She's lived through everything – life, death, life and more death! I think she truly is one of the most amazing characters on television." ❧

LINDSEY PROVED A THORN IN
TEAM ANGEL'S SIDE FOR QUITE
SOME TIME. HERE, ACTOR
CHRISTIAN KANE TALKS
ABOUT THE STARTLING
EVOLUTION OF HIS CHARACTER,
AND HIS GREAT JOY IN
BEING PART OF A SHOW
THAT CHALLENGED HIM
SO MUCH AS AN ACTOR
OVER THE YEARS.

BY TARA
DiLULLO

ONWAR

CHRI

From the moment Lindsey McDonald stepped into frame challenging Angel during the series pilot, "City Of," Christian Kane captured the hearts of fans with his portrayal of the ambitious but morally conflicted Wolfram & Hart lawyer audiences loved to hate. Over two seasons, Lindsey became an increasingly more powerful antagonist for Angel, clashing with the souled vampire over everything from nefarious business deals to winning the heart of Darla. By the end of the second season, a disillusioned Lindsey left the evil law-firm for parts unknown. It took two long seasons, but Lindsey finally returned to the series in the fifth season episode, "Destiny." Sporting a sexy new look, replete with long hair and runic tattoos, Lindsey craftily snuck his way back into town, setting in motion his mysterious plans that utilized an unwitting Angel and Spike as pawns for his ultimate goal. Together with his liaison-to-the-Senior-Partners girlfriend, Eve, Lindsey played a clever game of cat and mouse with the good guys, until his ultimate plan to take over the law-firm was revealed in the final episodes of the series.

Considering the shocking cancellation of the series this spring, Christian reveals he was doubly grateful to be able to return to the show so that closure could be given to his character. Not long after the series finale, Christian took some time out to talk to *Angel Magazine*...

ANGEL MAGAZINE: WHEN LINDSEY EXITED THE SHOW AT THE END OF SEASON TWO, DID SERIES CREATOR JOSS WHEDON LET YOU KNOW THEY MIGHT WANT YOU BACK SOMEDAY?
CHRISTIAN KANE: No, it was a done deal. I was leaving the show. I had no idea.

HOW WAS IT THAT LINDSEY CAME BACK INTO THE MIX AFTER THREE SEASONS?
Like I've said before, [David] Boreanaz and me are really close. We were close before I was even on the show, so we had talked about it all the time. We'd have a couple of beers and talk about me coming back. I think David put a little plug in there. Joss told me the [writers] were sitting around ask-ing, "Who are we going to make in charge of all this? Who is in control of Eve and responsible for bringing [Spike] back?" It wasn't even me at first, but Joss went, "How about Lindsey?" and supposedly the table kind of erupted, "Oh, that's perfect!"

YOU'VE BEEN BUSY DOING FILMS IN THE MEANTIME, SO HOW DID THEY GET YOU TO COME BACK?
I was in New York filming *Taxi* at the time and Joss called me and said, "Do you have any interest in coming back, because I'd love to have you back." I said, "Absolutely!" You just say yes when it's Joss Whedon, because he's so frickin' creative and you always want to work with him when he gives you a call. I told him though, and I made it really specifically

CHRISTIAN KANE
STATS AND FACTS

Christian Kane
Born: Dallas, TX
First gig: *Fame L.A* (1997)
Favorite role: Young Hub, *Secondhand Lions*
Next film: *Taxi* with Queen Latifah and Jimmy Fallon

Christian on his band, KANE:
"It's a nice release because while everyone else is out looking for other jobs, I get to sit and write music. I have another outlet so I'm not stressed out over tough times in Hollywood.

"We don't know a lot of the venues out there, so if the fans want to get together and tell us where to play, that would be great! Fans can go straight to my management, Brand-X at: www.kanemusic.com."

Christian on future plans:
"David [Boreanaz] and I are working on our own script now, so we can work together again. I think people would really enjoy seeing David and I on the same side of the ball."

clear, that I did not want to wear that damn suit and I wanted nothing to do with the [false] hand anymore. [*Laughs*]

WERE YOU UNHAPPY PLAYING LINDSEY WHEN YOU LEFT THE SHOW?
No, but the major point that I wanted to stress to [Joss] was that I was tired of getting beat up by every girl on the show. It started getting boring. Joss said, "No, it's a different Lindsey! He's going to kick a lot of ass." So I said, "Okay." I remember sitting once with [former *Angel* executive producer] Tim Minear, who is one of my favorite writers, and I asked him what he was doing and he said, "I'm writing the next episode. It's so awesome!" I just looked at him and said, "Just kill me, man." The hand was just too much. [*Laughs*] A show full of superheroes and here I was with no powers whatsoever. I was just a punching bag for these cats so that everybody on the show could look great. When Joss said I could come back and kick some ass, I was like, "I'm in!" Well, I was in before anyway, but I was happier.

DID THEY FILL YOU IN ON THEIR PLAN ABOUT EXACTLY

WHAT LINDSEY WOULD BE UP TO?
They gave me a little hint. When I was in New York, Joss told me a little bit about it and I trusted him. The first full episode I came back ["Soul Purpose"], there is a scene with Spike and me and of course, Spike's slamming me up against a strip club wall. I was like, "God dangit! It's starting again!" But Joss reassured me that there was a plan. It scared me a little bit, but I'm really happy with what they did. They gave me a lot of redemption and that was very cool.

YOUR EXIT FROM THE SERIES WAS VERY AMBIGUOUS AND YOUR RETURN IN "DESTINY" WAS VERY MUCH SHROUDED IN SECRECY. DID THEY GIVE YOU ANY CLUES ON HOW TO PLAY THIS NEW LINDSEY?
No, I couldn't even get anything from the directors. Matter of fact, that episode with Spike and I, David directed and I was like, "D, what is my motivation here? What am I doing?" He said, "I have no idea!" [*Laughs*] When I initially came back,

I walked into a very private set with just a skeleton crew to keep it away from all the leaks on Joss' crew.

WAS IT FUN TO TRICK EVERYONE SHOOTING THAT SECRET SCENE?
It was fun. I showed up at six in the morning and no one was there yet from the first unit crew. It was second unit with Skip Schoolnik directing. It was very much a compliment. I felt very privileged to be able to come back to a show like this and then be so secretive.

IT OBVIOUSLY WORKED BECAUSE FANS WENT CRAZY WHEN YOU WERE REVEALED.
I heard three or four message boards crashed! It was really nice.

LINDSEY'S RELATIONSHIP WITH EVE THIS SEASON SHOWED A SOFTER SIDE OF LINDSEY WE HADN'T SEEN SINCE DARLA. HOW WAS IT WORKING WITH SARAH THOMPSON?
It was very nice to walk into that first scene because I've known Sarah for a couple years. It wasn't awkward to get in bed with her and start kissing, which often, even as co-stars, it is. I had known her before, so that made it easier and I think we started playing off that immediately as a couple.

WHAT DID THEIR RELATIONSHIP SIGNIFY TO YOU?
I think it signifies the only little bit of

heart he had left. I think he loved her and used her as an outlet to still have a heart. Otherwise, he is just evil. It helped me out a lot because it let me show that I didn't come back totally evil – the old Lindsey is there. It was smart on Joss' part because you can still see a little bit of his heart but you still don't know what side of the fence he is going to fall off on.

WAS IT ODD TO COME BACK THREE SEASONS LATER, HAVING GONE ON TO DO DIFFERENT PROJECTS ONLY TO RETURN TO THIS FAMILIAR CHARACTER AND SET?
I've known James [Marsters, Spike] for a while and he is one of the nicest people I've ever met. I knew Alexis [Denisof, Wesley] and Andy [Hallett, Lorne]. J. August Richards [Gunn] is one of my dear friends. The only person I really didn't know was Amy Acker [Fred]. They were so warm when I came back. It's a different kind of crew there and it's also a *really* different kind of cast. We are pretty much a family and we all stick together. It's really rare. It's the fifth season of a show, and when we get done with a scene everybody still looks

at the person that was covered and says, "Great job!" That is really rare because it gets to be a machine after a while.

LINDSEY FACTORED HEAVILY IN THE 100TH EPISODE, WHICH REALLY FOCUSSED ON THE HISTORY OF THE SHOW – INCLUDING CHARISMA CARPENTER'S RETURN AND A REFERENCE TO GLENN QUINN. WAS IT IMPORTANT FOR YOU TO BE PART OF THAT EPISODE?
That episode was very important to me. You kind of figured out where things were at that point before it switched again for the final episodes. It was a blessing to come back and see all the press and all the fans still behind us after

{ "JOSS WHEDON CALLED ME AND SAID 'I'D LOVE TO HAVE YOU BACK.' I SAID, 'ABSOLUTELY!' YOU JUST SAY YES WHEN IT'S JOSS WHEDON. YOU ALWAYS WANT TO WORK WITH HIM WHEN HE GIVES YOU A CALL." }

SELECTED CREDITS

FILM

TELEVISION

a long time. It was very dear to me, and something that nobody can ever take away from us.

WAS THERE ANYTHING IN PARTICULAR YOU WERE LOOKING FORWARD TO EXPLORING WITH LINDSEY THIS TIME AROUND?

In "You're Welcome," I walked in and they said there would be a fight scene. At the time, they didn't know if it would be me and James or me and David. I had talked to Joss and told him that I had just gotten done with *Secondhand Lions* and that I'd gone through two and half months of sword-training with Anthony De Longis, who is one of the best sword teachers out there. Joss actually took that to heart and put it in the episode with David and I doing swordplay. This was very much an honor for me. Joss already has a path he is on, so for him to take time and let me play with a new skill that I had learned was a big compliment. I really felt like it was Joss saying he wanted me back and that was so great.

WHAT WERE THE HIGHLIGHTS AND THE LOWLIGHTS OF SEASON FIVE FOR YOU?

The scene where I was getting interrogated in "Power Play" and I say, "You gonna beat it out of me?" and Spike and I stand up to each other wasn't really scripted at all. I talked to

James and said, "Look man, you've never gotten any redemption for me playing you like a violin. I can't believe this thing is going to end without you and me going at it!" It was supposed to just be me sitting there and J. goes "No" and he steps back, but I know a lot of people on the websites were waiting for us to fight. I really wanted to do it and I know James did too because he really wanted some redemption. So I was like, "Let's just stand up and give them a little hint of what it might be like." James Contner was totally into it and he let us do it. I think it added a lot to the scene and it was cool because it was our idea.

I can tell you I didn't like the episode where I was in hell ["Underneath"]. I didn't feel comfortable with it at all. He was a nice guy and it was very awkward for me to play a good guy. [Director] Skip Schoolnik called me after he edited the episode and said what a great job I did and that was really important. It's very rare that a director calls you, but I was scared I didn't do a good job being this passive-aggressive guy. I saw the episode and I was really happy with it, so I'm glad I got to do it now. It was very scary at first because I had to be this really nice guy, but I'm still Lindsey, you know? If it had been a script for another movie, I could have gotten into that character, but to still be Lindsey and do that was very weird.

LINDSEY SHOCKINGLY MEETS
HIS END AT THE HANDS OF
LORNE, BY WAY OF ANGEL'S
ORDER. WERE YOU HAPPY
WITH LINDSEY'S FATE?

Yes and no. Joss was very nice in the fact that he killed me. I got to go in and kick some ass and then he takes me out. I'm not happy because the show has ended, so I don't think anybody is going to be happy with the way their character ends.

HOW IMPORTANT HAS THE FAN
SUPPORT BEEN TO YOU BOTH
PERSONALLY AND PROFES-
SIONALLY DURING YOUR RUN
ON ANGEL?

I've got a lot of fans from *Angel* and some of them have converted over to my films. Honestly, I don't exist without them. I really don't, so it's very important for me to keep in touch with them. I like doing it and it reminds me that I am doing something very cool that not a lot of people are fortunate enough to do. Any time you spend five years beating the crap out of a lead character that everybody loves and you still have people come up to you that are just as big fans as David's, then it lets me know that I am doing something right. [*Laughs*]

CHRISTIAN KANE, THANK YOU VERY MUCH! 🦇

we got the news to make sure he was all right. He was in good spirits and I know he was upset about the show getting canceled, but he wasn't down in the mouth. He was okay about it.

AROUND THE SAME TIME, YOU
GOT A PART IN A FILM IN
JAPAN THAT YOU HAD TO
LEAVE FOR. HOW DID THAT
FACTOR INTO WHAT HAPPENED
TO LINDSEY FOR THE REST OF
THE SEASON?

Nobody told me, because I never get the word until the last minute, but I was actually scheduled to finish out the season. I had to take off, so Joss wrote my last scenes and then I filmed them. What really made it tough on me was that I just had to read my lines and hope that I got them right because I actually filmed my parts of the last episode months before they filmed the finale. David and I just had to go with it. We knew it was our last scene together and it's a long, intricate, wordy scene in the boardroom, but it was fun.

WERE YOU ON THE SET WHEN
THE CANCELLATION NEWS
WAS ANNOUNCED?

It was me, David, James and J. August. We were actually in the dungeon scene. It was very dark and there was a lot of torture stuff around and my [prosthetic] hearts were all over the floor, no pun intended. They walked in and told us. I don't think it would have been easier in a lighted room with cake and flowers, but we were in a dungeon so it was a very morbid afternoon. It was like taking the rap for something you didn't do. The show was doing really well, getting really great numbers and everyone was tuned in and it just doesn't make sense. All the storylines were getting ready to take a turn and hopefully, they would have kept me on for another season. I went over to David's trailer right after

{ "ANY TIME YOU SPEND FIVE YEARS BEATING THE CRAP OUT OF A LEAD CHARACTER AND YOU STILL HAVE PEOPLE COME UP TO YOU THAT ARE JUST AS BIG FANS AS DAVID'S, THEN IT LETS ME KNOW I'M DOING SOMETHING RIGHT!" }

CATCHING UP WITH...
Stephanie Romanov

THERE HAVE BEEN DEMONS, VAMPIRES AND MONSTERS APLENTY ON *ANGEL*, BUT ONLY ONE HUMAN VILLAIN CUT THEM ALL DOWN TO SIZE WITH ONE GORGEOUS, STEELY-EYED GLARE — LILAH MORGAN. PLAYED BY STEPHANIE ROMANOV, LILAH WAS THE NASTIEST LEGAL SHARK AT WOLFRAM & HART AND WHILE SHE NEVER DID BEST ANGEL IN THEIR ONGOING BATTLE OF GOOD VERSUS EVIL, SHE SURE DID HAVE FUN MESSING UP HIS PLANS. *ANGEL MAGAZINE* TOUCHED BASE WITH STEPHANIE TO TALK ABOUT THE LAWYER THAT EVERYBODY LOVED TO HATE.

ANGEL MAGAZINE: DID YOU KNOW WHAT *ANGEL* WAS ALL ABOUT WHEN YOU AUDITIONED?
STEPHANIE ROMANOV: I had only just seen the show the day before I got the call. It was the favorite show of the guy I was dating at the time, and he said I had to watch it. So I did and the next day I got the call [*mocks the Twilight Zone theme*]. I was destined for Lilah! [*Laughs*]

WAS THE LILAH IN THE AUDITION THE SAME AS THE LILAH YOU PLAYED IN THE SERIES?
I think in the audition, I played it like they wanted it. I caught the director off-guard and made a joke he wasn't expecting. He was stunned. It was such a Lilah thing to do and I think that is what got me the job. Afterwards, I decided I wanted to play her like a film noir, femme fatale. I based her on actresses like Ava Gardner and Veronica Lake and Lauren Bacall.

DID YOU HAVE ANY SAY IN CREATING LILAH'S STYLIZED LOOK AND CALCULATING PERSONALITY?
I brought that all in and then they liked the way I did it and they started writing her more like that. I never talked to them about it. I just did it. I find if you try to talk too much, it gets diluted and they go back and forth so I just show up and do it. They wanted me to play her more afraid and I was like, "No! She's cool." So, I'd say, "Okay", and just do it my way!

LILAH WENT THROUGH SOME INTERESTING CHANGES, ESPECIALLY IN SEASON FOUR. DID THEY EVER SHARE THEIR PLANS FOR HER WITH YOU?
That year, there was some discussion but it looked like I wasn't going to come back. Then I got a call from Alexis [Denisof, Wesley] saying, "Do you want to work with me? We have a whole storyline." I had no idea!

THEY REALLY PUSHED THE ENVELOPE SHOWING THE AFFAIR BETWEEN WES AND LILAH!
I know! Shocking! [*Laughs*] And we hadn't really met as characters on the show. We had never been in a scene together before. It was so weird.

WHAT'S YOUR FAVORITE LILAH MOMENT?
I don't know if there is a favorite moment. I enjoyed when they broadened her and I got to play more aspects of her. It felt like the first few seasons, I was just playing the same scenes over and over again in a different setting with a different outfit. Then, when I got an actual storyline and they were doing something cool with her, it was much more interesting too.

WHAT ARE THE FANS' FAVORITE LILAH MOMENTS?
Oh, when Lilah shot Billy, because she was finally the hero. It was so fun, because she finally did something right! Fans and I loved when Lilah was mocking Fred. When I read it in the script, I was like, "Oh! Amy [Acker], it's nothing personal!"

JUST WHEN LILAH WAS GETTING A TEENY BIT OF A HEART, SHE WAS UNCEREMONIOUSLY KILLED. WHAT HAPPENED?
That really bothered me! I was hoping for a moment to milk it a little bit more. I was just dead and Angel is feeding on me and throwing me on the floor. It was a little insulting! [Laughs]

OF COURSE, THEY BROUGHT YOU BACK IN "HOME" – WERE YOU SHOCKED TO GET THAT CALL?
I got the call from my agent that they wanted to use me for another episode and I said, "They chopped off my head! What am I going to be – a headless Lilah?" Instead they drew a line [on my neck], so I was like, "Groovy! I heal well!" [Laughs] It was one of the most fun episodes.

WHAT WAS YOUR FIRST ACTING ROLE?
Mrs Hurry-Up in my first grade play. She was the lead and I thought everybody in class would want it and I was the only one who raised my hand. I got it by default. [Laughs]

WAS ACTING ALWAYS YOUR AMBITION?
My mother was a big movie buff, so I always loved movies. I started dancing at three and I always thought I would be a ballerina. I remember in second grade my teacher asked what I wanted to be and I said a ballerina and she said I needed a fallback career so I said an actress. So this is my fallback career. [Laughs]

WHAT ARE YOUR FAVORITE MOVIES?
The Sound of Music, *West Side Story*, *Oklahoma*.

WHAT'S YOUR NEXT PROJECT?
A film called *The Final Cut*, with Robin Williams. My character, Jennifer Bannister, is kind of creepy. It's a 'what-if' story about a technology where they can implant a camera in your eye that grows with you when you are an embryo and films your whole life. When you die, your estate hires a cutter to cut together a movie of your life. Robin plays a cutter and I play the wife of a lawyer who dies and I hire Robin to cut his life together. Otherwise, [my husband and I] are trying to have a baby. So for the first time, I haven't been concentrating on work.

LILAH IS DEAD, PROBABLY SUFFERING SOME ETERNAL DAMNATION. WHAT WOULD HELL BE FOR HER?
[Laughs] A real warm and fuzzy place where they dress bad, smell bad and are trying to hug you all the time!

> 'I WAS JUST DEAD AND ANGEL IS FEEDING ON ME AND THROWING ME ON THE FLOOR. IT WAS A LITTLE INSULTING!'

10 THINGS YOU NEVER KNEW ABOUT...

STEPHANIE ROMANOV

1 Stephanie Romanov was born on January 24 in Las Vegas, Nevada. At 15 years old, she was discovered by a modeling agent and Stephanie's career as a top fashion model began. Her first professional modeling job took her to Europe, shooting fashion layouts for French and Italian *Bazaar*. To further her career, Stephanie moved to New York. She has appeared in numerous fashion glossies, including *Vanity Fair*, *Elle* and *French Vogue*.

2 On December 26, 2001, Stephanie married film producer Nick Wechsler in Siem Reap, Cambodia, at the Bayon Temple at Angkor Thom. It looked just like a scene straight out of *Lara Croft, Tomb Raider*! It was a very traditional Cambodian ceremony, accompanied by five Buddhist Monks chanting in Sanskrit – even though apparently they didn't understand a word! Luckily, they did have a translator on hand, so at least they got the gist of it.

3 Stephanie was voted #44 in *Femme Fatales* magazine's 50 Sexiest Women of 2003 article.

4 In 1993, Stephanie decided to leave modeling behind for an acting career. Her first on-screen appearance couldn't have been more appropriate. She appeared in the short-lived Aaron Spelling series *Models Inc.* Subsequent television work included *Melrose Place*, *Due South*, *Early Edition*, *Seven Days* and *Homicide: Life on the Street*. She also had a part in the Leslie Nielsen comedy *Spy Hard* and appeared in the Joe Cocker music video for 'What Becomes of the Broken Hearted'.

5 Stephanie loves playing the part of corrupt, back-stabbing Lilah Morgan. When she auditioned for the part, she originally thought it would be for just one episode. She has a lot of fun with the role, especially since she couldn't be more different from her character. As Lilah, she gets to do some really evil things – and wear great lipstick and flashy suits.

6 Stephanie speaks many different languages. She demonstrated her Russian dialect when she appeared in *Early Edition* and *Seven Days*.

7 When it comes to the subject of future leading men, Stephanie would love to play opposite Brad Pitt. Not that we can blame her – although she's quick to point out that it's not for the obvious reasons! Stephanie thinks he has a lot of integrity as an actor, and she has a great deal of respect for the choices he's made career-wise. Never mind the fact that he's drop dead gorgeous!

8 Her all-time favorite film is *The Sound of Music*. Hmm, better not tell Lilah – she'd never live it down!

9 Fearless Stephanie performed her own stunts when she appeared in the movie *Menno's Mind*. So impressive were the stunts, Stephanie was made an honorary member of the Stuntmen's Association!

10 Stephanie is set to appear in *The Final Cut*, where she plays a wealthy, grieving widow. The sci-fi thriller also stars Robin Williams and Mira Sorvino and is due for release later this year.

Compiled by Kate Anderson

CALLING

Drusilla may be completely insane and terrifyingly lethal, but it's always a pleasure for us viewers to see her turning up every now and then in *Buffy* and *Angel*. And since her last appearances in *Angel* Season Five revealed shocking twists in the Spike/Angel/Dru relationship, we thought it was about time we caught up with Dru actress Juliet Landau for an insightful chat!

Part of the appeal for guest stars of *Angel* and the late *Buffy the Vampire Slayer* is the way that their characters can weave in and out of storylines as the tapestry of the Whedon-verse continues to evolve and expand. Actress Juliet Landau serves as a perfect

example of this.

Since debuting on *Buffy* as vampire Drusilla in Season Two's "School Hard" (which co-starred James Marsters as Dru's vampire lover, Spike), Juliet has reprised the role an impressive 23 times, most recently on the "Destiny" and "The Girl in Question" episodes of *Angel*. Along the way, the character has not only served as a tangible threat in the present, but in different time periods via flashback – all of which have played an integral role in Dru's evo-lution.

"Getting to work on a character for such a length of time is something that I liken to doing a run of a play," muses the daughter of *Mission: Impossible* and *Space: 1999*'s Martin Landau and Barbara Bain. "When you work on a play and you do, say, eight shows a week from

opening night through 40 shows later, this other sort of thing starts to happen where you gradually begin to find so much more in the character. Playing Drusilla has been the same kind of experience, except that the text is different every time as opposed to a play where it's the same text night after night. But getting to live with this character and bringing her out over six years – well, I've never really had the longevity of that kind of experience before as a character. It's so great and I've been so busy doing other things, too, so it's this balance where I get to play this great role and I get to do many other things as well.

"I love this role," Juliet continues. "There's just so much dimension and it's really a great time working on this part. In terms of history, you're dealing

Interview by Edward Gross

with characters who are 200 years old, so there's quite a bit of lineage there. The cast and creators are wonderful –both *Buffy* and *Angel* have been great shows to work on, and working on [*Angel* Season Five] was wonderful."

In "Destiny", Angel and Spike vie for the virtual Holy Grail of the vampire world: the Cup of Perpetual Torment, which will supposedly transform a vampire back into human form in fulfillment of the Shanshu Prophecy. Along the way, the episode flashes back to the 1880s where we discover that the rivalry and antagonism between Spike and Angel has often been over their feelings for the same woman: Buffy in the present and Drusilla in the past. "The appeal," Juliet explains, "is that it sort of takes place right after I've made Spike a vampire, and investi-gates that love triangle between Angel, William and Drusilla. That's the theme of it, and it's always great to come back and work with the boys and to explore new colors and dimensions in the role."

This is an opportunity that presented itself to Juliet from the beginning. "For the first six episodes of *Buffy*," she reflects, "my character was weak and dying.

Then I got renewed strength and became powerful. When I came to Los Angeles and teamed up with Darla [on *Angel*], it was this little bit of a different side – and I got to spread more of my evil wings. Then filling in the flashbacks is some-thing I've always loved, because I've always wanted to do a period movie, so we get to do some of that. The nice thing is that this is not just a straight black and white, 'Oh, she's the villainess' kind of role. So much had happened to the character in terms of her life before she was turned into a vampire, that I hope it creates some sympathy for her as well. She's a little crazy, but, as we've learned, she was also victimized."

In that regard Juliet recalls a flashback sequence on *Buffy*, in which a still-human Dru is suffering from bizarre visions, and turns to the church for answers. Unbeknownst to her, the "priest" she's talk-ing to in the confessional is actually Angelus, who more or less pushes her over the edge of sanity before turning her into a vampire. "What was interesting about that scene," she says, "is that we usually get scripts about a week in advance, but for some reason on that particular episode for that particular

sequence, I really only got it a cou-ple of days ahead of time. It seemed like such an important piece, because it was the first time I got to work on Drusilla prior to her becoming a vampire, and I felt that this was important and we had to get it right. For that reason, it was an intriguing scene."

Just as intriguing about the character of Drusilla is the fact that she seems to be extremely sensual, which Juliet attributes to a combination of the character as writ-ten and what she's attempted to bring to it as an actress.

"When I first got hired for the role," she says, "I had never actually read for it ahead of time. I came in for a meeting and Joss had seen my work in *Ed Wood* and a movie I did with Whoopi Goldberg [*Theodore Rex*], where I played an upper class English character. I went in and we had this incredibly creative meeting where it was [the WB's] Gail Berman and David Greenwalt and Joss, and we bounced ideas off of each other and I thought, 'This could be so much fun.' When I got hired, I went in for a creative meeting and Joss and I sat down. He sort of filled me in on all the vampire lore of the show and he told me the objectives he wanted for Drusilla – and they were quite a spectrum of things. A little bit Ophelia, but diabolical. Sensual, but

{ "I LOVE [THE DRUSILLA] ROLE. THERE'S JUST SO MUCH DIMENSION. IN TERMS OF HISTORY, YOU'RE DEALING WITH CHARAC-TERS WHO ARE 200 YEARS OLD, SO THERE'S QUITE A BIT OF LINEAGE THERE." }

ethereal – things that seemed like a big spectrum. I thought to myself, 'How am I going to put all of these pieces together?' Then I did a lot of work on it and it all fell into place. She is definitely sexualized.

"There's a lot of it that's twisted," Juliet elaborates with a laugh, "because there's also the fact that the relationship with Angel is kind of an incestuous love affair, as he's kind of my father figure. I remember talking to Joss about a movie called *Night Porter*, with Dirk Bogarde and Charlotte Rampling, which was about Nazi Germany but was also very dark and interesting and has that murky sexuality as well. So I think it's a combination of what was given and and how it's taken off as well. Definitely collaborative. That's one of the things that's so great about working on these shows."

For those who wonder how much of Dru is informed by the actress, she's quick to point out that there is actually very little that connects the two. "It's funny," she smiles, "there's someone I've been friends with since we were kids, and she hadn't seen a lot of *Buffy* or *Angel*. But she called me one day after she did see an episode and said, 'I recognize you, but I don't recognize you. Drusilla is so *not* like you in terms of mannerisms and physicality.' I actually took that as a huge compliment. Of course, in terms of choices, as an actor you use yourself. I really don't feel that I'm like that character in pretty much any way, but in terms of adding to my life, I feel like I get to make some really bold choices as an actor and get to have a certain freedom that has been an

incredible experience."

Although Juliet has made an impressive career for herself in such independent films as *Life Among the Cannibals* (1996), *Carlo's Wake* (1999), *Freedom Park* (2000), *Repossessed* (2002), *The Toolbox Murders* and *Shopping* (both 2003), it remains her work in Tim Burton's *Ed Wood* (1994), in which she played Loretta King, and, naturally, as Drusilla that she continues to be most recognized. "When I was working on *Ed Wood*," she says of the movie for which her father played Bela Lugosi, "a lot of people responded to that film and loved Tim Burton, but I would say that Drusilla has a different kind of life, definitely. I have an action figure, which is kind of surreal and pretty wild. I am one of the few people on the planet who doesn't have a computer, but I've been told that there are quite an extensive amount of sites devoted to the characters from *Buffy* and *Angel*. The thing that's really cool about the fans is that there's such a wide spectrum of them. It seems like the show appeals to a wide range of people in terms of ages. I get fan-mail from really interesting parts of the world.

"It seems that people respond to the writing because it's really intelligent," Juliet adds. "The thing that made it terrific as an actor is that there's an element to the shows that is fantastical, obviously, but Joss has always been really clear that everything is rooted in something. The whole initial concept of high school as a nightmare and using evil forces to pull that metaphor to the extreme is a perfect example. 🦇

Crazy For Dru

Drusilla's always had a way with words, so we decided to reflect on some of her most memorable and, well, maddest sayings...

"Do you know what I miss? Leeches."
(*Buffy*: "Halloween")

Drusilla: "I'm naming all the stars."
Spike: "You can't see the stars, love. That's the ceiling. Also, it's day."
Dru: "I can see them. But I've named them all the same name. And there's terrible confusion."
(*Buffy*: "Innocence")

"I didn't like that barkeeper. Hmm, can't get his eyes off my fingers."
(*Buffy*: "Crush")

Drusilla (*to bird*)**:** "You sing the sweetest little song. Won't you sing for me, hmm? Don't you love me anymore? Come on. I'll pout if you don't sing. I'll give you a seed if you sing."
Spike: "The bird's dead, Dru. You left it in a cage, and you didn't feed it, and now it's all dead, just like the last one."
(*Drusilla cowers and whines*)
(*Buffy*: "Lie to Me")

"I think sometimes that all my hair will fall out and I'll be bald." (*Buffy*: "School Hard")

Drusilla: "These flowers... are wrong. They're all... wrong! I can't abide them!" (*screams and rips at them*)
Spike: "Let's try something different with the flowers then."
(*Buffy*: "Surprise")

"You'll kill [the Slayer], and then we'll have a nice celebration. With streamers... and songs."
(*Buffy*: "School Hard")

"Do you like daisies? Hmm? I plant them, but they always die. Everything I put in the ground withers and dies. I'm a princess."
(*Buffy*: "School Hard")

Drusilla: "I was dreaming."
Spike: "Of what, pet?"
Dru: "We were in Paris. You had a branding iron. And there were worms in my baguette."
(*Buffy*: "What's My Line", Part Two)

(*to Angel*) "Shhh! Grrrruff! Bad dog."
(*Buffy*: "What's My Line", Part Two) 🦇

ANGEL
MAGAZINE

The Vampire Chronicles

A History of Vampires in *Buffy* and *Angel*

VAMPIRES: VICIOUS, BLOOD-SUCKING CREATURES — BUT IS THAT ALL YOU NEED TO KNOW ABOUT THEM? *ANGEL MAGAZINE* EXAMINES AND INVESTIGATES THEIR MYSTERIOUS WORLD...

BY K. STODDARD HAYES

Vampire Trivia

- Vampires kill by exsanguination: they suck your blood until you die of blood loss.

- If a vampire makes you drink some of his blood before he kills you, you will rise from your grave as a vampire (unless your head is cut off before they bury you).

- Vampires look like ordinary humans (apart from a tendency to dress in out-of-date clothes), except when they're going to attack someone, when they vamp into a monster face with fangs.

- Vampires can't enter a home unless invited by someone who lives there: but they can enter any public place without an invitation.

- Vampires have no souls, but in rare circumstances, a vampire can regain his soul.

- Vampires can be harmed or repelled by certain mystical objects: Holy Water, crosses, garlic, the Vampire Slayer.

"Are you still... Grrr?"
"Yeah. There's not actually a cure for that."
Cordelia to Angel, "City Of"

Two of the major heroes in the *Buffy*/*Angel* universe are vampires. Angel and Spike have supernatural strength and agility, plus a near invulnerability to wounds that would kill an ordinary human. These fighting abilities make them powerful champions of good, who can take out any number of monsters, and save the world from Beasts, goddesses, evil vampire armies and law-firms.

But in *Buffy* and *Angel*, vampires are the bad guys. Before they got their souls back, Spike and Angel were demonic creatures that lived by sucking the blood of human beings, and got their jollies from remorseless cruelty and the terrorization of humankind. Spike earned his nickname by torturing victims with railroad spikes, while Angelus was such a vicious monster that all of Europe feared him. Despite the recent good deeds these two might have done, they're still vampires. As good guys, they've even had to save the world from each other.

Still, considering the personal histories of Angel and Spike, and their lovers Darla and Drusilla, it's hard not to wonder whether even the nastiest vampires might have good reason for behaving badly. Darla was a 17th Century prostitute – a notoriously destructive profession – and was dying of syphilis when the Master sired her into her new life. Angelus was a despised son, who could do no right in his father's eyes. Spike was the butt of contempt and humiliation from his genteel society and the lady he adored. And Drusilla was deliberately driven mad by Angelus, who murdered her family and a convent of nuns before taking her into his vampire family. No wonder these people entered vampire life with a thirst for tormenting the living!

Vampires may have no soul or conscience, but they do have their own set of moral – or rather, *immoral* – standards. Their highest value seems to be making humans suffer. After Angel regains his soul, Darla despises him for his mercy

The Ultimate Vampires

The Master: Darla's sire and one of the oldest and most powerful of vampires, the Master meets his match in Buffy, who dusts him and smashes his bones to powder, after he fulfills a prophecy that says he'll kill her.

Dracula: The legendary Count turns his charms on Buffy – but she eventually dusts him (although he's still not dead!).

The Turok Han aka The Ubervamp: The primeval vampire, the main soldier of The First Evil's army, seems almost indestructible – until he meets the Slayer and her army, and a mystic talisman that brings sunlight into the Hellmouth itself.

Angelus: The most vicious vampire in Europe for a century and a half, Angelus could only be vanquished by a gypsy curse that restores his soul; and a certain red-haired witch, who puts back that soul every time Angel loses it. Still a threat as long as there's any chance that Angel could lose his soul again.

Darla: A centuries-old evil who served her sire, the Master, and helped make Angelus the monster he was. Right up to the last days of her second vampire life, she still hoped to bring "her boy" back to her side. Only the miraculous birth of Connor saves her soul and redeems her somewhat.

Drusilla: Angelus' masterpiece of torment, she's psychic and more than a bit mad, with her obsession for dolls, caged birds, and kinky sex. Hardly anything in the *Buffy/Angel*-verse is as creepy as her quiet little voice.

Spike, aka William the Bloody: The final member of Angelus' family of chaos, has killed two Slayers and is always ready to kill or torture, or to provide useful information, in return for a bit of cash – until he falls in love and wins back his soul.

in only feeding on criminals instead of the innocent. The Master's perfect vampire world, seen in "The Wish," involves vampires harvesting humans at will, in a factory of blood, while the human social order completely disintegrates. The Master also expects his followers to serve him in devoted loyalty and obedience, and to be willing to die if they fail him, like samurai committing suicide rather than suffer disgrace. This seems a peculiar code of honor for creatures who ought to be more interested in terror and chaos than in loyalty and service.

The Vampire's Nemeses

But despite their talent for causing mayhem, don't get the idea that vampires can't be good with people. In fact, they excel at certain relationships – like seduction. For all the vampires we've seen hunting and terrorizing their prey in dark alleys, we've seen just as many luring their victims with a promise of seduction. The very first scene of *Buffy* shows Darla enticing a boy to a quiet corner of the deserted school, where instead of kissing him as he expects, she feeds on him. And both Darla and Drusilla sired "their boys" Liam and William, by seducing them in dark alleys. Though male vampires seem a bit more likely to resort to terror than to temptation, the most seductive vampire of all is a male – Dracula himself. His long hair, bedroom eyes and smokey voice work their spell even on the Slayer – for a little while. But by the time Dracula meets Buffy, she has outgrown a teenage girl's longing for the validation of a man's love. She's had too many hard lessons in love, and she can see right through a man – or a vampire – who wants to use her. Just when he thinks she has succumbed to his wiles, he learns that he has fallen victim to her. So much for seduction.

As much as they rejoice in bloodlust and terror, vampires also rejoice in their immortality and near-invulnerability, which they find as intoxicating as fresh blood. Some mortals are also seduced by the thought of vampiric immortality. The human Darla talks as if the life of a vampire, with its unending youth and passion and freedom from disease, were a gift that she gave Angel. Buffy's friend Ford and the other young people in "Lie to Me" worship the vampires' immortality; and the has-been actress Rebecca in "Eternity" wants to be a vampire to extend her

The Slayer: While Slayers usually die at the hands/fangs of vampires, another Slayer always rises. And ever since Buffy and Willow did their mojo with the Scythe, vampires don't have to worry about the Slayer. They have a whole army of Slayers to hunt them across the globe. Curses!

Modern Vampire Hunters: Gunn, his gang, and his big truck. While Gunn makes a specialty of vampires, his former gang extends their vigilante violence to demons of all sorts.

Antique Vampire Hunters: Daniel Holtz, the most famous vampire hunter in 18th Century Europe, pursued Angelus and Darla from Yorkshire to Rome and finally all the way to the 21st Century – all in revenge for their brutal murder of his family.

Evil lawyers: Wolfram & Hart has vampire alarms all through their offices, and sics their nasty lawyers on any vampire who isn't actually a client.

Most Enterprising Vampires

Russell Winters ("City Of"): Corporate giant, Hollywood power broker, and Angel's first Los Angeles bust. Winters: "I pay my taxes. I keep my name out of the paper. And in return, I can do anything I want." Angel: "Can you fly?" (Pushes him through a high rise window into the sunlight)

Doug Sanders, motivational vampire ("Disharmony"): Sanders teaches vampires how to "turn a blood bath into a blood bank" with his simple pyramid scheme for harvesting human victims: "Turn two, the rest is food."

Holden Webster (*Buffy*: "Conversations With Dead People"): The moment he rises from his grave, the former psychology student sets himself up in counseling practice. His first and only patient: The Slayer.

Harmony Kendall: She never gives up trying to make it as a successful vampire, whether she's leading a vampire gang ("Real Me"), joining Doug Sanders' pyramid scheme ("Disharmony"), or fighting her way up the corporate ladder at Wolfram & Hart ("Harm's Way"). Even after proving her disloyalty to her CEO, Angel, she still walks out of Wolfram & Hart with his personal recommendation for her next job.

"It's Dead, Jim!"
Facts about our favorite undead critters

Because they are dead, vampires...
- Have no breath or heartbeat
- Are cold-blooded like most reptiles, with body temperatures determined by their surroundings
- Cannot have children, no matter how many times they do the deed, nor who they do it with (except for one miraculous exception)
- Are immortal, in the sense that they cannot die a natural death, and heal rapidly from injuries that would kill a living person
- Have superhuman strength and agility
- Don't care for the taste of any human food; they only relish fresh human blood
- Turn to dust the instant they are killed — probably catching up on years or centuries of decomposition from the date of human death

career and preserve her youth without Botox.

But no matter how young and immortal they seem, vampires are not symbols of life in the *Buffy*/*Angel*-verse. They represent Death, and they are its most prolific Reaper. In "The Harvest," Giles tells Buffy and Xander that a person turned into a vampire is dead, and his body is inhabited by a demon. This is a good argument for staking many a vampire, from Xander's friend Jesse in "The Harvest," to Gunn's sister Alonna in "War Zone," to Spike's beloved Mum in "Lies My Parents Told Me." According to Giles, you're not staking your beloved (no matter how much it feels that way to Gunn, especially); you're killing the monster that killed her and took her place. This argument makes all the difference to Spike, who realizes that his mother's vicious rejection of him after he turned her, was not his beloved mum speaking, but a hateful demon. He's able to believe that his mother never stopped loving him, and to free himself from the painful memory of her rejection.

But this same premise is also the biggest unresolved issue in the vampire mythology of *Buffy* and *Angel*. If a vampire is a soulless demon merely occupying the body and memories of a dead person, then what are we to make of the choices made by Darla, Spike and Angel, about their eternal souls? When Darla, resurrected as a human by Wolfram & Hart, learns that she is mortally ill, she begs Angel to give back to her the immortal life of a vampire. If a human dies when a vampire sires him, and is replaced by a demon, then this is a very strange thing for Darla to ask, because she could not save her life by becoming a vampire again. She can only believe she is saving her life, if she knows that her first

Six Ways to Kill a Vampire:

- A wooden stake driven through the heart (a near miss won't do it).
- Beheading.
- Exposure to sunlight.
- Holy Water (a bathtub full, not just a splash).
- Fire (if the vamp is completely burned up, otherwise they'll heal to bite again).
- The Scythe in the hands of a Slayer (using either end).

vampire life was something she herself – the real Darla, not a demon – experienced.

Then there's the matter of free will and conscience. Most of the time, we're told that vampires are without a conscience or compassion or the capacity to love. The love that the members of Angelus' vampire family profess for each other is often revealed to be possessive and selfish, as when Darla takes the only horse and abandons Angelus to Holtz, or when Drusilla leaves Spike because he's gotten soft. But Spike begins to feel genuine, self-sacrificing love for Buffy, after a while. He's willing to let Glory kill him, rather than see Buffy suffer the loss of her sister. How does a demon without a conscience do that? There's no human replacing a vampire who replaced a human here. There's only Spike winning back his soul to make himself worthy of Buffy, and to become a champion.

The Angel/Angelus duality at first glance makes this question still more confusing. Angelus always speaks as if Angel is a different person, an enemy and an opposite, by whom Angelus is trapped in his own body, and tormented by watching Angel's sickening good deeds. When Angelus comes face to

face with Angel in "Orpheus," he sees the moment as his opportunity to finish off his rival and take back 'his' life for good.

But the conflict between Angel and Angelus isn't a battle between two distinct individuals. When Angelus complains about having to remember Angel's good deeds, Angel snaps, "It's not about you, jackass!" Though Angelus thinks of Angel's life as separate from his, Angel never speaks or acts as if he thinks Angelus is a separate entity, a demon who possessed his body. Everything Angel has done, and everything Angelus has done, is all one life – his life. He lives by the belief that he personally is responsible for the atrocities committed by Angelus, atrocities for which he can never entirely atone, no matter how long he lives or how much he sacrifices. Angelus is a part of Angel, a destructive second personality that he must keep forever locked away in his psyche. And when Willow puts Angel's soul back, the Angelus of the dream world is drawn back into Angel, the true personality – unless some cosmic mischance frees him again from Angel's control.

If we look at the vampire heroes, and especially at Angel and Spike, it seems there's no departing human life; only a

transformation from human to vampire. So if you should be turned into a vampire, don't give up hope. You may be dead and demonic, but at least you're immortal, and you could someday win back your soul and become one of the good guys again. All you need is a miracle, or a good spell!

Further Research

A few unanswered questions about vampire biology:

- If vampires have no blood circulation, why do they bleed? And how do they heal themselves, or digest the blood they drink, or carry out any other bodily function that requires blood circulation?
- If vampires have no taste for human food, why does Spike like onion flowers? And why does Angel care whether Cordelia makes bad coffee? We can only assume that they do have some taste, but it is very dulled.
- If you have sex with a vampire, are you committing necrophilia? Is it still necrophilia if the vampire has a soul? And isn't it awfully chilly cuddling up to a dead person?
- Do vampires need to use the toilet?

Angelus' Guide To Being Evil

By Kate Anderson

During five years, the *Angel*verse has been home to some truly nasty individuals. Who can forget the killing machine known as The Beast? Or seemingly kindly brainwasher Jasmine? Or how about when Wesley went pear-shaped for a bit?! Still, being evil does seem to have its perks. But just what does it take to be evil? What qualities does one need to possess? Well, to get the lowdown on being bad, we've examined the life and crimes of the ultimate Big Bad – Angelus – in order to provide a few tips...

1 Don't Have A Conscience

Conscience? What conscience? Never ever show any kind of remorse – it's the ultimate sign of weakness. Being a sociopath will make the job a lot easier. You can't be evil if you have even the slightest bit of humanity in you, and showing any form of emotion will just get in the way and cloud your judgement. There's no point doing bad deed after bad deed and then suddenly getting a severe case of guilt! Evil-doers wouldn't know guilt even if it came up and bit them on the butt!

2 Torture Is Fun

Being evil means you get to have all sorts of fun. It means you get to cause mischief and mayhem, go on bloody rampages and wreak havoc simply for pleasure. And there's no better way for deriving pleasure than inflicting pain, be it physical or emotional. You could torture your friends/family with chainsaws, snap a few necks, kill your neighbors' fish or perhaps turn your victim mad after killing off their entire family one by one. As the saying goes, if a job's worth doing, it's worth doing properly. But whatever your preferred modus operandi, having a strong stomach is essential – after all, you can't be evil and faint at the sight of blood! If you haven't got a cast-iron constitution, being evil probably isn't the ideal career choice for you.

3 Mess With Their Minds

Evil has many faces. And being evil doesn't always have to involve inflicting physical pain – no sir-ee! It's amazing what damage you can do when you take the time to mess with someone's thoughts and feelings. You just have to have a little patience; put in a little overtime. Better still, find someone with a troubled soul – someone like that would be the perfect candidate to manipulate and have your wicked way with – that way half the damage is already done. You could then put an end to their suffering, too – but where would the fun be in that?

4 Stay Away From Gypsy Curses

These days, it pays to choose your victims carefully – perhaps do a little detective work beforehand. After all, one minute you are out enjoying yourself, offering an ugly death to pretty much everyone you meet. And then, lo and behold, you discover one of your victims just so happens to belong to a clan of Romany Gypsies! And then you find yourself cursed with a soul! From that day forward you find yourself suffering because of all your evil deeds – highly inconvenient.

5 Keep Your Friends Close But Your Enemies Closer

In other words, trust no one – except yourself! It's all well and good to team up with other evil-doers – there's strength in numbers, after all. But you can't always rely on other people, let alone trust them. Let's face it, honesty and trust aren't exactly top of your personal agenda – for all you know, when the going gets tough, your partner-in-crime could suddenly decide to switch sides! One minute there you are, fighting side by side, and the next they team up with the enemy! Talk about being stabbed in the back! So, why give them any ammunition? Unless of course, you beat them to it... ✛

The Slayer is a disciplined young woman who takes her calling seriously and is dedicated above all to the unending struggle against vampires and demons. So we learn from watching Buffy and Kendra, and so we believe, until Faith walks out of The Bronze and dusts her first vampire. From the minute Faith appears in Sunnydale, she challenges all ideas about who or what a Slayer is supposed to be.

First, Faith's style and personality are very different from Buffy's. She enjoys being a Slayer; she loves the thrill of the violence and rejoices in the kill. To her, life is one big party, and nothing should be taken too seriously, especially rules. Second, and worse, Buffy's friends and family all admire Faith when she first appears, so much that Buffy feels she is being elbowed aside in favor of this new Slayer. The Scoobies eat up Faith's Slaying stories, while Giles tells Buffy

that if Faith is whaling too hard on the vamps, it just means she's "a plucky fighter." And protective mother Joyce wants Buffy to retire from Slaying and let Faith take over.

Unsettling as this may be for Buffy, it's only the beginning of the disaster that is Faith. Faith's primary role in the third season of *Buffy* is to show us what happens when a Slayer goes bad. Her addiction to violence is more than just the adrenaline rush of a thrill seeker. No matter how plucky she seems, Faith has come to Sunnydale because she is fleeing from the demon Kakistos, who gruesomely murdered her Watcher, and plans to do the same to her. The demon made her feel terrified and helpless, and she only knows one way to make herself feel powerful and brave again: by letting out the strength and killing lust of the Slayer. She becomes so addicted to the rush, that she

sometimes forgets the goal is to kill vampires, because she's having so much fun beating them up.

When Faith mistakes a man for a vampire and kills him, she can't admit her mistake; and when she realizes that Giles considers the killing a serious matter, she tries to frame Buffy for it. She insists that a Slayer doesn't have to live by the world's rules, because Slayers are better than everyone else. It's an easy rationalization to escape the responsibility that comes with being a Slayer – a responsibility that feels to Faith like a trap that will snare her and get her killed like her Watcher. As far as she's concerned, there's only one reason why Buffy is trying to get her under control: "You need me to toe the line because you're afraid you'll go over it, aren't you, B? You can't handle watching me living my own way, having a blast, because it tempts you." ("Consequences")

KEEPING THE

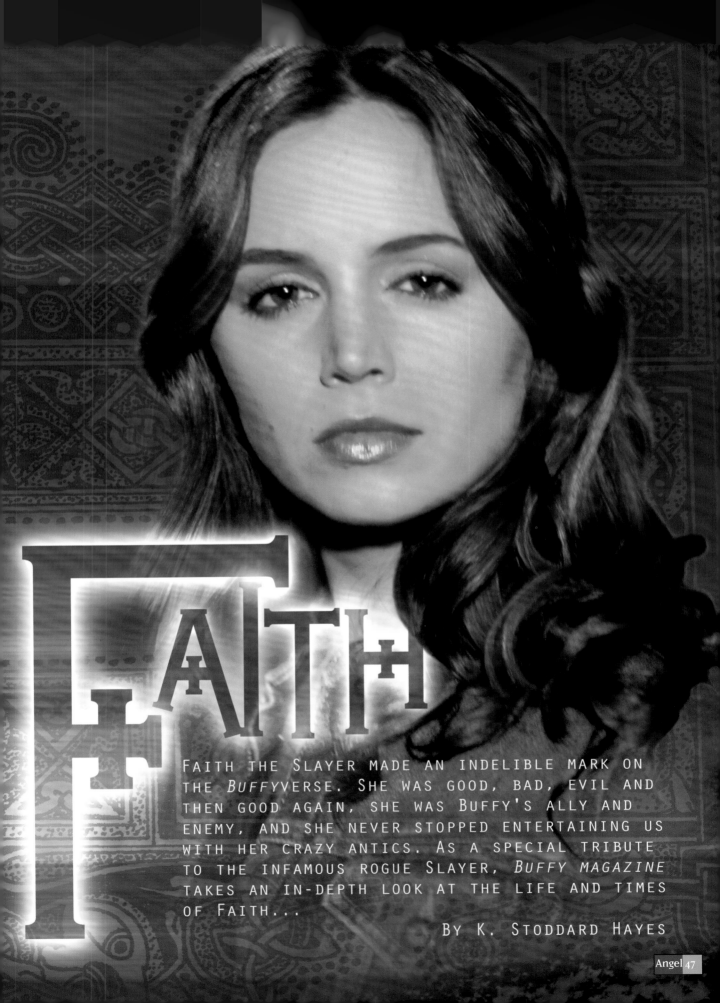

FAITH

Faith the Slayer made an indelible mark on the *Buffy*verse. She was good, bad, evil and then good again, she was Buffy's ally and enemy, and she never stopped entertaining us with her crazy antics. As a special tribute to the infamous rogue Slayer, *Buffy magazine* takes an in-depth look at the life and times of Faith...

By K. Stoddard Hayes

Faith differs from Buffy in another essential way, too. While Buffy has a close-knit group of friends and family to help her through the tough choices of being the Slayer, Faith has no one. She shows us what can happen to a Slayer who chooses to be alone. Though Buffy, Giles and the Scoobies try to befriend Faith and help her, she rejects their friendship at every turn. Buffy assures her "I'm on your side," but Faith can't bring herself to rely on anyone, even Buffy. She turns her back on Buffy, telling herself, "I'm on my side. That's enough." ("Revelations")

When Faith is embroiled in the Mayor's plans to rule the world (plans which will leave Faith in a coma) Willow tells her bluntly what she has thrown away: "You made your choice. I know you had a tough life, I know that some people think you had a lot of bad breaks. Well, boo hoo! Poor you! You had a lot more in your life than some people. You had friends like Buffy. Now you have no one. You were a Slayer, and now you're no one. You're just a big, selfish, worthless waste." ("Choices")

After Faith revives from her coma, she uses a gadget given to her by the mayor to switch bodies with Buffy so she can escape the desolation she's made of her life. In Buffy's body, she takes her first chance to buy a plane ticket to get away from everyone who's hunting her. But in the interval between buying the ticket and getting on the plane, Faith has to spend some time pretending to be Buffy, and it's much harder than she expected. At first it may seem to Faith a sweet payback to watch Buffy (in Faith's body) be arrested and taken away like a criminal; and it's a kick to make Buffy's mother, her friends, and especially her boyfriend, Riley, think that she is Buffy. Having sex with Riley is fine, but she can't handle Riley's sincerity when he tells "Buffy" that he loves her. She pushes him away, demanding, "What do you want from her?" To keep her own armor of self-reliance she has to believe that all love is selfish.

To her own surprise, Faith herself is still selfless in one critical way. She's still a Slayer. When she hears about Adam's vampires taking hostages, she leaves the airport, abandoning her escape, and goes to fight them. This brings her face to face with Buffy, who's in Faith's body, in a confrontation that forces her to look at how far she has fallen from her calling as the Slayer. When she beats on Buffy and screams at her, the words and the blows

are meant for the face that she sees looking back at her: her own. "You're nothing! Disgusting, murderous bitch! You're nothing! You're disgusting!" ("Who Are You?") The conflict between a Slayer's calling and Faith's guilty conscience is ripping her apart.

Faith reaches the end when she arrives in Angel's world in the *Angel* episode "Five by Five." Just as her *Buffy* episodes explore the nature of the Slayer, her *Angel* episodes explore the primary theme of *Angel*: finding redemption. Faith joins with Wolfram & Hart to assassinate Angel, supposedly because he's one of the good guys, who has defeated her before. Once she comes face to face with him in that battle in the rain, we learn what she really wants from him. She wants him to kill her, so that she can be free from her torment.

Angel refuses. He understands the misery of a guilty conscience, and he also knows how to heal. He fights her

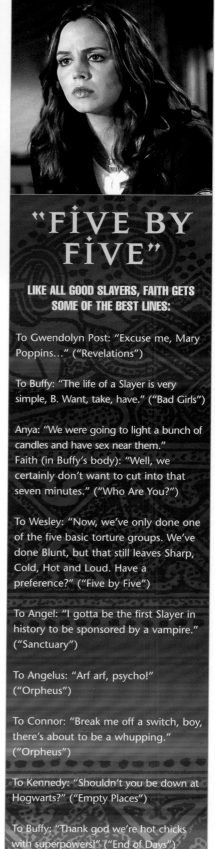

LIKE ALL GOOD SLAYERS, FAITH GETS SOME OF THE BEST LINES:

To Gwendolyn Post: "Excuse me, Mary Poppins…" ("Revelations")

To Buffy: "The life of a Slayer is very simple, B. Want, take, have." ("Bad Girls")

Anya: "We were going to light a bunch of candles and have sex near them."
Faith (in Buffy's body): "Well, we certainly don't want to cut into that seven minutes." ("Who Are You?")

To Wesley: "Now, we've only done one of the five basic torture groups. We've done Blunt, but that still leaves Sharp, Cold, Hot and Loud. Have a preference?" ("Five by Five")

To Angel: "I gotta be the first Slayer in history to be sponsored by a vampire." ("Sanctuary")

To Angelus: "Arf arf, psycho!" ("Orpheus")

To Connor: "Break me off a switch, boy, there's about to be a whupping." ("Orpheus")

To Kennedy: "Shouldn't you be down at Hogwarts?" ("Empty Places")

To Buffy: "Thank god we're hot chicks with superpowers!" ("End of Days")

until she collapses in tears, begging for release, then he takes her home. And what he teaches her shows us a lot about his own redemptive journey, which has happened mostly off camera and long before we first meet him. When he explains to Faith what atonement will be like, he's describing his own life: "I won't lie to you and say it'll be easy. It won't be. Just because you've decided to change doesn't mean the world's ready for you to… No matter how much you suffer, no matter how many good deeds you do to try and make up for the past, you may never balance out the cosmic scale. The only thing I can promise you… is that you'll probably be haunted, and maybe for the rest of your life." ("Sanctuary")

Faith accepts the consequences at last, by turning herself in to the police, and going to prison for murder. Two years later, Wesley breaks her out of prison to help him catch Angelus, and puts a reverse spin on the redemption theme. Just as Angel refused to give up on Faith's redemption, she refuses to give up on restoring Angel's soul, and she won't let anyone kill Angelus, least of all Connor.

The Faith who saves Angel, then returns to Sunnydale to help Buffy battle The First Evil, is in some ways the same Faith we've always known, who loves good fights, good sex and good times. But she's also much more mature, focused and responsible, as a true Slayer should be. In returning to Buffy's universe as a good Slayer, Faith now has

a different thematic role. She shows us the difference between an ordinary Slayer and a champion.

Faith is willing to join the fight, to offer advice on strategy and the training of the Potentials (like the need for them to blow off a little steam by relaxing at The Bronze). She's even willing to support the gang's challenge of Buffy's leadership, when Buffy is about to lead a reckless attack against The First. But she's nearly as shocked as Buffy when the Scoobies and the Potentials depose their Slayer and ask Faith to take over as leader. Though she does her best, she's not at home in the role, and her leadership is just as disastrous at first as Buffy's. Later, when Buffy has returned, Faith tells her what it was like to try to fill her shoes: "There I am, everybody's looking to me, trusting me to lead them, and I've never felt so alone in my entire life. And that's you every day, isn't it?" ("End of Days")

Faith is ready to fight any battle that comes her way, but she's not ready to go looking for the big conflicts, and to take the weight of the world on her shoulders. That's the work of the champions, like Buffy and Angel. They take life and the struggle seriously, and look to the future. Faith takes life as a thrill ride, and lives in the present, moment to moment. She may someday grow to be a champion or she may remain an ordinary Slayer, a soldier in the fight against evil. No matter what, she'll always be a hot chick with superpowers! ✛

CLASSIC SCENE

"In the dark"

"Quickly, to the Angel-mobile, away."

The Story so far...

In a dark alleyway in downtown L.A. at night, an angry boyfriend confronts his terrified girlfriend. Accusing her of seeing other men, he starts to lay into her, before producing a gun. But out of the darkness, Angel suddenly appears to rescue the girl from her abusive partner.

The Scene...

A DARK, DESERTED BACK STREET, SOMEWHERE IN DOWNTOWN LOS ANGELES.

(On a rooftop, Spike stands watching the scene unfolding below him. As Angel steps in to save yet another damsel in distress, Spike decides to make up his own dialogue...)

SPIKE: (In a high, girly voice.) How can I thank you, you mysterious, black-clad hunk of a night thing?
(In a low, manly voice.) No need, little lady, your tears of gratitude are enough for me. You see, I was once a bad-ass vampire, but love and a pesky curse defanged me. Now I'm just a big, fluffy puppy with bad teeth. (Rachel steps closer to Angel, and Angel steps back, warding her off with his hands.) No, not the hair! Never the hair! (High voice.) But there must be some way I can show my appreciation. (Low voice.) No, helping those in need's my job, and working up a load of sexual tension, and prancing away like a magnificent poof is truly thanks enough. (High voice.) I understand. I have a nephew who is gay, so... (Low voice.)

Say no more. Evil's still afoot! And I'm almost out of that Nancy-boy hair-gel that I like so much. Quickly, to the Angel-mobile, away!

(Spike lights a cigarette while he watches Angel lead the young woman away.)

SPIKE: Go on with you. Play the big, strapping hero while you can. You have a few surprises coming your way... The ring of Amarra... A visit from your old pal, Spike and, oh yeah, your gruesome, horrible death. (Smiles wickedly.)

EPISODE CREDITS

Angel Season One,
Episode Three

first aired: 10/19/99 (U.S.)
& 01/21/00 (U.K.)
written by: Doug Petrie
directed by: Bruce Seth Green
Main actors this scene:
Spike: James Marsters
Angel: David Boreanaz

WHY SO COOL?

Who'd have thought a scene involving a bleached-blond vampire making fun of the brooding, hunky one – and his hair – could be so entertaining?! A successful teaser manages to grab the audience in seconds, and this does just that. Spike mimicking the scene unfolding between Angel and the latest girl he's just rescued is so hilariously funny and engaging, it sets you up for what turns into a corker of an episode.

EPISODE TRIVIA

- This is James Marsters' first appearance on *Angel*, before he joined as a series regular in Season Five.

- This is the very first *Angel/Buffy* crossover. This episode is the second part of a story that began in the *Buffy* episode "The Harsh Light of Day." Originally, the two episodes were aired back-to-back in the U.S.

- Despite editing more than five minutes' worth of footage, "In the Dark" still roused the anger of the ITC in the U.K., with viewers complaining about the violence and adult tone. It wasn't long before the show was switched to a much more suitable, later, time slot, than the original time of 6pm.

NO HOLTZ BARRED

Angel's third season introduced a unique adversary for the show's central bloodsucker-turned-hero, in the form of 18th century vampire-slayer Daniel Holtz. Actor Keith Szarabajka discusses Holtz's quest for justice...

Interview by David Bassom

He may have been the principal villain last year on *Angel*, but Keith Szarabajka never viewed Daniel Holtz as a bad guy. "Personally, I always saw Holtz as a hero avenging his family's death," says Keith of his time-traveling, vampire-slaying alter ego. "Holtz was a family man who lost his family to Angel and Darla, and sought justice. He was an honorable man, but his pursuit of justice led him to act in ways that could be interpreted as dishonorable.

"Holtz and Angel actually had a lot in common," he continues, "although they came from opposite ends of the emotional spectrum to that common ground. Angel used to be evil and now possesses a soul, while Holtz was a decent man who put his

show's casting director, who showed it to David. David called me immediately and asked if I wanted to do it. And I said, 'Absolutely!' I'd watched *Angel* on and off and I really like the show. So the idea of working on it was intriguing."

Although Keith wasn't given any advance info on Holtz's back-story or his place in *Angel*'s third season, he insists that the role came fairly easily to him from the moment he began working on the show – once, that is, the show's makers had decided what dialect would best suit the character.

"There was some debate over Holtz's accent," he reveals. "At first, David [Greenwalt] thought it might be Dutch or German, but that sounded too campy. And

then we talked about an Irish accent, but I guess Angel was Irish in flashback scenes and that would have been too confusing. So they settled on this British accent.

"They didn't want it *too* British," the American actor stresses. "They didn't want a Cockney accent, which I've done a lot

> "THE ONLY THING I DIDN'T LIKE ABOUT HOLTZ'S ARC WAS THAT HE DIED, BECAUSE I WAS OFF THE SHOW!"

soul in jeopardy to achieve his aim.

"I thought Holtz was a great character," adds Keith with an infectious enthusiasm. "I loved playing him and I really enjoyed working on the show. I miss it terribly."

Keith's one-year stint on *Angel* began in the summer of 2001, when he launched Holtz's mysterious quest for 'justice'. Unusually, the prolific stage and screen actor was handpicked for the prestigious role by *Angel* co-creator/executive producer David Greenwalt, and joined the show's recurring cast without even an audition.

"I worked with David a number of years ago on a show called *Profit*, which was a short-lived but wonderful series on Fox," explains Keith. "It was a great disappointment for everyone who worked on the show when it was canceled, but we've all had something of a bond since then. When the producers of *Angel* were looking for someone to play Holtz, my agent submitted my [acting] videotape to the

of, or a Yorkshire accent, which I could easily have researched. They wanted it much more mid-Atlantic."

With his character's mid-Atlantic British accent in place, Keith was free to develop Holtz's back-story and pursue his masterplan over the course of 11 episodes of *Angel*'s third season, starting with the season premiere, "Heartthrob." In those episodes, viewers learned that Holtz's quest for justice began in 1764, when Angel (as the soul-less Angelus) and his lover Darla brutally killed the noble vampire-slayer's wife and transformed his daughter into a bloodsucker – who Holtz was then forced to murder. In the wake of this tragedy, Holtz made a deal with a demon, SahJhan, and was transported to the early 21st Century. Once there, he promptly embarks on an elaborate

David because his stuff was good too, but I believe Tim's work was the strongest and most heartfelt, and it portrayed the duality and ambivalence of Holtz's character the best. It really seemed to explore whether Holtz was pursuing justice or vengeance, and it asked whether it's worthwhile for someone who loses their family to then go and take someone else's family. Do you get your family back? No, you don't. And I think that's something that Holtz actually learned during the course of the series, though he still carried through with what he did. But I think that was a bit of improvisation at the end on Holtz's part.

"Apart from 'Lullaby,' I enjoyed the episode where I actually stole the baby and leapt through the portal into Quor-toth ['Sleep Tight'], and 'Benediction,' where I come back as an

old man and I have Justine kill me."

The aforementioned "Benediction" required Keith to don extensive old-age prosthetics for the second time in his career, following his portrayal of a 72-year-old man who started to age backwards in the Stephen King-penned 1991 mini-series, *Golden Years*. "I think that was something David Greenwalt had in mind at the beginning of the season, although he didn't reveal that to me or Tim, who wrote and directed the episode," muses Keith. "I actually told Tim I think David knew I could play both a regular character and being old really well, and that was probably one of the reasons why they hired me. It makes sense."

Looking back at his time on *Angel*, Keith reports that he was always made to feel welcome on the show's sets, and

{ "I REALLY LIKED WORKING WITH DAVID BOREANAZ. I ALWAYS FOUND OUR SCENES TOGETHER INTERESTING." }

scheme to destroy Angel – a scheme which ultimately leads him to kidnap Angel's son, Connor, and try to destroy their relationship. Unsurprisingly, Keith was more than satisfied with Holtz's pivotal role in the season.

"I was very happy with it," he states. "David Greenwalt originally planned for me to do eight episodes and I did 11. That was really nice. The only thing I didn't like about Holtz's arc was that he died, because I was off the show. But in Joss Whedon Land, just 'cos you're dead it doesn't mean that you're dead!

"I think the episodes that stood out for me were 'Lullaby,' 'Sleep Tight' and 'Benediction.' 'Lullaby' is the one in which I have to kill my daughter and I sing this little lullaby to her when I discover she's a vampire. That was intensely emotional for me. Tim Minear wrote and directed that, and his stuff was just *so* good. I don't mean to take anything from

thoroughly enjoyed working with its cast and crew. Ironically, despite their adversarial on-screen relationship, he particularly savoured his scenes with the show's leading man.

"I really liked working with David Boreanaz. After my first episode I said to David Greenwalt, 'Gee, I really like working with David. I think he's a very good actor.' And David said, 'Yeah, he comes up to the level of the competition', which I guess was a sort of backhanded compliment for both of us! But I always found our scenes together interesting.

"There was no one on the cast I didn't like either," he adds. "I particularly liked Andy Hallett [The Host]. And I liked working with Jack Conley, who played SahJhan. We did a lot of scenes together."

Away from the world of *Angel*, Keith has played countless stage and screen roles over the past three decades. In addition to the aforementioned small-screen productions *Golden Years* and *Profit*, he has appeared in such films as *We Were Soldiers*, *Missing* and *A Perfect World*, and famously spent four years as Mickey Kostmayer in the hit 1980s action series *The Equalizer*. Keith has also guest-starred in numerous TV shows, including *The X-Files*, *Babylon 5*, *Early Edition*, *Roswell*, *Star Trek: Voyager* and *Enterprise*. Yet despite the wildly diverse nature of his prolific career, Keith fully appreciates how his work on *Angel* seems to have had an unusually strong impact on the viewing public.

"People walk up to me all the time and say, 'Oh, you're that guy from *Angel* – you're Holtz,'" he notes. "And I say, 'Erm, yes,' and they normally say, 'God, I love your character!' I'm surprised how often that happens."

Since concluding his work on *Angel* in the spring of 2002, Keith Szarabajka has shot guest roles on the TV shows *ER* ("I played an angry biker"), *Crossing Jordan* and *She Spies*, and is currently working on two screenwriting projects. While there's no sign of any further appearances on *Angel*, Keith would certainly be very interested in working on the show or its parent series, *Buffy*, and doesn't rule out the possibility of reprising the role of Holtz one day.

"I have no idea if Holtz will ever come back," he admits. "No one's contacted me or said anything to me about it. But I think it would make sense if he did come back, because he seemed to be a popular villain. And I'd love to come back.

"I did say to David Greenwalt, when Holtz went in and left Quor-toth, it wasn't just a portal we went through – we actually ripped the fabric of space and time, and there could very well be an infinite number of Holtzs wandering around in different dimensions. And David said, 'Oh, I like that idea.' But then he left the show," he notes with a chuckle. "So much for that idea. I should have had that conversation with Joss!" ✛

CATCHING UP WITH...
Laurel Holloman

TOGETHER, JUSTINE AND HOLTZ MADE IT THEIR MISSION TO BRING ANGEL TO HIS KNEES IN THE THIRD SEASON. THREE YEARS LATER, *ANGEL MAGAZINE* FINDS LAUREL HOLLOMAN MORE THAN HAPPY TO REFLECT BACK ON HER BAD GIRL DAYS AS JUSTINE...

DID YOU KNOW ABOUT *ANGEL* WHEN YOU GOT THE AUDITION?
I'd never seen *Angel* or *Buffy*. I didn't even want to go in to audition. I didn't know the show and I was really busy. It was my manager that was like, "You are making a big mistake. This is a great show and it has a wonderful following." They had described the character like Ripley from *Alien*. She was a cold, military type and I did find that interesting. So I walked in and read, and then as I was driving home my manager called and said they wanted me to do it.

DID YOU WARM UP TO THE IDEA ONCE YOU WERE CAST?
It was so much fun and I would do it again in a second. I think Joss Whedon is so creative. I never got offered stuff like that before. I loved the stunts and the fighting and the people. I've always been athletic and it was fun to have that challenge. It's hands down one of my favorite jobs I've ever done.

WAS JUSTINE TO BE PITIED OR JUST PLAIN EVIL?
Well, a vampire killed her sister! In the beginning, she was all about the rage. Towards the end, there was more sympathy. She's also kind of co-dependent. She doesn't stand

"I LIKED ALL THE WESLEY STUFF AND I LOVED SLITTING HIS THROAT."

Photo © Sue Schneider

WRITT

up on her own, but rather she was more dependent on Holtz. But I think cutting Wesley's throat was the part where most people were like, "God, she is really dark!" Almost everything I'd played up to her was a lot lighter or more maternal, so it was fun to just be angry. I think she is really angry, but also sitting on top of a lot of grief, so there was a sadness, too. She is like the warrior that would die on the battlefield.

FANS SAW HER AS A BAD GUY. AS AN ACTOR, DID YOU LIKE OR UNDERSTAND JUSTINE?
Everybody has layers. Even the hero has some dark sides. I'm working on *The L Word* with Jennifer Beals and she's watched every *Buffy* and every *Angel* and she was like, "I'd love to be on one of those shows!" Actors are excited because of the layers and all the fun stuff to play. It's never black and white. It's about the degrees of darkness and pain we deal with every day.

SO WHAT WAS UP BETWEEN JUSTINE AND HOLTZ? THERE WAS A CREEPY VIBE THERE.
I was wondering where they were going with it! I think they wanted to play around with it. When her sister died, there was a loneliness, so she attached herself to him in a father figure way. But it had some *other* layers, too. [*Chuckles*]

YOU APPEARED IN NINE EPISODES. WAS THERE A FAVORITE MOMENT FOR YOU?
Some of the fights were great. They worked with the best stunt people. A couple of the fights were very choreographed, like dance steps. I had a stunt double a couple of times. There was a huge stunt where I got thrown against a wall... I didn't do that one. [*Laughs*]

YOU HAD AN INTERESTING, ALBEIT VIOLENT, RELATIONSHIP WITH WESLEY, TOO.
I liked working with Alexis. I liked all the Wesley stuff and I loved slitting his throat. "Sleep Tight" was a rollercoaster ride. It was really fun because all this manipulation was going on and it was one of the darker things I've done. We always tried to create this angry, evil, weird energy between each other. His character had this way of understanding really angry people. I think his character had the most compassion on the show.

AFTER JUSTINE HELPED CONNOR SINK ANGEL TO THE BOTTOM OF THE SEA, YOU ONLY MADE ONE MORE APPEARANCE. WAS THAT PLANNED?
It was really complicated because I had already booked *The L Word* and I was shooting it when [*Angel*] was ready to pick up where [it] left off. I was happy to go back, but I wasn't sure if I would be able to go back. *The L Word* worked it out. [The *Angel* producers] had to fly me down from Canada and work on a Saturday. But they were really cool about it. I was even platinum blonde at the time and I had to get a wig made.

YOU'VE DONE TWO SEASONS OF *THE L WORD*. WHAT ATTRACTED YOU TO THE SERIES?
I just read the script and it was so great. It's a very emotional-based show. It was so cool because my character, Tina Kennard, is so positive and maternal. She was so different, so that was great. We just shot our second season. I just had a baby a few weeks ago and they incorporated my pregnancy into the show. It was one of those times when my work was working out with my life. Now I'm taking a break to be a mum.

THE LAST TIME WE SAW YOU ON *ANGEL*, WES HAD JUSTINE TIED UP IN A BROOM CLOSET!
I think that was when I was in a closet with a ball in my mouth. [*Laughs*] I was like, "Wow! What are we doing now?" I loved it because I definitely needed to get punished for what I did.

WESLEY THEN LET HER GO, SUGGESTING SHE BE A SLAVE OR LIVE HER LIFE. WHERE DO YOU THINK JUSTINE IS NOW?
Yeah! I thought they would be more definitive and someone would get rid of me, but they just let her float somewhere out there in the universe. I would hope that she has moved on and is in a real relationship and dealing with her grief. It's not about revenge anymore. But of course, you could go either way with her and she's probably putting an army together and is going to fight full force.

REVENGE FOR THE BUCKET?
Yeah. [*Laughs*]

Believe it or not, David Boreanaz is not actually a vampire. Nor is James Marsters. And neither of them have the ability to morph their face into the visage of these creatures. For that matter, Amy Acker cannot bend time at her will, and, as talented as the stunt people who work on *Angel* are, they cannot make themselves turn to dust on command. So when an *Angel* script requires an effect that cannot be achieved practically, the Emmy Award-winning visual effects wizards at Zoic Studios are called upon to create the impossible out of thin air (or thousands of hexagons and ones and zeros.) Week in, week out visual effects supervisors Loni Peristere and Rocco Passionino, along with a small team of CG artists, fill in the fantastic world that Angel and company inhabit,

and make that world all the more believable. *Angel Magazine* chatted with both Loni and Rocco recently about their time on the show…

ANGEL MAGAZINE: WHAT IS YOUR BACKGROUND? HOW DID YOU GET STARTED IN SPECIAL EFFECTS?
ROCCO PASSIONINO: I grew up in the early 80s, which was heavily steeped in video game technology. Movies like *Tron*, *Young Sherlock Holmes* and *The Last Starfighter*, which incorporated computer renderings, fascinated me. I did a little research and realized I needed to get a degree in Computer Programming if I was ever going to get into that field. I

graduated from Binghamton University with a bachelor's degree in Computer Science, then leapt into Defence Industry programming. A few years later, I met a friend who was heading up a joint venture between a couple of unknown film industry people [James Cameron, Stan Winston and Scott Ross] and IBM. A year into that and I got an interview and started working at Digital Domain as a Software Programmer for the Renny

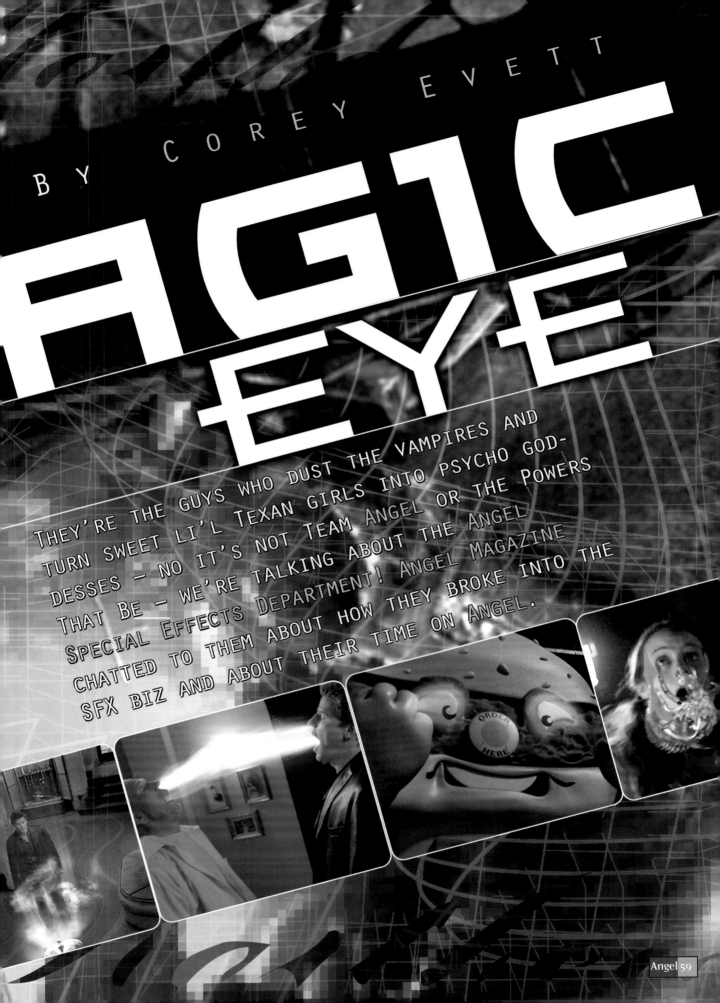

BY COREY EVETT

MAGIC EYE

They're the guys who dust the vampires and turn sweet li'l Texan girls into psycho goddesses – no it's not Team Angel or the Powers That Be – we're talking about the Angel Special Effects Department! Angel Magazine chatted to them about how they broke into the SFX biz and about their time on Angel.

ROCCO PASSIONINO OVERSEES THE SFX WORK. ALSO PICTURED, RACHEL KEYTE.

ROCCO AND ANGEL EXECUTIVE PRODUCER JEFF BELL ON SET

Harlin version of *Godzilla* which was shelved one week in, due to budgetary concerns. Ten years later and here I am!

LONI PERISTERE: I started in stop motion at the age of 10 with some *Empire Strikes Back* action figures, ships, and a super eight camera. Then I moved over to video in high school, and back to film in college at UMASS Amherst. I continued making movies and directing theater through graduation. I moved to Los Angeles permanently in 1996 after graduating, and got a job as a production assistant at Digital Magic. I learned the craft of visual effects and animation on the job while working with VFX Supervisor Ralph Maiers. While under his direction, I had the opportunity to work on *Volcano, The Long Kiss Goodnight, Powder, Mortal Kombat 2, Sphere* and others. Then there was television and commercials, where Ralph allowed me some creative control, and then the introduction to the great Joss Whedon.

WAS VFX YOUR PRIMARY AREA OF INTEREST?

LONI: No, telling good stories, but the craft of visual effects made me a better storyteller.

ROCCO: There was never a doubt

in my mind that I wanted to do [computer generated] effects in movies and television. Now, the connection between what I wanted to do and what was available to me was always in question. There usually aren't a lot of opportunities to do what you want to do in your life.

WHO WERE THE MAJOR INFLUENCES ON YOU IN TERMS OF VFX? WHAT SPURRED ON YOUR INTEREST IN THE AREA?

ROCCO: Like almost anyone in this industry, there are directors that tend to continually reach above and beyond our expectations and these tend to be the favorites and influences in our careers. James Cameron is a big one, Steven Spielberg, Ray Harryhausen, Robert Zemeckis. Their work is the cornerstone for this industry.

LONI: As well as John Knoll, John Dykstra, Richard Edlund, Phil Tippet, Dennis Muren and a host of other craftsman.

HOW DID YOU BECOME INVOLVED IN *ANGEL*?

LONI: Joss created the show and asked me to work on it. I loved the idea of a deeper, darker, action hero.

ROCCO: I was the digital effects supervisor on the *Firefly* pilot back in 2002, which was part of the Whedon family. When an opportunity arose in Season Four to help out Loni, whose time was being consumed by the *Firefly* series, I stepped in and picked up the show from him.

LONI, IS IT TRUE THAT YOU CREATED THE DUSTING EFFECT THAT HAS BECOME A STAPLE OF THE *BUFFY/ANGEL*-VERSE?
LONI: I was the pain in the ass creative guy who forced some hard-working artists to continually go back into a concept, which only existed, in the deep recesses of my imagination.

WHERE DID THE IDEA
COME FROM?
LONI: A chemical reaction between wood and soft tissue, which causes all the moisture in a vamp's body to evaporate and fall to pieces. The idea came from a feigned logic.

WAS IT DIFFICULT TO
ACHIEVE? HOW IS IT DONE?
LONI: Yes. It included years of revisions and additions. Today, it basically includes a 3D character who is match-moved to a live actor. Once the character is animated to match, we project the live action photograph onto a 3D form. This form is eroded through a series of [mattes], which emit dust and reveal the layer beneath it, finally resting on the skeleton, which breaks apart.

THE OTHER MAJOR EFFECT THAT CARRIED OVER FROM *BUFFY* WAS THE VAMP EFFECT, HOW IS THAT ACHIEVED?
LONI: Two make-ups, same actor, twice the fun. The success of this effect rests on the performance of the actor. If the actor is able to repeat his actions on cue in the two make-ups, the effect is really a dissolve between two pieces of photography, with a little help of a digital bend done in the pasting stage.

WHAT IS A TYPICAL
EPISODE LIKE? TAKE US
THROUGH PRE-PRODUCTION,
PRODUCTION AND POST.
ROCCO: For us, the show begins with a writer's beat sheet [a rough outline of the script in paragraph form broken down scene by scene]. From this we get a general idea what they are planning on doing for an episode. If something is going to be a little bit more complicated than average, we give production a heads-up that it is going to take us more time – and ultimately more money – than average. Next comes the Writer's Draft, which leads to the Shooting Draft. That is usually when we start putting more concrete bidding numbers to the visual effects they are going to need. If storyboards are necessary for more complex visual effects we work with the writers and directors to nail down the look and camera angles to make the effect work.

Next up is the actual shooting of the plates we are going to need. Typically, any shots that are going to need visual effects, I'm there to supervize what is being shot [to ensure] it is going to work for us. After the plates are shot, editorial makes a first pass at editing the show together. Once the director, the executive producers and creators are happy, they bring us in for a spotting session to make sure everyone is on the same page [as far as] what the visual effects should look like. Then the actual work begins. Models are made, textured and rigged. Plates are delivered to us, tracked and rotoscoped. Then CG is animated, lit and rendered. Everything

is composited together and handed back to post production for changes and comments. After a couple of iterations to nail exactly what [executive producer] Jeff Bell and Joss are looking for, the shots are finalized and we move on to the next episode.

HOW LONG DOES IT TAKE
USUALLY TO COMPLETE THE
VISUAL EFFECTS FOR AN
ENTIRE EPISODE?
ROCCO: Once the plates are delivered to us, the visual effects can take anywhere from six weeks to a couple of days. Plates are things that have been filmed, such as backgrounds and other elements – green screens, pyro, smoke or other effects. The average is about three to four weeks for the typical 15 visual effects in a show.

WHAT KINDS OF EFFECTS DO
YOU DO THAT MAYBE PEOPLE
DON'T NOTICE?
ROCCO: A considerable amount of our effects involve more or less an in-your-face look to them. Portals, spells, people vamping, dusting and exploding are all some of the more gratuitous effects, but sometimes there are effects that when they are hidden give you a kind of thrill. In Season Four, I pitched an effect where the camera had to float down a set of stairs and pass through a set of bars that caged Angelus. Dave Funston, one of our animators did a fantastic job of rendering the CG bars to look like they were part of the scene. If you don't think about it you'd never know it was an effect.
LONI: Set extensions. [Production designer] Stuart [Blatt] builds the bottom and we do the top.

IT SEEMS THAT, BY AND LARGE, VISUAL EFFECTS HAVE BECOME VERY CARTOONY, BUT ZOIC HAS MANAGED TO AVOID THAT. IS REALISM AN IMPORTANT FACTOR WHEN YOU APPROACH AN EFFECT?
ROCCO: Definitely. If you don't base an effect on realism, people tend to see right through it. When a character turns to dust after being staked, if the dust particles and skeleton don't behave [as physics would

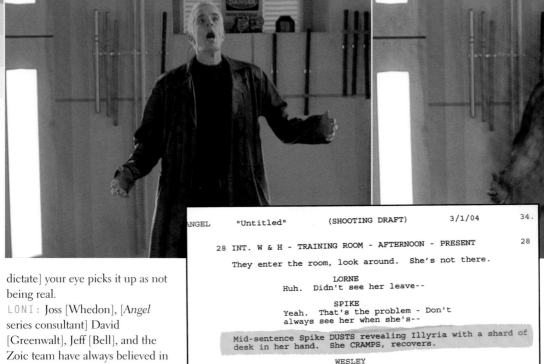

```
ANGEL     "Untitled"        (SHOOTING DRAFT)        3/1/04      34.

28  INT. W & H - TRAINING ROOM - AFTERNOON - PRESENT        28
       They enter the room, look around.  She's not there.
                           LORNE
          Huh.  Didn't see her leave--
                           SPIKE
          Yeah.  That's the problem - Don't
          always see her when she's--
       Mid-sentence Spike DUSTS revealing Illyria with a shard of
       desk in her hand.  She CRAMPS, recovers.
                           WESLEY
          Illyria--
       Angel rushes at her--
```

dictate] your eye picks it up as not being real.

LONI: Joss [Whedon], [*Angel* series consultant] David [Greenwalt], Jeff [Bell], and the Zoic team have always believed in the less-is-more factor. We also like to come up with a legitimacy and realism in the story for what happens on the effects side.

I THINK THAT THIS IS ILLUS-TRATED BY, WHAT LOOKS TO BE, A VERY SIMPLE SHOT AT THE END OF EPISODE 15, WHEN FRED'S EYE FREEZES OVER. HOW WAS THIS EFFECT ACHIEVED, AND IS IT ALSO IMPORTANT TO KEEP EFFECTS SUBTLE LIKE THIS?

ROCCO: There are a lot of questions we ask ourselves when we create these effects. Some are answered by doing a lot of research, the rest we kind of just make up. For this shot,

we had to ask ourselves: what does ice look like when it is forming? The crystallization patterns. How do we recreate that digitally? The answer was we had to create a fractal pattern in Maya [a computer graphics software] that mimicked the effect. Rachel Keyte did a great job of matching the CG to what real life looks like. We also had to take into consideration things like what would the specular highlight on the wet eye be versus the frozen digital eye? How would that change in reality? Ice gets duller and therefore the gleam in her eye would soften. For this effect a huge consideration

was how close we wer the actual actor. The you get to a human be the more difficult it becomes to trick the audience into believin the CG is real.

SPEAKING OF FRED/ILLYRIA, TELL US ABO THE EFFECT IN EPISODE 16 HER COSTUME MATERIALIZES. APPEARED TO BE A VERY COMPLICATED EFFECT.

ROCCO: Yes it was. We started with tw separate passes shot on film, one of Fre naked and the second of Illyria in full c tume. Next came the full body scan of Acker] as the Illyria character. The sca ated a digital representation of the char for us to begin working with. Next the was textured with the colors of the Illyr costume. Once the plates arrived, both

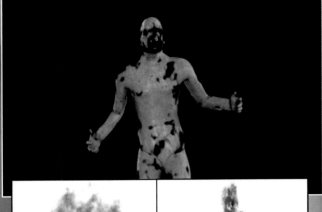

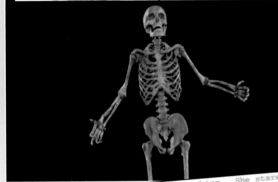

He buries his face in her neck, succumbing. She stares out into nothing, sees nothing. Ceases.

                    WESLEY
            Please... please...

A moment more, holding her, and he realizes that she is dead. He remains motionless, wrapped in her.

There is a pause.

EXTREME CLOSE ON: HER EYE. Open, dead. A blue frost suddenly, cracklingly covers the whole eyeball.

She bucks like a greenbroke horse, throws him off in the power of it, thrashing and twitching on the ground for a few moments -- he reaches for her --

ANGLE: She rises into an empty frame, all the fear gone from her face. Her new face.   CONTINU[

camera and the character need to be tracked [tracking is a way to create a digital version of not only the live action camera but also objects in the scene]. For this shot, the moving camera added a little bit of complexity to the shot. Next came creating a series of transition elements that could be applied to the digital version of the character. Much like the eye effect in Episode 15, the design of the Illyria effects all had to revolve around ice and freezing. One of our animators, Seth Hall, created a series of elements of ice forming and freezing all across Fred's digital body. These were layered together along with the digital version of Illyria to create the effect for both of the shots.

LONI: Our team loved designing this "Venom-esque" shot.

YOU HAVE ALSO BEEN CALLED UPON TO CREATE A FEW REALLY BEAUTI-FUL DIGITAL MATTES IN THE LAST FEW EPISODES OF SEASON FIVE, SPECIFICALLY THE DEEPER WELL, AND ILLYRIA'S TEMPLE, HOW ARE THESE CREATED?

ROCCO: The Deeper Well was actually a CG environment created by the masterful hand of our CG supervisor Michael Leone. All of the upper cave, bridge and actors were shot on green screen with tracking markers scattered within the CG sections of the shot. Once the plates arrived, Mike tracked the shot. It sounds a lot harder than it actually is. After generating the digital camera came the task of modeling and texturing each of the stacks of coffins that make up the columns in the infinite well along with the cavernous walls. The whole look and feel of the unearthly light was a challenge because realistically the well should get darker as it gets deeper. Joss wanted not only the environment to look dark and cavernous but be illuminated from below. This was not an easy task, but one that turned out to be a highlight visual effect for the show.

Illyria's decimated temple was great because we got the chance to hire one of the great matte painters in our industry Rocco Gioffre. Based on drawings from the Art

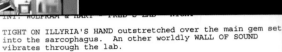

Department, he was able to create an amazing painted wasteland of a once-powerful goddess now fallen into collapse and decay. The film plates were shot with a wide lens with the actors against green screen. We intentionally shot a wider shot than what was going to be used to add a post move to the plate and the matte painting. The result allowed us to reveal the aftermath as the shot progressed.

WHAT OTHER EFFECTS OVER THIS LAST SEASON STICK OUT IN YOUR MIND AS MEMORABLE, OR THAT WERE JUST A PAIN TO GET RIGHT?

LONI: Spike's return [in Episode One]!
ROCCO: That was a treat. It was a chance to not only bring back the dead but a character you liked. Having killed him off in *Buffy* it was fitting we would have to do it in reverse. Pavayne's effects from "Hell Bound" [Episode Four] were fun. The inky abyss, the materialisation effects, the machine explosion… these were all fun effects. The destruction of Los Angeles. Who wouldn't love to destroy L.A. in a fiery blaze? And, of course, the "Smile Time" puppet effects. We got to vamp a puppet. Very cool.
LONI: And Spike's bloody stumps.

IN RETROSPECT, LOOKING OVER ALL FIVE YEARS OF ANGEL, ARE THERE ANY EFFECTS THAT YOU ARE PARTICULARLY PROUD OF, OR STAND OUT IN YOUR MIND AS REALLY MEMORABLE?

ROCCO: Everything from the last two years is memorable, because I worked on them.
LONI: We really liked the "Slucks" [in episode 19 of Season Three], and Connor's digital stunt work in 20 [of the same season].

THANKS VERY MUCH, GUYS!

A FINE NECROMANCER

W R I T T E N   B Y   T A R A   D I L U L L O

killed, fall off horses and have glorious death scenes and I got some of that on *Angel*. Hainsley was a pretty bad guy and I *really* liked it," he chuckles.

As Magnus Hainsley, Victor was a tricky first adversary for Angel and his new ghostly sidekick, Spike.

Victor remembers it was interesting not only for him to get accustomed to the set, but also to watch his fellow leads, David Boreanaz and James Marsters, do the same with one another. "They work very differently and [James] was worried if he was going to be able to put himself in the *Angel* culture having come from *Buffy*. I found *Angel* to be a very friendly set, with a very nice crew and cast," he offers.

Victor says the staff were key in helping him find the core of Magnus Hainsley. "The thing [the producers] really knew about was what a necromancer was. I knew the word loosely but they knew their stuff. They were able to lay out the history of necromancy and what a necromancer does. Also the show's 'bible' was very useful to me in understanding Angel's arc and who he was at the moment.

"They wanted him to be more overtly, demonically evil than my choices," he continues. "But I had admired Anthony Hopkins as Hannibal Lector and he is an example of a bad guy in great control, and it seemed to me Hainsley went that way. Once they made it clear to

me who the man was, they didn't interfere with me in how I presented him. There was also a lot of support both from James and David and the stuntmen around for the fight scenes."

Victor loved the climatctic battle between Hainsley and Angel: "While I did have a stunt double, they taught me how to fight and I did [the stunts] all myself. It was the *best* fun! Now some of the things, like when I kick, I can't get my foot above my head so the double did that, but I did everything else," he chuckles. "It was wonderful."

While Hainsley ultimately gets a big dose of *Angel*-style justice, Victor hopes the role lingers long after his brief appearance as it has happened on so many other shows. "I still get recognized for my one-time appearances on *Seinfeld*, *Saved By the Bell: The College Years*, and *The Wonder Years*," he shares. "I'm hoping the same happens for *Angel*. It was a neat experience for me."

W ith his gravelly voice and working man appearance, Victor Raider-Wexler has spent the bulk of his career playing characters that colorfully accentuate the edges of a story. The Ohio native worked for years doing New York theater, before finally transitioning to the West Coast 25 years ago. Since then, Victor has been making his mark as a character actor, amassing over 100 film, television and voice-work roles on his resume. Yet with all that to choose from, he still regards his turn as the necromancer, Magnus Hainsley in "Just Rewards," as one of his most fun roles. "I really, really liked shooting it," Victor enthuses. "Mostly because having spent so many years on stage, I'm not as comfortable in film and television as I am on stage. There have been a few exceptions, where I thought something was great and this was one of them. It was just fun. When I was a kid, that's always what I wanted to do – get

"I had admired Anthony Hopkins as Hannibal Lector and he is an example of a bad guy in great control, and it seemed to me Magnus Hainsley went that way."

Jas PLAYER

As an actor, Gina Torres has displayed many different facets in her genre roles – from the ass-kicking heroine of *Cleopatra 2525* and the no-nonsense Zoe on *Firefly*, to the seemingly charming (but maggot-faced!) Jasmine in *Angel*'s fourth season. Paul Simpson caught up with her during the final week of shooting on *Serenity*, the first movie featuring the characters from the short-lived *Firefly* series...

**ANGEL MAGAZINE: What's the filming on *Serenity* been like?
GINA TORRES:** It's been wonderful. It's been really quite extraordinary. It's been great fun working with everybody again – we all came back. Joss wrote a brilliant story. Fans of the show will not be disappointed, and people who have not yet discovered the show will not be alienated. It pretty much covers all bases. I was actually amazed that he could do it – it took him a while, but I read the script, and I couldn't believe that he had done it. He did a beautiful job of walking that tightrope, and I think that if people who did not discover the television show come and see the feature, they will go out and buy the DVDs to spend more time with these people.

In a sense, this is the third introduction for the characters, since Joss had to create a second pilot for *Firefly* with "The Train Job" anyway...
Yes, unfortunately Fox, the network, did not believe that the pilot was flashy enough and did not contain the elements that would grab an audience straight away. They were really on the fence about picking us up as a series at all having viewed the completed pilot, because they didn't understand it. It wasn't what they had in mind when they thought of science fiction – a bunch of good-looking people running around. We weren't all sleeping with each other! They were trying to figure out how they could sell this, and they just didn't know. So Tim Minear and Joss Whedon got together over a weekend and wrote "The Train Job" and hoped that they had inundated it with enough of the elements that Fox were looking for to jump-start this television show – and upon reading that script, Fox went ahead and picked up the show.

Did you think that Joss would be able to bring *Firefly* back?
I know that he fought very hard to get the series moved to another network. He met with quite a few different networks, and at one point, he said, 'I'm not done with these characters, and if I can figure out a way to present it as a low budget feature, that's what I'm going to do'. I don't think that realisation came until perhaps a good seven months after the show was cancelled, and we all

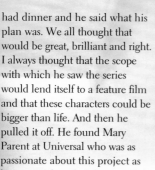

had dinner and he said what his plan was. We all thought that would be great, brilliant and right. I always thought that the scope with which he saw the series would lend itself to a feature film and that these characters could be bigger than life. And then he pulled it off. He found Mary Parent at Universal who was as passionate about this project as he was, and made it happen. I think we were all relieved – we felt like it was an interrupted haven. We had all started to really reach and hit our stride as a cast, as a writing team. It was all really starting to gel. You can see from the episodes that it just got better and more interesting. It was great to revisit, and put a bow on it. That was more than any of us expected, and we were more than willing and happy and joyful to come back.

COULD THERE BE FURTHER ADVENTURES AFTER THIS?
Oh yes. There's room for one more caper! One more heist!

WHAT WAS THE ATTRACTION OF THE PART? YOU'VE DONE A NUMBER OF ROLES WITHIN THE GENRE...
Isn't that odd? It was not my intention. I've often felt that I am the Alan Rickman character from *Galaxy Quest*. 'I've done theater – how did this happen?' I was actually quite done with my time in the genre, and my agent called with the outline of the pilot with character descriptions. She said it was Joss Whedon, and I said I don't care, I don't want to do this any more. I wanted to go back and do other things, closer to what I was trained to do. She said, 'I think you should

read this'. It was about eight pages long, and I read the character description of this woman, who was engaged in these very complicated relationships. She had a husband, and she was second-in-command to a captain that she was undyingly devoted to, and committed to, but there was no sexual aspect to it. Mal and Zoe understood each other in a way that Zoe and Wash could never understand each other and the reverse was also true. The human aspect of that, and the emotional challenges of that was what ultimately sold me. Then I thought, 'okay, what else is going on in this world?' It was so unlike anything else I had ever envisioned or read, that it kept me turning the page, and finally at the very end of the synopsis was a sentence that simply read, 'In this future, there are no aliens or mutants...' I thought, okay, that's it. It's us. It's human people, it's survival at a basic level. I thought that was great. I met with Joss and read with him and the rest is history. I think he said that he thought I was his Zoe when I walked in the room, and that makes me happy!

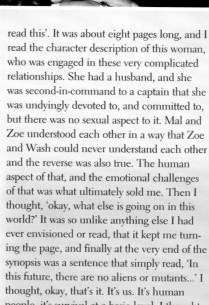

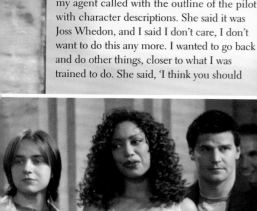

GINA TORRES
SELECTED CREDITS

 TV

24 (2004) – JULIA MILLIKEN
C.S.I. (2004) – WARDEN
THE GUARDIAN (2003) – SADIE
ANGEL (2003) – JASMINE
THE AGENCY (2003)
FIREFLY (2002) – ZOE WARREN
ANY DAY NOW (2002) – STACY TRENTON
ALIAS (2001) – ANNA ESPINOSA
CLEOPATRA 2525 (2000) – HELEN
HERCULES (1999) – NEBULA
ENCORE! ENCORE! (1998) – OPERA PATRON
LA FEMME NIKITA: "OPEN HEART" (1998) – JENNA VOGLER
XENA: "KING OF ASSASSINS" (1997): CLEOPATRA

PROFILER: "FTX: FIELD TRAINING EXERCISE" (1997) – MICHELLE BRUBAKER
NYPD BLUE: "E.R." (1995) – DOMINICAN WOMAN
LAW & ORDER: "PURPLE HEART" & "SKIN DEEP" (1995 & 1992) – CHARLENE & LAURA ELKIN

 FILM & TV-MOVIES

FIREFLY: SERENITY (2005) – ZOE WARREN
HAIR SHOW (2004) – MARCELLA
MATRIX REVOLUTIONS/RELOADED (2003) – CAS
THE HARRY LEE PROJECT (2003) – VICKI LEE
THE UNDERWORLD (1997)
THE SUBSTANCE OF FIRE (1996) – MAITRE D'
DARK ANGEL (1996) – LAMAYNE
BED OF ROSES (1996) – FRANCINE
M.A.N.T.I.S. (1997)

HOW LONG WAS THERE BETWEEN FINISHING ON *FIREFLY* AND STARTING ON *ANGEL*?

A couple of months. *Firefly* was 'Merry Christmas, you're canceled' and I think I got the call for Jasmine around March.

HOW WAS JASMINE PRESENTED TO YOU?

They made me an offer I couldn't refuse. It was very funny. I started getting these calls; Jeff Bell, one of the head writers on *Angel*, called me directly, and I think I also spoke with Tim Minear as well. Part of this was fueled because Tim wrote a few of the episodes on *Firefly*, and there was one episode in particular, "The Message", where it looked like Mal and Zoe might have had a date. We're at a carnival, picking stuff up. I had always wanted one scene where you see Zoe just completely femmed out, with a dress or a skirt, and her hair down. Just not how you're used to seeing her – it could happen, on a day off. It would shock the audience – oh wow, there really is a woman in there! They fitted me with a skirt and a really beautiful top, and I showed up on set – and both Tim and Joss went, 'We can't do it. It isn't going to work – you and Mal picking up this coffin with you in a skirt. Sorry, you're beautiful...' so they brought out my regular costume, and I pouted for a few minutes for their benefit.

So when they called me about Jasmine, they pitched her as having all the attributes that we weren't allowed to show with Zoe! 'She has great, sexy clothes, her hair is always down. She speaks several languages, we might get you to sing a song, and she's worshipped by the world. She has all these acolytes...' So when I show up for my first day at work, and the cast kneels before me, I thought, 'Alright, we're even!' Of course she ends up being evil, but how delicious for me!

WHAT DID YOU THINK OF HER AS A CHARACTER?

What was wonderful about playing Jasmine – and when you play anybody you have to firmly believe what your goal is, what your reason for being is – was that she believed with every fibre of her being that she was doing the best thing for the world. Everybody was enamored and happy and loving each other and living together – okay, so people get eaten along the way... What a commentary on world events! We sacrifice our young every day for the sake of peace – this is what we have to do.

I thought her fate was hilarious. It's like the classic Bill Cosby joke – 'I'm your father, I brought you into this world, I can take you out!' A fist through the head... well alright. The jig was up, she really had nowhere to go after that, it all sort of went wrong. It was fine!

YOU'VE DONE A LOT OF ATHLETIC ROLES – IS THAT SOMETHING YOU ENJOY OR IS IT SOMETHING THAT COMES WITH THE TERRITORY?

It certainly comes with the territory. There is a therapeutic aspect to it, pummeling people and what-not. It's fun. When you reach the end of a physical scene like that, whether it's a fight or running down the hallways, there's a great sense of accomplishment. Nobody got hurt. There's just as much acting involved in a fight sequence because you have to sell those punches, and really make people believe that there's damage being done. That's challenging because you're really trying not to hurt anybody, and you're trying not to make a whole lot of contact. It's tricky, so I take quite a bit of pride in the fact that I can do it, and do it well, but it is exhausting.

How did this happen? How did I arrive at this place where people have come to know me as this strong action chick? It's very odd but it's fun, and liberating. Most importantly, it gives young women a sense of strength and emancipation, and it speaks to the possibility of a life outside of their own. I think that's what makes active women, physical women, so attractive to the world. It's a fantasy to some degree. Who doesn't want to witness that kind of strength?

WILL YOU LOOK FOR SOMETHING MARKEDLY DIFFERENT ONCE *SERENITY* IS OVER?

Always. Always. I'm an actor so I look for things that I haven't done yet. I look for ways in which I can grow and hone my craft. Every situation is a learning experience and so that's what I look to do. I look to go back on the stage, I would love to do a musical again. I would love to play a mother, somebody's wife – someone that doesn't carry a gun! All these things. There's a lot to do out there. I think part of the reason why I've been cast in the roles that I have been is my physicality – I'm quite tall and quite strong, so they go, 'Okay, Gina looks like she can kick some butt, so let's put her in this role.' But I've always tried to play these women with many layers so you know that there's a lot more going on in there than just getting the bad guy, and I hope that that comes through. ❧

BEAST WARS!

He's one of the nastiest enemies to ever crop up in the *Angel*-verse - he's big, he's bad, he's The Beast! Jenny Lynn discusses the making of a monster with Jeffrey Bell and the guys at Almost Human.

O ne of this season's darkest villains on *Angel*, very aptly named the Big Bad, from conception to life, took less than two months. Sometime around the shooting of episodes three and four, *Angel*'s co-executive producer Jeffrey Bell approached the make-up effects team about creating the monster –

also known as The Beast – that would make its first appearance in episode seven, "Apocalypse, Nowish."

Robert Hall and his make-up effects shop Almost Human have created many memorable creatures in recent episodes of *Angel* and *Buffy the Vampire Slayer*, among them Sweet from the *Buffy* episode "Once More, With Feeling" and Skip from *Angel*'s "That Vision Thing." This time, Jeffrey asked them to top them all. "We didn't want it to look like any other demon we've ever had or had been out there," Jeffrey explained, "and between this and *Buffy*, there've been a lot of them."

Though there were merely three episodes left to shoot before the appearance of the Big Bad, Robert considered it ample time. "Jeff Bell gave me a nice heads-up, which is something we don't get a lot of the time. We normally have a week and a half from the time we hear about something to the time it has to be on set."

Ideas floated back and forth between the writing team and the make-up FX group, and from those, they were able to narrow down the aspects they wanted this creature to exhibit. As Jeffrey explains, "we thought it should be a very traditional, demonic character. There should be a diabolic, devilish aspect to him. We thought it had to be as smart as anyone Angel had met, and so we felt his face should be intelligent and regal and wise. And we talked a lot about what these qualities look like. We've done more designs with this guy than we've ever had for anything." Even before an actor was cast to play the Big Bad, Almost Human had already gone through eight or nine designs with the producers. However, as Robert relates, these designs never strayed far from the original mandate nor varied too much at the different stages. All the elements were variations on the same idea, tweaked until the creative powers at *Angel* were satisfied.

One of the biggest projects was to get the horns just right. "We started drawing and said, 'Okay, these are too much like antlers, too much like antennae, these are too goat-like, these are too big, too small,'" recalls Jeffrey. With all the specifics given to the horns and every other part of the body, Robert and his team decided to create a clay model of the Big Bad, called a maquette, to facilitate the creative process. "The three-dimensional maquette is basically just to give everyone involved an idea of what it's going to look like 360 degrees around." At close to a foot tall, the maquette was green and stood on a spindle-like device that let the make-up FX people rotate it and allowed the viewer to see it from every angle.

Every little moment for Robert Hall and his team was precious, and they worked as quickly as they could. So it was a surprise to learn that everything came to a halt once the designs were approved. They needed to wait for the actor to be cast. "What a lot of people may not know is that our hands are completely tied until they cast someone and send him to us. Every square inch of that person, we have to mold – their hands, their body, their feet… their teeth, their head. These appliances fit them specifically and they're custom built for them. So until we have those molds of their head or whatnot to work with, we can't do anything."

Fortunately, *Angel* casting directors Barbara Stordahl and Angela Terry found the search for the Big Bad a relatively quick process. "We were actually thinking that it could be a few sessions, like we had with casting Alexa Davalos (**Gwen – Ed**)," says Angela. Barbara illustrates, "If they want just a female who's 20-something, there are so many different ways you can go." The casting team was given specifics to work with to limit their search. "They wanted someone as tall as possible," says Barbara, "and kind of old-world." Terry

notes, "We were looking for men who had a classical-sounding voice, a theatrically-trained voice."

Overall, the casting department looked at over 100 men, and nearly 60 came in to audition. They eventually went with Czech-born actor Vladimir Kulich, who had not only the body-type, but also a body of work (*The 13th Warrior, The X-Files*) that gave the cast-

ing directors notice. "When we read him, it was like, 'Oh, my God, that's it,'" recalls Barbara.

With the role cast, Almost Human could get back to work again. Mold-makers and sculptors worked arduously over a weekend to get casts of Vladimir's head, body, hands and feet. As is typical to making a body suit, Vladimir wore a spandex suit and was positioned to stand still for 20-30 minutes. A mold of the actor's entire body was made in two pieces – front and back – out of plaster bandages. A fiberglass core was tapped out of the plaster body mold. From there, a life-sized version of the maquette design was sculpted in clay over the fiberglass core.

The producers made further changes after seeing the life-sized rendition. "We said, 'we think this thing is made of magma. It's from the earth,'" says Jeffrey. "In the big movie version of this, in his molten cracks, you would see molten lava running through there." The producers were looking for a proper texture that wasn't so flaky that they looked like scales, and not too rough like armor.

After final approval of the clay sculpture, a mold was made of that. From this mold of the sculpture and the mold of the actor's body, Almost Human was able to make a full, latex body suit. The same process was done to create a demon suit for the stuntman, who was to double Vladimir.

Finally on set, Robert Hall brought both stunt and 'hero' (worn by Vladimir) suits in all their various parts: the hands, feet, horns, head (also called the cowl), and face pieces. It took a total of four hours to make-up the actor on days the beast appeared before the cameras.

All in all, everybody was happy with how the Big Bad came to being. The casting directors gleam, "It's exactly how you would picture the devil if you were ever to meet the devil. He's such a good opponent for [Angel] because overall this season, [Angel's] come up against a lot of big bads, and this is like the ultimate big bad." ✛

Photos © Almost Human

The make-up ladies dab powder on Alexa Davalos (Gwen). David Boreanaz puts Fred's glasses on, trying to make J. August Richards laugh. Alexis Denisof sits on the couch reading the paper. The *Angel* cast is between camera set-ups, and as director of photography Ross Berryman tells it, there will be at least 29 more today. No wonder the actors are trying to amuse themselves.

However humdrum this scene may look to a visitor, episode nine, "Long Day's Journey," is certainly not that. The electric femme fatale Gwen returns, the Big Bad continues to wreak havoc, and well, let's put it this way, the episode ends with the sentence, "We need Angelus." When have they ever *needed* Angelus?!?!

Executive story editor Mere Smith, who wrote this season's "Ground State," which introduced Gwen, is the writer of this episode. "We wanted to bring another woman in and we wanted her to be cool," Mere reveals. "The archetype we were going for was Catwoman – slick, sleek, sexy."

The idea of Gwen was in the works since the end of Season Three. Given that, Mere was able to spend her summer hiatus trying to come up with the various characteristics that would identify Gwen. "We came up with 'Electro Girl,'" says Mere. "Then, it was up to me to decide how that manifested itself. With her bending the lasers, her being able to tap into surveillance cameras… they evolved out of what the story needed." Aside from her extraordinary powers, Gwen's personality was derived from Mere's love of old-fashioned, fast-talking, Howard Hawks' films. "I wanted this woman to be sharp and witty and clever," she reveals.

Report by Jenny Lynn

IT'S
THE
EN

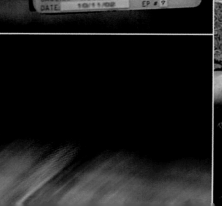

D OF L.A.
AS WE KNOW IT!

THE BEAST IS DESTROYING L.A. AND THE ANGEL INVESTIGATIONS TEAM ARE PRETTY MUCH DESTROYING EACH OTHER — Y'KNOW, IT'S A SCARY TIME TO BE AROUND THE ANGEL GANG. HOWEVER, OUR REPORTER BRAVELY VENTURED ON SET TO GET THE BEHIND-THE-SCENES LOWDOWN ON

"Long Day's Journey" also gave the art department an opportunity to create what the script calls "Gwen's Fabulous Swank Pad." "The idea was, here's this run-down tenement or warehouse, but it's really stately Wayne Manor [inside]," production designer Stuart Blatt describes. "Gwen opens the door into this fabulous wood-trimmed, marble-floored, columned, chandelier, old-money kind of a lair." Based on the script, Stuart decided that Batman's Wayne Manor would be a fitting template for what Gwen's apartment should be like.

Stuart, along with set designer Andrew Reeder and assistant art director Leonard Harman, carefully selected which aspects would best bring the script descriptions to life. To that end, they decided that the space would not have windows because it was a top-secret location. The rooms were also designed to be unusually tall so one would feel enveloped in the secret space. Aside from those practical considerations, "There's dark wood, dark marble floors and dark red on the walls because red is kind of a signature color of Gwen's," says Stuart.

On this particular day, only the walls of Gwen's apartment are up, but Stuart describes how the walls will be textured to add richness to the general feel of the place. Construction coordinator Ted Wilson and paint foreman Steve Bishop work very quickly to erect this grand set, which might not be used again after this episode. Even so, every detail undergoes the scrutiny of set decorator Sandy Struth to make sure the apartment looks like a place Gwen would inhabit. Stuart notes, however, that no matter how great the sets look, their primary purpose is to further the story. "We could make sets that look great all day long, but if they don't help the story along, and if the crew can't shoot the scene there, then it's just a nice photograph."

The production designer's comment is best illustrated by what's happening over at Connor's Place. The stunt crew, led by stunt coordinator Mike Massa, spends all morning rehearsing and rigging Connor's residence at a warehouse belonging to the fictional Southern California Museum of Natural History. All of the props that make it Connor's (and Cordelia's) are pushed to the side. Taxidermy animals (yes, they are real) are on the floor. The bed is moved out of the way. Two large windows are missing panes. A huge fight between Connor and the Big Bad will be shot the following day, which means the room is busy with activity and there is much deliberation on what is needed.

Mike approaches Stuart about obtaining more breakaway crates than were budgeted for the episode. "The Big Bad – you can hit him, but he can't hit us," says Mike. He's referring to the overwhelming strength of the Big Bad, where The Beast can crush an opponent with one blow. Therefore, Angel and his team need to dodge his blows or they'd "be toast." "What could we do besides him always missing us that would be cool? What if he just missed us and hit a crate, so you know how massive his power still is?" Mike explains later that this was a last-minute idea that ended up not happening.

With that said, there is still plenty of action in this show, due in no small part to the larger-than-life Big Bad. Veteran *Angel* director Terrence O'Hara was working on other projects after directing this season's opener and hadn't caught up to the storyline until prepping for episode nine. Just to familiarize himself with the Big Bad, Terrence watched the fight sequence in episode seven, "Apocalypse, Nowish." "Holy cow! You can't defeat it!" was Terrence's first reaction. "Our guys are gonna fight this guy? We gotta find another way!" he laughs. "They've shot it. They've stabbed it. They've done everything possible, so it affected how all of our action was staged and what went on with the story.

As Mike Massa points out, because of the nature of the Big Bad's incredible strength, it gave Mike and his stunt team something different to work with. "We got to experiment with some wire gags. A lot of the stuff that we did with Connor was new. You know, throwing him over the monster," says Mike. Mere had written some comic book type moves in the script and Mike, in turn, added wired kicks and throws. Adds Terrence, "I think we'll have a nice bit at the beginning of Act Four, where Connor tries to fight [the Big Bad] but gets thrown around like a rag doll."

The biggest anticipated stunt occurs at the end of the week on a location in Downtown Los Angeles. This is an exterior shot of Connor's place and calls for a stuntman to take a free fall out of a seven-story window. Strangely enough, Connor's regular stunt double, Chris Daniels, happened to take another assignment on a feature film, so Mike Massa ended up calling on stuntman Andy Shehee.

Meanwhile on terra firma, crewmembers eagerly await in anticipation. Before long, first assistant director Ian Woolf announces over a megaphone that he will do a three count backwards to signal the fall. "Three! Two! One! Action!" Andy bursts through the window and flies through the air surrounded by window shards going down with him. He smacks onto the bag and everybody whoops and applauses. When he emerges, he bounces down from the bag and hugs the director. Terrence O'Hara recalls later, "[Andy] was pumped after that. He was like, 'Wow! Wow!' His heart was probably beating about 200 beats per second. He liked it and that guy used to be a high diver."

What the stunt team is accomplishing on *Angel* is a huge feat. We all know how spectacular it looks on the screen, but the pace in which they prepare and choreograph – all the while making it safe – is astounding. "We're really doing feature [film] stuff on this show," comments Mike Massa. "I've talked to the

and jibes. Charisma Carpenter approaches Mere Smith before the shot where Cordelia and Gwen first meet. And both Charisma and Mere concur that Cordelia should try to appear reserved, even though her feelings may be stewing underneath.

The character drama plays out in several large populated scenes. "There are so many scenes with so many people," says Terrence O'Hara. Just the hotel lobby scenes take an entire day of filming. All of this is not lost on Mere, however. "Because I knew we were going to have so many scenes where there are eight people talking," says Mere, "you've got to have a different personality show up." From this need, Mere created the character of Manny.

"When I typed up a beat sheet for [producer Kelly A. Manners], I just put Manny as 'Nebbishy Man,'" Mere recalls. "As I got into the story, I was like, 'Okay, well we've got Gwen and she's all sexy and hot and we've got all this angst and pain going through all

{ ANGEL:
FROM HERE ON OUT, WE'RE ON THE OFFENSIVE. WE'RE GONNA FIND THIS THING'S WEAKNESSES, GO IN PREPARED, AND FIGHT SMART.
(THEN)
IT'S TIME TO TAKE THE BEAST DOWN. }

Mike and Andy get together earlier in the day to take a run-through, which means placing the 20x30 feet airbag in location where Andy is comfortable having it. Also, seeing that the bottom of the windowsill is two feet above the floor, Mike adds a 4x8 steel deck on which Andy can stand to eliminate any risk of tripping on the leap out. Mike says, "I told him, 'Look, you got to have a lot of energy coming out the window because you're going to have some resistance. So do it like you're going to run out the window.'" The special effects team then puts in candy glass and scores it so the window would shatter upon impact.

Mid-morning on a Friday, the *Angel* crew congregates at a safe distance away from the airbag. Four cameras are set up at different angles (including one for slow-motion) so that the stunt only needs to be done once. Andy Shehee dons a wig to look more Connor-esque. He checks all four sides of the airbag before he goes into and up the building.

producer Kelly and said, 'Look at the stuff we're doing! Normally, shows get six to eight weeks to practice what we're doing in a couple days.'"

The action in "Long Day's Journey" isn't limited to the fight sequences. "I think the show is going to play very well, just simply because of the drama," says Terrence O'Hara. Surprisingly, the director mentions the lack of physical action in the show's first two acts as being a challenge for him. The drama lies in the interpersonal relationships among the characters and Terrence's task is to keep the dramatic action interesting and flowing.

Similarly, Mere Smith also cites the complexity in setting up the character dynamics in the script. "For the first draft of episode nine, Cordy and Gwen were a lot more overtly catty. Joss [Whedon] basically made a very good point, which was, I had nowhere to go," she recalls. Thus, in the shooting draft, the tension between the women starts as digs

of our characters. I figured, why not create a character who's just a guy, and a funny guy too?" Though creator Joss Whedon suggested that the humor be toned down, Manny is still pleasantly offbeat. "Manny was terrific. Jack Kehler [who plays Manny] is a terrific actor, very funny," adds Terrence O'Hara.

Manny was not solely created for comic relief. Mere had a larger goal in trying to create a story that would move the Big Bad arc forward. "We've proven how strong The Beast is, we've proven that he's evil. Now, we have to prove how smart and how stealthy he is," explains Mere. "This episode was about showing those qualities of the Big Bad rather than just his brute strength."

The writing team worked together to produce a story that would exemplify the Big Bad's intellect by showing he was capable of carefully calculated strategy. "We constructed a look-door mystery of Manny and the vault," tells Mere. Angel and his friends discover that

SCRIPT

{
CORDELIA
So... (LONG AWKWARD PAUSE)
ALL THIS TIME ALONE TOGETHER.
COULD BE GOOD FOR US. (BEAT)
MAYBE WE SHOULD TALK.
ANGEL
(BEAT) MAYBE WE SHOULDN'T.
}

built and then moved to the Stocker Oil Fields in Los Angeles. This set is used for the scene in which Angel and Gwen first encounter Manny. "In the time frame we have now, we'd like to make the cave out of foam because it's lightweight and more sculptural. We can carve them and make them into many more accommodating shapes for us." However, the director and writers want to use torches in the cave, which is forbidden by law on a set made out of foam. "If we did one out of plaster, or if we did one out of cement, it takes a lot longer and we can't make it transportable," says Stuart. Eventually, on the day of the shoot (Halloween to be precise) everyone is placated. The set is made out of foam and the actors use candles instead of torches.

Back on set, Ross Berryman and his team are getting all the camera angles to cover the seven-person conversation in the hotel lobby. Several takes are done: Sometimes a shot needs to be re-framed, sometimes an actor's position is moved, and sometimes an actor has a different suggestion. Through it all, it looks like the actors are having a blast as they share laughs between takes. Their camaraderie is probably what makes this ensemble look so good and work so well onscreen. "There are always good surprises on this

the Big Bad is after seemingly ordinary citizens, Manny among them, who turn out to be the Five Totems or the Ra'Tet. In destroying these five, The Beast blocks out the sun so that creatures of the night can rule the Earth. To prevent this disastrous deed, the gang tries to keep Manny safe, but is unsuccessful. Needless to say, the gang is duped.

"Most of the mythology in episode nine is based on some version of Egyptian myth," explains Mere, though she confesses that she took liberties. "I kind of took features of Egyptian myth and wove them into a tapestry that suited my needs." Mere borrowed from the Egyptian Sun God Ra's journey across the sky. To illustrate the mythology more clearly for the audience, Mere Smith and Terrence O'Hara decided that a book prop would be useful to the audience as a visual aid. So now, Wesley shows off a book depicting the Order of the Ra'Tet.

No matter how dense this episode seems to be – the Angel/Connor/Cordelia tension, The Beast fights, Gwen and Manny – producer Kelly A. Manners considers this one a "normal" one from his budgetary standpoint.

"This actually, for me, is pretty much a standard episode. In the rankings of my job, it's one that I'd like to make over and over again because it's not breaking our backs."

The trick is to use the budget wisely. For this episode, most of the money is allotted for construction on Gwen's apartment and the cave where Angel finds one of the dead totems. Gwen's apartment is, by all means, all decked-out, but Stuart Blatt, who is also budget-conscious, ended up recycling Professor Seidel's office from the "Supersymmetry" episode as Gwen's study. On a tour of the sets, Kelly Manners' assistant Matt Partney points to several more recycled sets, mainly the hotel hallways and rooms. In fact, he mentions one fact that sounds titillating, which turns out not to be. "Cordelia's room is Angel's room," says Matt, which sounds as if he is commenting on an evolving romantic situation between Angel and Cordelia. Alas, he is not. The set merely doubles as both rooms.

Returning to the tricky balance of money, time and practicality, Stuart decides to construct a cave out of foam, as it needs to be

show, where you just see how relationships turn, and what the actors bring to it individually," shares Terrence O'Hara.

Everyone agrees that this season of *Angel* is spectacular. "I'm very happy with the storyline," says Mere Smith. "I feel like the story arc this season is the strongest one we've ever had. This year, the shows have been very, very large so we've been spending oodles and oodles of money. The trick for me is to make the very best damn *Angel*, the most exciting *Angel* we can make."

Now what about that Angelus thing? Just stay tuned; you'll want to see for yourself.

ACCESS ALL AREAS

THEY SAY MOVING PLACES IS ONE OF THE MOST STRESSFUL TIMES OF YOU LIFE — SO IMAGINE HOW STRESSFUL MOVING TO A DEMONIC LAW FIRM MUST BE! AND A NEW ABODE MEANS BRAND NEW *ANGEL* SETS! WE TAKE A GUIDED TOUR THROUGH THE NEW SETS AND DISCOVER SOME OF THE THOUGHT PROCESSES THAT WENT INTO THEIR DESIGN.

BY MATT PARTNEY

PHOTOGRAPHY BY STUART BLATT

WOLFRAM & HART
ATTORNEYS AT LAW

Welcome to the 18th floor of Los Angeles' most powerful and prolific law firm. 10,500 square feet on two levels, three elevators (one private), five offices and more than 20 other doors that go who knows where. Complete with conference room, ancient art and sweeping vistas of Los Angeles (visible through the safest necrotempered glass money can buy), this is the new Wolfram & Hart – the Season Five home of Angel and the gang.

The overall style of the new Wolfram & Hart set is best described as modern-Japanese/high-end industrial with a Californian twist. From the redwood and birch to the Japanese floral arrangements visible throughout the office, the design is set in its natural elements of wood, stone and flora. Upon entering the office commons, visitors are greeted by two monolithic, two-storey-tall concrete walls flanked by green horsetail reeds (thought to be the oldest plant in the world). It is a subtle reminder of the power and archaic age of the evil law firm. You just feel small.

Stuart Blatt, production designer for *Angel* since Season One, was charged with the task of creating the new look for the show. "I was asked to create something that would show a sense of power and a side of L.A. that we've come to expect from Wolfram & Hart, which is a kind of glitz, power and prestige, without tipping our hand as to what might be going on behind closed doors." Many local and not-so-local offices were looked to for inspiration, from ad agencies and law firms to record labels, and even the Seattle-based corporate offices of a certain global coffee shop conglomerate that begins with an 'S' and ends with a 'tarbucks.'

The natural design of the new Wolfram & Hart continues into each of the three offices, but each has its own décor and theme. Wesley's office features a subtle arts and crafts period décor that matches his apartment. Gunn's office is more modern and slick with a splashier sense of color – inspired by Gunn's new position in life this season. "He's kinda like a kid in a candy store," says Stuart, "and we are going to develop this idea that he has expensive toys, expensive hobbies and expensive tastes, whereas Wesley's more rooted in his studies and research."

Although the offices reflect the diverse tastes of their inhabitants, they share one sweeping view of L.A. toward Beverly Hills and Hollywood. That differs from the downtown

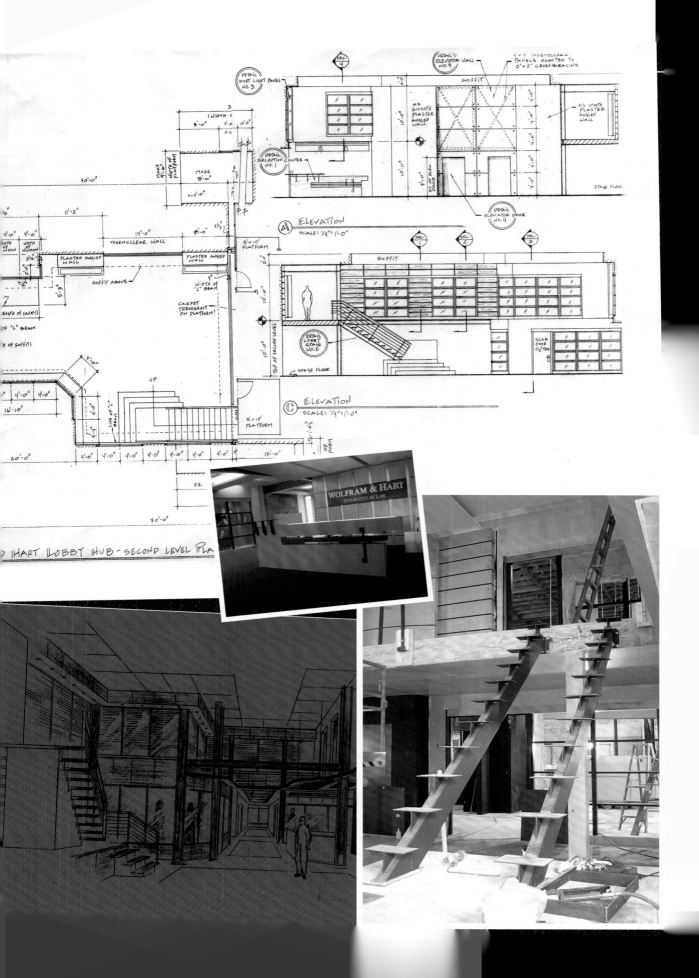

L.A. view of Angel's office. Stuart is quick to note that the two backings, also known as translights, were custom made and feature actual vistas of the L.A. area. (Ironically, during the past four seasons, backings used outside of Wolfram & Hart's offices were from cities such as Chicago, Miami and San Francisco.) "Using [these random urban/metro translights] has given Wolfram & Hart an odd, sort of everywhere-at-once, big feeling," says Stuart. "And it saved us a lot of money!"

The office commons is marked by the desk of Angel's assistant, Harmony. Beneath the Wolfram & Hart marquee, it resembles your typical corporate reception area – but what's behind the desk is pure kitsch. A keen eye may spot the ridiculously funny collection of unicorn figurines, many of which came from the Magic Box set on *Buffy*.

Moving beyond the reception area will naturally bring you to the centerpiece of the new Wolfram & Hart set: Angel's expansive and extravagant office. His office features a conference room and private elevator, which – Stuart would like fans to know – has four buttons. One goes to Angel's penthouse suite, one to his office, another to his private garage stocked with muscle cars and lastly, one goes to the sewers. "We weren't asked to have that last one in there," confides Stuart. "We did it as our own little private aside. Once in a while we try to add little things that only mean something to us." Stuart cannot wait to use that fourth button…!

One button that was addressed by the producers was the elevator call button, which has become the source of some on-set and on-screen comedy. Stuart, at the request of the producers, did not include a call button for Angel's private elevator, opting instead for an implied high-tech automatic sliding door. However, no one told David Boreanaz that before he attempted to access the elevator while filming one day. As a result, Angel can be seen nervously standing in front of his new private elevator wondering just how to open the door. It has become a bit of an on-set joke that has translated onscreen.

With hard ceilings that rise a full two feet taller than all the other offices and large, floor-to-ceiling windows (necrotempered of course), the space is dynamic and oozes power. "Angel's is more a custom-designed office," Stuart says. "[It] was set up for him by

PICTURE OF THE HYPERION HOTEL: Angel may have left it behind, but it's not forgotten.

DESK LAMP: Matches the lamps in Angel's penthouse. The *Angel* crew can easily use these lamps to light actors from off-screen.

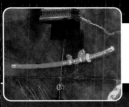

SAMURAI SWORD: From Angel's travels in Japan. "He displays weapons like this as a reminder of the violence and terror he was responsible for in the past as Angelus," says David Boreanaz.

CHINESE DRAGON: Presumed to be another piece of 'loot' collected by Angelus.

SUNSHINE AND GLARE: You'll see a lot more sun this season now thanks to the necrotempered glass that allows Angel and other vamps to enjoy the sun without bursting into flames.

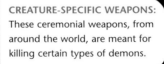

CREATURE-SPECIFIC WEAPONS: These ceremonial weapons, from around the world, are meant for killing certain types of demons.

ANGEL'S SWORD: This Celtic sword symbolizes Angel's Irish heritage and has been with him and the show since Season One.

CEREMONIAL TUSKS: These tusks are so invaluable they're pulled from the set and locked up every night!

into taking their offer."

And just where does Angel get all his cool antiquities and relics, like those perched on the slate wall behind his desk? Vampire Storage. "Vampire Storage is a place that Sandy Struth, our set decorator, has concocted, where Angel has stored all the things he's collected over his several hundred years around the world," Stuart jokes, "And we generously pull from that during the course of the season as Angel needs other artifacts and reminders from his past."

The new set features dozens of windows that allow a flow from office to office. Stuart explains: "[Series creator] Joss Whedon asked specifically to be able to do steadicam shots like those seen on *West Wing*. He liked the fact they can go from room to room, down corridors, in and out of offices and sort of explore the space on camera without having to cut away." This is evident in the Joss-directed Episode One, which features a five-minute, continuous, steadicam 'oner'.

There is one problem with a set full of windows on a show that features no fewer than three 'creatures of the night': reflection. Stuart jokes, "although the glass in Wolfram & Hart is necrotempered to cut down on harsh UV rays, it doesn't take away a vampire's reflection… or an actor's! The solution: spending extra money on customized windows that gimble, which is production-designer-speak for "windows that swivel left-to-right in order to avoid the reflections of actors and crew."

In addition to the size and flow of the office, Joss Whedon wanted to see ceilings. "Ceilings convey a sense of power and reality," says Stuart. "That's something we've always wanted to do in the art department, but we run up against the fact that we are a stunt and action-based show and there's a give and take between design and practicality." And that is where designing an office for a typical show and designing an office for *Angel* differs. Most production designers don't need to anticipate the huge fights that have come to be expected by *Angel* fans. All designs and features of the new set

LOS ANGELES AT NIGHT: A false view which looks just like downtown L.A. The flick of a switch can turn night into a bright, sunny day.

END TABLES: Actually from Angel's mansion set on *Buffy* Seasons Two and Three.

ORNATE BATTLE SHIELD: A favorite of set decorator Sandy Struth and co-executive producer Jeffrey Bell, this shield is symbolic of the many battles Angel has been involved in.

CEREMONIAL CHINESE DRAGON MASK: Another prop pulled from Angel's 'vampire storage'.

BLOOD-RED FURNITURE: An obvious color choice for a vampire. The lush red tones have been a recurring color in many of *Angel*'s sets.

STONE SLATE WALL: One of the key designs that remain from the original W&H office in the Season Four finale.

EGYPTIAN CAT STATUE: Depicts the Egyptian goddess Bast in feline form. This is just another piece from Angel's collection – apparently, he once spent time in Egypt as well!

MINERAL WATER AND BLOOD: For entertaining clients, alive or undead.

NECROTEMPERED GLASS WINDOWS: Engineered by the unlimited resources of W&H, these windows allow vampires like Angel and Harmony to work during the day without bursting into flames.

CONFERENCE TABLES: Lit from underneath for aesthetic reasons and also for quick and convenient cast lighting.

CHINESE SEAL: Borrowed from the set of another Joss Whedon show, *Firefly*.

WIDESCREEN PLASMA TV: Concealed behind this intricate monkeywood-carved screen from Thailand which depicts two guardian angel deities that are half-woman, half-animal.

BULLDOG ASHTRAY: This art deco piece was first seen in Season Two ("Are You Now or Have You Ever Been?") in the 1950s and was later kept in the Hyperion Hotel's office in the present day.

WOLFRAM & HART RECEPTION DESK: Through the window, Angel can easily see his vamp-assistant, Harmony.

LILAH'S RED OFFICE PHONE: This is the actual phone used in Lilah's office in the first four *Angel* seasons.

ANGEL'S PRIVATE ELEVATOR: Angel's route to his penthouse, personal garage, office and the LA sewer system.

HARD CEILINGS: A first for an *Angel* set. They convey a sense of power and realism.

had to accommodate the inevitable smackdown between Angel and some demon or vampire that would see walls being smashed and ceilings being cracked. "A set can be an amazing design," quips Stuart, "but if it doesn't work for the shooting of a scene, then all it is is a neat set and it doesn't serve the show."

Stuart designed the offices as realistically as possible, complete with real lighting and hard ceilings, while the office commons, or 'hub', outside the elevators features a 22-foot-high space with no ceilings. This approach may limit the magnitude of fights and wirework that can be done in the offices, but that loss is made up for by the hub. The large open space there, which is almost reminiscent of the Hyperion Hotel lobby, allows for an all-out brawl if the writers happen to call for it. Keep your eyes out this season!

Another consideration Stuart had to give to the function of the design was lighting. In order to have the ability to shoot from all angles while walking all over the set, the set had to be designed with a clever lighting solution. For all intents and purposes, the new set has a realistic lighting system. The crew can enter, flip a switch and begin shooting. Stuart worked closely with the director of photography, Ross Berryman, and construction coordinator Ted Wilson to create three different lighting scenarios, and went to great lengths to achieve them. There is a working-hours, an after-hours, and a spooky, power-outage, 'zombies-coming-to-getcha' scenario, which on this show could actually get some frequent use – remember Wolfram & Hart's zombie-filled visit by The Beast last season?

Stuart started designing the new sets during Episode 20 of Season Four. He and the producers went through four different passes on the general layout and four different models before everyone agreed on one they liked. "Some had four offices, some had a smaller hub and a raised office for Angel," he says. One model even had one large conference/meeting room the size of Angel's entire office, where the gang were to spend most of their time. Angel's office, likewise, went through four different designs as well. In fact, Angel's office in the Season Four finale is not the same as the one featured this season. Some elements, such as the slate walls and hidden plasma-screen TV console, remain. With guidance and input from Joss Whedon, co-executive producer Jeff Bell and producer Kelly Manners, Stuart had a working blueprint

just weeks before shooting began on Season Five.

Construction lasted a short three weeks, right up to the morning of the first day of shooting – a feat which seems more impressive when you consider that construction on the Hyperion Hotel, a set half the size of Wolfram & Hart, took more than five weeks. "It takes an enormous amount of coordination," reflects Stuart, "especially when you are working with a truncated construction schedule. It became controlled chaos on the last few days." In fact, construction, lighting and dressing on much of the set had still not been completed as the cast and crew filmed the first day's work in Angel's office!

Like the Hyperion, Stuart sees the new Wolfram & Hart surroundings as another character within the show: "Wolfram & Hart has come to represent an evil, big-brother-type-entity that has arms that reach far and wide." With the Senior Partners nowhere in sight, the set's mysterious surroundings become an adversarial player in the search for just why the gang was put in charge in the first place. While the Hotel was spooky and dark, the new set is bright, foreign and ambiguous. Stuart says, "the idea was that Angel and the gang were a bit like fish out of water that were thrust into this bright, corporate environment. On the surface, it will have a different look, but it has yet to be seen how that new look will translate itself on the show."

And just what's become of the gang's old home and headquarters, the Hyperion Hotel? "I'm not at liberty to say," says Stuart with a laugh and long pause. "The set itself is in a landfill, unfortunately."

"TRUST NO ONE" GOES THE OLD T.V. SAYING. WELL, TEAM ANGEL AND *ANGEL* VIEWERS ALIKE CERTAINLY WEREN'T READY TO TRUST NEW WOLFRAM & HART LIAISON EVE WHEN THEY FIRST MET UP WITH HER — AND IT LOOKS LIKE THOSE SUSPICIONS WERE WELL PLACED! ACTRESS SARAH THOMPSON DISHES THE DIRT ON EVIL EVE!

Angel might feature a male-heavy cast this season but fans were quickly introduced to a fresh-faced addition to the new Wolfram & Hart offices. Eve, the petite and appealing liaison to the Senior Partners, appeared in the premiere, "Conviction", and has since served as a lovely, albeit mysterious presence, providing key information to Angel and his team. Despite her pleasant disposition, no one in the Fang Gang trusts her, considering that her bosses are evil. It also hasn't helped that her motives have been shrouded in secrecy – until the final stunning moments of the episode "Destiny", where Eve's true colors were finally revealed along with her silent partner, Lindsey McDonald (the returning Christian Kane). It was a moment that shocked fans, as well as the actress, Sarah Thompson, who plays her. "I didn't know what the new season was going to hold," she shares. "I was actually going on face value up until we actually shot that scene, so it was so much fun to finally figure out what is going on with her."

A native of the Los Angeles area, Sarah realized her

BY
TARA DiLULLO

Eve of Destru

ct ion!

calling early. "Since I was a little girl, I just knew I was going to be an actress even before I'd ever acted in a school play. I had this feeling, knowing that was what I was meant to do." Despite being painfully shy, she auditioned for a part in a stage production of *The Music Man* when she was 10. "I got in the chorus and that started it all. When I got on stage, I was a different person and I kept doing school plays and musicals until I did it professionally." She moved with her family to New York City when she was in high school, "so I was exposed to some amazing acting teachers and I studied on my own. I got an agent and started doing commercials."

After high school, she attended Barnard College at Columbia University for a year and a half until she got her big break. "My plan was to finish college and then pursue acting full time, but it just so happened that while I was in college I got a pilot for Fox and it got picked up. It was called *Manchester Prep*. I was 19 and I got the job so I left school with my parents' full support. I moved to L.A. by myself and I didn't really know anyone except the people on the show. We shot about four episodes and it was canceled before it aired but they cut it into a movie and released it as *Cruel Intentions, Part II*."

She stuck it out in L.A. and not long after, she landed the recurring role of Dana Poole for two seasons on *Boston Public*. "That experience was so special because I had been a fan of David E. Kelly's for years and I wanted to work with him so badly," she enthuses. She followed that stint with more episodic guest appearances and small film roles until she got the audition call for *Angel* in the summer of 2003. "I got [some lines] faxed to me from my manager for

"I'm actually starting my seventh [Angel] episode next week and they called and said I will be doing some of the back nine episodes so for the time being Eve is here."

a recurring role," she explains. "I was so excited because Joss Whedon is another guy that I wanted to work with in the television world. I wanted to nail it, so I worked really, really hard. I was specific in every choice I made, down to my nail polish and my wardrobe for the audition.

"My first audition was with [executive producer] Jeffrey Bell and casting. The second audition was for the same people and then I auditioned for Joss. I was very nervous," she laughs. Nerves or not, she won the part and immediately got to work getting caught up on the series. "I don't watch a lot of television but I had watched *Angel* off and on for the four years so I was familiar with the show. Once I got the role, I started watching the re-runs every week. I wanted to learn as much as I could about the history and the characters so I felt more comfortable."

Stepping into the established cast was another cause of stress for the actress. "I was just so nervous because these people have been working with one another for four years and I was the new kid on the block." Her fears quickly disappeared when the cast greeted her with a big "Welcome" on her first day. "I immediately felt part of the family and my nerves were calmed. It is such a remarkable group of people. Even after four seasons, everyone is down to earth with great attitudes. The first day I was there, Andy Hallett came out and showed me around. He was showing me where everyone's trailer was and the rundown on everybody. He was so funny.

"By the second episode I felt settled," she continues. "The first episode, I was still learning names and I was so focused on doing a good job. A new environment can be scary but by the second episode, I knew everyone's names and I felt right at home. It's so much fun and I love going to work everyday."

So far, the biggest challenge for Sarah in playing Eve has been her lack of knowledge of what exactly this woman is all about. Not only has the audience been in the dark about the character, so has the actress playing her. "I was working just off what I was given on the page, from script to script, from episode to episode. So, I played her like she is trying to help and every once

Sarah Thompson Facts!

Birthdate:
October 25
First professional role:
'Beth' in *The Ice Storm*
Favorite female villain:
Catwoman
Favorite noir film:
Double Indemnity
Acting inspiration:
Meryl Streep
Song she would sing at Caritas:
Etta James' "At Last"

in a while I injected a little mystery." But as the season progressed, Sarah picked up hints in the scripts that gave her more insight. A big clue for her was the dark look she delivered at the end of "Life of the Party". "That look was actually in the script so I thought, 'That's a clue of what is going on with this girl!' In the following episode ["Lineage"], there is a scene with Spike in the elevator where he says there is more to you than you're letting on and when I read that scene, I knew there was definitely something going on."

That revealing elevator scene gave Eve a chance to go toe-to-toe with Spike [James Marsters], which was a highlight moment for Sarah. "We were supposed to shoot that scene a few days later. They were so ahead of schedule one day that I wrapped work and went home and they called me about an hour later and said, "Is there any way you can shoot that scene today?" I didn't even know my lines yet and neither did James because it wasn't for a few days. So I said, 'Sure' and rushed back to set. James and I stepped aside and we rehearsed it a bunch because we wanted it to be really, really good."

But it was in "Destiny" that Sarah finally got to prove her suspicions right when Eve is revealed to be working behind-the-scenes against Angel. "What's funny about the big reveal was that nobody got that scene until the last minute. When we first got the script, that scene wasn't in it because it was top secret. I didn't even have it. We shot it as a Second Unit scene after that episode had already wrapped," she shares. "I had heard a rumor about a secret scene and I tried to ask everyone about it but all I got was, 'I don't know, I don't know.' One day, I notice in my trailer there is an envelope marked 'Confidential' and I was like, 'Wow!' but I couldn't tell anybody about it. Not my friends or the other cast-members because they wanted to keep it such a secret that Eve is evil and Lindsey is coming back. I had to keep my mouth shut but it was so exciting.

"In 'Destiny', because I shot all of the other scenes before I got that last scene, they kept directing me to play Eve very, very sincere. They said, "We can't exactly tell you why but it's very important you play this scene very sweet and sincere." So any mystery that I injected into the character in that episode, they pulled me away from that because they wanted such a reveal at the end. I had to really trust the director but I felt a little blind because I knew it was going somewhere with a reason but I didn't know what it was."

While a lot came out in that reveal, there is much that still remains to come to light about Eve and her plans. "Honestly, I'm still going from script to script but now I have more information so when I'm playing my scenes at Wolfram & Hart with the people there, I have to play against what I know because I don't want to be too obvious." Working with Christian Kane is another plus for Sarah, as the duo will feature prominently in future episodes. "All I was told is that he is pretty much my boyfriend and [he] is the one person with whom I can let down my guard."

That implied intimacy came through loud and clear with Eve's strip scene and their cuddle in bed; a potentially uncomfortable moment that Sarah says was difficult for altogether other reasons. "Initially, it is sort of awkward but you get over it. What was tough was the timing of that scene. My lines were timed with taking off different pieces of clothing and the camera movements and I had to focus on taking this off, at this line. It was all very choreographed. I had to hit my mark, say my line, make sure the camera was in the right place... But that scene was a couple days before my birthday so at the end they brought me out a birthday cake so it was a fun day after all that work," she laughs.

Another highlight for Sarah is David Boreanaz' directorial debut on Episode 10, "Soul Purpose". "He did such a great job," she enthuses. "I had a wonderful experience working with him. It was fun to see him in a different role. Usually, he is my co-worker so to have him direct me was fun. I think because he is an actor he knows how to talk to actors. He lets you do your own thing and then offers his ideas. He was great."

Sarah was signed for six episodes this season but happily, she recently got word that Eve will be around for more episodes. "I'm actually starting my seventh episode next week and they called and said I will be doing some of the back nine episodes so for the time being Eve is here," she smiles. "I don't know how many more it will be but it's more than my guarantee of six."

In that time, she hopes to get more action scenes under her belt. "I was excited by the strangling scene in 'Destiny'," she laughs. "It was cool and it was fun to watch. It's funny – when you do a scene like that it's kind of scary and it gets emotional so I found it very easy to access those emotions and convince myself of the reality." Her attacker, J. August Richards, was less enthused. "J is such a great guy and he is so aware. He was trying very hard to be very careful. It was all very co-ordinated with a stunt co-ordinator but the end of every take, he would ask if I was okay because I would be crying, but I was acting. That has been my only real action scene, but I'd like to get in a fight with somebody," she laughs.

Looking over her efforts so far this season, Sarah has a clear favorite episode. "I think 'Destiny' is now my favorite because I really loved everything about it, not just the things I did. I thought the whole episode was phenomenal. It was fun to do the reveal and I had some fun lines, which I enjoyed."

As if playing an evil liaison wasn't enough, Sarah will also be appearing on another series this winter. "I have another arc on an ABC show that starts in December, called *Line of Fire*. They have been co-ordinating the schedules and I have been able to do both. I play a prostitute. I don't know how I get these roles because in real life I'm really shy and quiet but somehow I get the vixen roles," she laughs. "Things happen at once and as they say, when it rains it pours but I welcome it!"

MONSTERS & *Angel*

ANGEL — EPISODE 20 — OLD ITALIAN FEMALE DEMON

ANGEL — EPISODE 20 — LACKEY DEMON

ALMOST HUMAN

ROB HALL FROM ALMOST HUMAN - *ANGEL*'S MONSTER MAKERS - TALKS ABOUT THE CREATION OF THOSE CRAZY LITTLE ITALIAN DEMONS FROM SEASON FIVE'S "THE GIRL IN QUESTION"

Although she showed up two episodes from the end of the series, the little old Italian lady demon in "The Girl in Question" is one of *Angel* make-up designer Rob Hall's favorite creations. "That was actually the last prosthetic make-up that I physically applied myself for *Angel*," Rob recalls, "so she was kind of bittersweet for me. I knew that I wanted to take it back to the beginning of when we started doing the prosthetics work. The very first make-up that I did at Almost Human for *Angel* was the Old Codger demon [in 'Heartthrob'] and we did that as a silicone sort of old age demon make-up. And then this came up, and it was reminiscent of the very first thing we did, so I knew I wanted to do a very flabby skin texture like we did on that Codger demon."

Despite their short stature and nationality, Rob says that the little old lady demon and Alfonso, the male Italian demon who keeps thwarting Angel and Spike, are not meant to be the same species. "Alfonso was a very traditional, more comic book kind of demon; we tried to go a little more realistic with the old Italian demon lady."

Rob notes that series co-creator/episode director David Greenwalt was delighted by these demons. "David S. Lee, who played Alfonso, is a really good actor," Rob says. "He's really funny, and he really helped bring it to life with the performance."

Photos and Artwork Courtesy of Almost Human

Interview: Mercedes McNab

Perfect HARMO

BY BRYAN CAIRNS

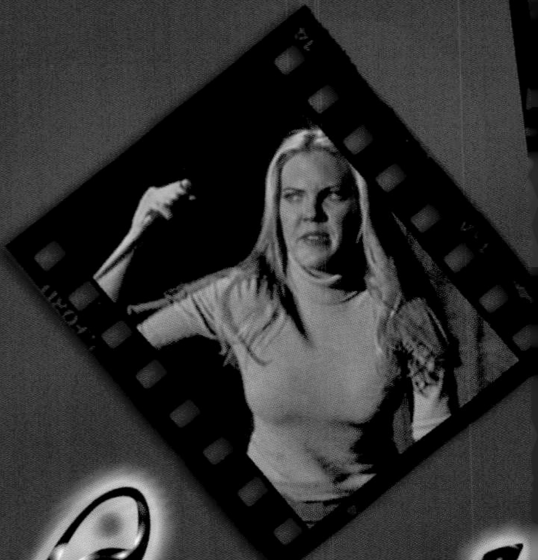

From her debut in the first episode of *Buffy*, to her final, treacherous appearance in the last episode of *Angel*, the ditzy Harmony Kendall was a character that fans were always pleased to see. We caught up with actress Mercedes McNab to talk about her latest big screen projects, from romantic comedies to horror flicks, and the legacy of playing Harmony...

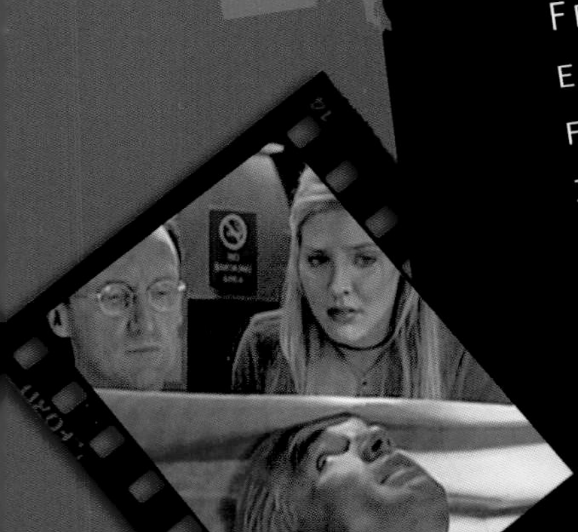

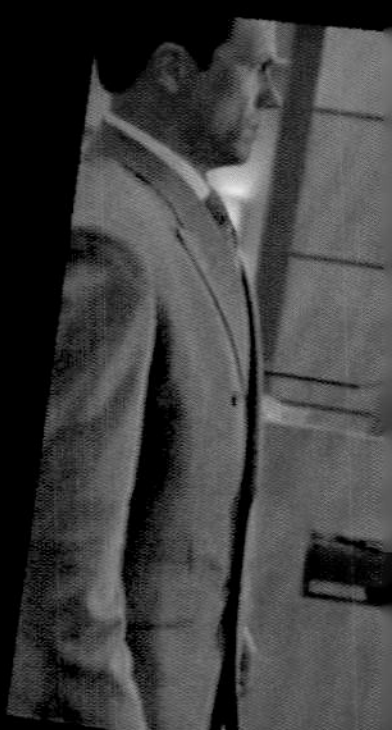

Photo: Albert Ortega

No one can accuse actress Mercedes McNab of being squeamish. Whether it be on *Buffy the Vampire Slayer* or *Angel*, her character Harmony Kendall was constantly serving up or drinking blood, and with no less than four horror movies on the horizon, the popular actresse's future looks red.

"The fans for this genre are so committed and you build relationships through that," enthuses Mercedes. "It is more of a community than any other genre. And to be honest, I just like the gore and guts of it all. In one movie, I get to be degloved, which is basically when they tear the skin off your face. That was my favorite day. It is also fun to play such a heightened sense, whether it is being scared or anything else."

There is certainly plenty of that in this fall's *Hatchet*, a fright flick about tourists on a haunted tour in the bayous of Louisiana. When their little boat gets swept up in a storm and they become stranded, the group finds themselves at the mercy of sadistic madman, Victor Crowley. Caught in the grisly mayhem is Mercedes' unsuspecting character, Misty.

"*Hatchet* comes out September 7, now," Mercedes explains about the release date shift. "We didn't want to compete with *Spider-Man 3*, obviously. Kane Hodder, Robert Englund, and Tony Todd are also in *Hatchet*. It has a huge cast and it is really funny, gory, and scary. I liked the writing a lot because you actually care about the characters. They are making you laugh, so you didn't really want anyone to die.

In some horrors, you are like, 'Please get rid of that person! I can't stand them any-more!' The acting is solid all around

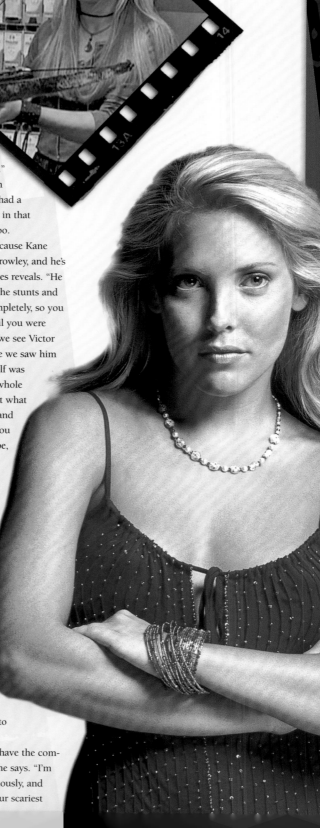

which is rare for horror films. It was an enjoyable experience."

Director Adam Green and actor Kane Hodder had a few tricks to get the cast in that terrified state of mind, too.

"It was really nice because Kane plays the killer, Victor Crowley, and he's a method actor," Mercedes reveals. "He was also doing some of the stunts and would cover himself completely, so you could never see him until you were shooting. The first time we see Victor on screen is the first time we saw him in real life, so that in itself was scary. You build up this whole thing in your mind about what he is going to look like, and no matter how horrific you thought it was going to be, it was worse! And the director would tell us Victor was coming from one way, and it would actually be the other. Nowhere was safe. The only place you could go where you weren't going to get attacked was catering."

Hodder, who played killer Jason Voorhees in four *Friday the 13th* movies, has a reputation for being a joker, and Mercedes fell victim to one of his pranks.

"You know how they have the commentary for the DVD?" she says. "I'm in my trailer taking it seriously, and they asked, 'What was your scariest

> **"MY FRIENDS MAKE FUN OF ME NOW. THEY JOKE, 'MAYBE PEOPLE JUST WANT TO KILL YOU... WHO DO WE WANT TO KILL? PUT MERCEDES IN A FILM SO THEY CAN KILL her!'"**

Victor Crowley moment?' And I say, 'Probably the first time I saw him,' and at that moment, he jumped out of the bathroom. I screamed! He scared the crap out of me and it's on tape. It was in good fun and my reaction was perfect. And I'm pretty gullible. They wouldn't even tell us when he was or wasn't on the set. Sometimes they would have people in the bushes and I hadn't seen him yet. I was really nervous and I already had it in my mind he was there during a pivotal scene, and I was like, 'I don't want to go! I don't want to go!' Then it turns out he wasn't even there."

Any blonde beauty in a slasher movie is bound to die, but Mercedes wasn't overly pleased with her demise.

"Honestly, no I wasn't," she states. "I didn't get to die on screen. My Dad and I used to watch horror, or Bruce Willis movies, and pick out who had the best death, but I get killed off screen. You figure out what happened to me afterwards, and then see the damage that had been done. I made up for it on the next two [films], that is for sure."

Before those, Mercedes turned to something more light-hearted with the comedy *The Pink Conspiracy*.

"This script wasn't so emotionally intense, because *Hatchet* was running around being scared for your life," sighs Mercedes. "It was nice to be able to relax and play a crazy character. I am kind of the leader of the Pink Conspiracy, which is girls destroying boys' lives. She's another loveable character. It is really over the top and a dark comedy."

The project also reunited her with *Angel* alumni Sarah Thompson [who played Eve].

"That is always fun, because after you wrap, everyone assumes you hang out everyday when you are on set, but it is generally not the case because you are working on different things," Mercedes reveals. "It is nice when you get to work with [a former colleague] and the comfort level is there. Sarah is this nice person in the movie, and I am always trying to beat her up."

In her next horror outing, *VII*, Mercedes surfaces as one of 12 jurors targeted after convicting a man to jail.

"My friends make fun of me now," she chuckles. "They joke, 'Maybe people just want to kill you. Who do we want to kill? Put Mercedes in a film so they can kill her!'"

To date, *VII* provided Mercedes with her favorite on-screen death.

"This one was cool because I had a prosthetic head, but it had animatronics in it, so when you peel off the skin, you can still see my eyes and tongue moving," she explains. "That was really neat from an outside perspective, but it is weird to do fake dying. You don't really know what you are doing, but you go with it. When I had my animatronic head, I asked if I could be one of the people that shoots the blood in. It doesn't freak me out."

Although Mercedes is yet to film

> "I WOULD HAVE LOVED TO BE ABLE TO PLAY HARMONY AGAIN. THERE WAS SO MUCH SPECULATION [ABOUT THE SPIN-OFFS] EVEN BEFORE THE SHOW GOT CANCELED, [BUT] NO SCRIPTS WERE EVER WRITTEN. I WASN'T SURE IT WOULD EVER REALLY HAPPEN."

Medium Raw, in which she plays an investigative reporter, she still had to rely on her lung power in the completed *Dark Reel*.

"This is more of a horror film inside a horror film," reveals Mercedes. "We are all actors inside a horror film, and then we start getting picked off. It is interesting because one minute you'd be pretending to be getting killed, as if you are filming a movie, and then in the next part, you are actually getting killed. It was fun because if you are playing a bad actor, then you get to die really badly, and then in real life, you get to do it again."

Mercedes may be keeping busy but there's no denying she truly cut her teeth on *Buffy the Vampire Slayer*. Once a member of the popular clique at Sunnydale High, Harmony was transformed into one of the undead after being bitten by a vampire during the final showdown with Mayor Wilkins in Season Three. Initially, she plagued Buffy and the Scooby Gang before packing up and eventually

joining Wolfram & Hart as Angel's secretary. For Mercedes, the transition was smooth and stress-free.

"It was easy for me because I pretty much knew everybody," states Mercedes. "I knew David [Boreanaz] and James [Marsters] so for me, I didn't even think about it; it just seemed a natural progression. It was fun and I liked my character. There was more to do, and I was happy they brought me instead of somebody else. Harmony was finally trying to be good, and there was that inner battle. She made a commitment to it in *Buffy*, but never really stuck to it. Then at the end, when you have no soul, how good can you really be? I liked that I got to be this humorous character. With all the dark stuff that was happening, I got to come in and break that ice."

It has been noted that Harmony spent more time as a bloodsucker than a human, and Mercedes still has vivid memories of her inauguration to the make-up process.

"It was with Willow and Oz, and it was when the audience found out I had been vamped," the actress recalls. "It was the first time I had to wear those prosthetics, and it was kind of scary. I thought, 'How am I going to play a vampire and be this bad ass?' I was glad the prosthetic and teeth were on, because it helped me get into character."

Mercedes enjoyed plenty of Harmony-esque moments, most notable in the *Angel* episode "Harm's Way," and like most of her castmates,

was shocked when *Angel* didn't get picked up for a sixth season.

"Thank God I wasn't there when they announced it," she says. "I would have been crying. I found out the next time I was there. My manager told me. It came out of the blue. We thought we were pretty golden after our 100th episode, which was obviously not the case."

There were rumors a series of *Buffy/Angel* TV movies were in the works, and while fans were anticipating revisiting those lives, they appeared to stall in developmental hell.

"I would have loved to be able to play Harmony again," confirms Mercedes. "Again, there was so much speculation even before the show got canceled, and no scripts were ever written. I wasn't sure it would ever really happen. I knew it was pretty much

time to move on."

Luckily, creative mastermind Joss Whedon is currently penning what he considers the eighth season of *Buffy the Vampire Slayer* in comic book form.

"I think it is awesome!" exclaims Mercedes. "I love that due to the fan response, they keep on going with the characters, so whatever medium that may be, whether it is television or comic books, it is because of the fans."

Outside of entertainment, the actress recently grabbed the headlines when she appeared nude in the pages of *Playboy*.

"It came about from a random call one day, and that they were interested in shooting me for the cover," she explains. "I was kind of confused. My Mom even said, 'Why are they calling you?' 'Thanks Mom!' The experience was amazing. I went to Italy to shoot it, which was my first time there, and my best friend

came to join me. We shot for three days and after that, we stayed for another two weeks. To get to go there for free was pretty nice. The photographer was amazing. I had a lot of control with the pictures, what was chosen, and what I would be willing to do. All in all, it was awesome!"

Still actively attending conventions and interacting with fans, Mercedes will probably always be remembered as the conflicted Harmony, and she's grateful for that

continued recognition.

"It is surprising to me because generally people are so fickle," she concludes. "The commitment level with the fans is so surprising and amazing. It is weird that people are still passionate about us, and it is really flattering!" ✛

L.A. LIAISON

BY TARA DILULLO

Move over, Eve —
there's a new
Wolfram & Hart
employee in town!
And he's just as
mysterious as Eve
used to be — and
maybe a little
more deadly too...
Actor Adam Baldwin
discusses his
Angel role.

When you ask actor Adam Baldwin how he's been able to sustain such a successful acting career over the past 25 years, he smirks and answers in his uniquely concise manner, "I kept at it. I'm like a fungus; you can't get rid of me." It's a humble answer for a humble guy who has always been more blue-collar about his career than typical Hollywood glitz and glam. It's a strategy that has served Adam well as he's worked on more than 60 films and television projects over the years, making for an eclectic and varied resume. Yet arguably, his recent involvement in the Joss Whedon projects; *Firefly* and *Angel*, are now getting him some of his biggest notices and a surge of new fans.

On the short-lived *Firefly* series, Adam played the cranky, gruff mercenary-for-hire, Jayne Cobb, who was always up for a fight or making a quick buck. It was a role Adam completely embraced. "Jayne for me is the role of a lifetime," he says. "He could be good, funny, bad, selfish or a slob – that guy can do no wrong!" Meanwhile, Joss Whedon-fans get to see another side to Adam in the final arc on *Angel*. Starting with the episode "Underneath," he appears as Hamilton, the mysterious replacement for Eve as the new liaison to the Senior Partners

at Wolfram & Hart and a key player in the end-game of the series.

It's been a long road from acting in school productions as a kid in Chicago, Illinois to where he is now, but as Adam says, "I never complain about the work." Originally, acting was just something fun for Adam to do. "I was involved with drama departments since the 5th grade. I played at it. It was an escape. My brothers and I would watch *The Three Stooges* or shoot-'em-up Clint Eastwood movies and pretend we were in them, but it never reared its ugly head as a profession until I lucked into it."

That 'lucky' break came in 1980 when he was plucked from obscurity to play Ricky Linderman, the most feared kid in the schoolyard, in the film *My Bodyguard*. "I was one of three or four thousand kids to try out for *My Bodyguard*. I just happened to be that [*affects creepy voice*] 'disturbed' child. It was kind of who I was in my misspent youth. Teenage years will do that to a kid," he laughs. "1979 was the summer of Hollywood in Chicago. *My Bodyguard*, *Ordinary People*, *The Hunter* and *The Blues Brothers* were all shot there around the same time and I got parts in two of the four [including *Ordinary People*], so I guess it was a trend."

After appearing in those two critically acclaimed films, Adam was truly bitten by the acting bug. He decided to pursue it professionally and moved to New York in the early '80s with friends. "It was right about then that crack hit the streets and New York City got really nasty and dangerous, so we all got scared and headed to Los Angeles!" he chuckles. He transitioned to the much more mellow West Coast and proceeded to work steadily as an actor in a wide variety of projects and films like *Full Metal Jacket*, *Predator 2* and *Independence Day*, always remaining busy in his chosen profession. "The only people who have control over their careers are the ones you see on the covers of magazines. Everyone else is just plodding along making a living. The key is not to live over your means and overdo it with the 'bling, bling'," he smiles. "It was never the fame or fortune that drove me to act. It was something I love and I enjoy doing. A lot of people identify who they are by what they do and that's not me. It's what I do but not *who* I am. Who I am is a parent. I'm a family man," he confides.

Over the years, Adam has also made many guest appearances on genre television shows like *The Visitor*, *Stargate: SG-1*, and *The X-Files*, even though he finds it challenging to jump in and out of existing shows. "I don't prefer the guest star, one-shots. The arcs are more interesting because they give you more time to work through the character and they tend to give you more close-ups, which is what television is all about. I've done a couple of guest shots on shows, and I like to go and experience other people's working atmospheres as much as I can. I like to see how they are behaving and what they are doing. The top-notch shows have pretty good crews and I'm a big fan of hard-working camera crews. They make our jobs so easy."

Of course, Adam's television experience changed radically when Joss Whedon hired him for *Firefly* in 2002. "A lot of the television industry is so cookie-cutter. In general, there are so many shows that are easy and bland to watch. You can tune in at any time and know exactly where you are in the story arc because it's pretty much the same every week. But the shows that Joss writes, you have to pay attention or you get lost. That's good and bad because you will lose a large percentage of people who aren't willing to focus so that can be a drawback, but I don't care about them," he laughs devilishly.

"That's not why I'm here. I'm here because good writing is fun to do. He's a really good writer so that is my blessing at this time."

Adam ended up appearing in seven of the 13 produced *Firefly* episodes and was just as upset as the rapidly forming fanbase when the show ended so quickly. "When it was canceled, we were all heartbroken. It was a heartbreaker because we all understood how many stories there were to be told. Unfortunately, we didn't get launched as well as we would have hoped. Business is business and we didn't get the numbers so off you go and I understand that, but as the artists, we all said, 'Nooo, there is so much more to tell!'" Obviously, Joss agreed as he worked tirelessly to keep the show's concept alive, getting Universal pictures to green-light the *Firefly* film, *Serenity*, which will reunite the cast and crew this summer. "I know the main cast is in, so it will be a family affair.

"It is a redemption that we are able to keep it going and all to Joss' credit and Mary Parent [supervising producer] at Universal, who saw the show, liked it and thought it was a no-brainer to make it into a feature film. I believed very strongly it would come back because Joss said he was going to get it done. He said he wasn't done telling the story and the man is nothing if not tenacious. He went and wrote a great script and they bought it. Woo hoo! I actually just came back from the lot today

and I looked at some of the artwork and the sets they are beginning to build and it's just great. I took my son with me and as we were walking out of the studio, my seven-year-old son goes to me, 'Dad, I'm so happy for you.' He was there and saw me cry when they canceled it, so he knows."

In the meantime, as Joss has been known to do with his *Firefly* cast in the past year, Adam was brought onto another Joss Whedon show, appearing on *Angel* for the final episodes of the season. "I think [Joss] liked working with me and didn't want me to run off and do something else. I'm lucky that I've been able to convince and trick Joss into thinking I'm good at what I do," Adam chuckles. His turn as the imposing Hamilton, is the kind of liaison to the Senior Partners that Eve never quite lived up to during her tenure. Asked to describe the part, Adam smiles and offers, "Joss wanted a big guy to come in and kick David Boreanaz' ass, and seeing how I'm so reliable and so scary, he went with me. Joss also said, 'Now Adam, this is the anti-Jayne,' and I said, 'Great!'"

Despite being part of the Joss family now, Adam had some brushing-up to do when it came to getting to know *Angel*. "Well, my kids watched it here and there. We don't watch too much TV, but they knew it. I'd seen several episodes over the years. Not having committed to the arcs, it was hard to jump in, but I certainly get the pacing and the rhythm of the dialogue and the timing of the jokes." He then describes how he immersed himself into the actual day-to-day culture of the show. "You're professional and quiet and occasionally drop little humor bombs and let them get to know you. You get a sense of how the show works and then let your personality take over." His overall assessment of the

show now is typically brief. "Pretty girls, handsome men and a really good crew."

Pressed more on the role that Hamilton takes in the show, Adam is cagey with the details but does offer, "He's representative of pure capitalism – he's all about business. Those that aren't willing to play the game get left behind and there are all kinds of ways to get left behind on this show. Let's just say I'm involved with the violently climactic stuff at the end of the season," he laughs sinisterly.

"I like the timbre of the guy," he continues. "He is very calm and has a nice suit. I think that some of the dry humor that comes out and playing the writing that Joss gives us; just playing it straight comes out so funny. I'm also liking the fact that the character is as powerful a force as Angel is and he's fearless. I'm fearless when I try to go in and play this stuff. Plus, the key to playing a heavy for me since I am so big is to just be nice. Play nice. Do evil things."

Adam is pleased he was able to share time with another of Joss' casts, who he

says were all in good spirits despite the show ending. "At this point, they are all ready to move on and they are looking forward to their next things. Five years running is a great accomplishment. They are blessed and hopefully, they invested their money wisely," he chuckles. For his part, he says, "I'm honored to be a part of a series that will carry on. I just consider myself a piece of the puzzle and I'm lucky enough to be asked or invited to the party, if you will. I hope I can bring some laughs and grimaces to the fans."

His five-episode stint on *Angel* ended in mid-April and Adam reveals he has been auditioning for some new television series again. "I tested for a couple pilots, but they said I was too tall," he smiles. Regardless, his next gig on *Serenity* began on June 1, and it is his total focus for the time being. "I'm looking forward to it big time. It's going to be great." ✦

{ "WHEN [*FIREFLY*] WAS CANCELED, IT WAS A HEARTBREAKER BECAUSE WE ALL UNDERSTOOD HOW MANY STORIES THERE WERE TO BE TOLD. WE ALL SAID, 'NOOO, THERE IS SO MUCH MORE TO TELL!'" }

THE FACTS

HEALTH AND SAFETY
THE WOLFRAM & HART WAY

We all think we know about health and safety – however, in the past couple of years at Wolfram & Hart:

⚠ Our *entire* LA office was *wiped out* by The Beast.

⚠ One member of senior staff was *taken over* by an extra-dimensional entity.

⚠ Countless more were *beheaded* and *shot* – some even by members of staff! By following the appropriate measures we can make Wolfram & Hart *safer* for *everyone*.

SECTION 1

HOW TO HANDLE ANCIENT ARTEFACTS

Items of great mystical power come through the Wolfram & Hart doors *each and every day*. There is a way that we can all help each other deal with them *safely* and *appropriately*. There is a *right* way and a *wrong* way to handle ancient artefacts of immeasurable evil.

WRONG: *Do not* touch the artefact with your bare hands or inhale any dust that may emerge.

RIGHT: Handle the artefact with *care* and *consideration*. (Also, *bend your knees*.)

SECTION 2

THE BUILDING

Wolfram & Hart has a specially designed building with windows made from necro-tempered glass to assist our undead employees. **PLEASE DO NOT LEAVE WINDOWS OPEN**. This could lead to crispy co-workers and extra vacuuming for the cleaning staff.

More and more staff seem to be thrown out of windows every day. This has led us to form some guidelines about the correct procedure when being thrown out of a window.

TIPS ON HOW TO BE THROWN FROM A WINDOW:

RIGHT: Try to keep your arms and your legs *tucked in*.

RIGHT: Try to avoid *hitting* other members of staff on the way down.

WRONG: Don't *wave your arms or legs wildly*, you could damage them on the way down.

WRONG: Don't try to *re-enter* the building immediately. There was probably a reason you were thrown out of the window in the first place.

ALWAYS REMEMBER THE WINDOW RULES: First, *do not approach* any vicious/powerful entities in the vicinity of a large glass window. And most important of all, *duck and cover*.

SECTION 3

THE WHITE ROOM

The White Room is the conduit to the Senior Partners. It is *completely off limits* to staff without proper clearance. Any attempts to access it without proper clearance will be dealt with very severely.

SECTION 4

THE BASEMENT

Wolfram & Hart is an *equal opportunities employer* and has many undead members of staff. Many of our non-corporeal members work in the basement, along with some of Wolfram & Hart's permanent zombie security force. As a result of this, employees are *discouraged* from visiting the lower levels. Wolfram & Hart accepts no responsibility for anyone dismembered and consumed by a zombie.

SECTION 5

DEMONIC POSSESSION

Sadly, possession by unwanted demons has become a regular part of life at Wolfram & Hart. But there are ways to avoid it.

WAYS TO AVOID DEMONIC POSSESSION:

⚠ *Do not draw* strange pentagrams on the floor.

⚠ *Do not read aloud* mystical chants or incantations.

⚠ If you are sent any strange packages, *think twice* before opening them.

⚠ *Do not drop blood* on or into unknown artefacts.

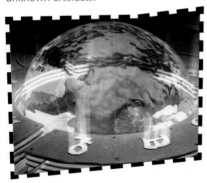

IF YOU THINK YOU ARE BEING POSSESSED BY A DEMON

⚠ Try to find your *nearest exorcist*. The Exorcism Department is located on the sixth floor.

⚠ Try to *fight* the demon yourself. Some demons are weak and can easily be *fought off*. Holy Water can be found on the first floor.

⚠ If you cannot find an exorcist or fight it yourself then leave the building in a *calm and collected manner*. Please *do not* jump out of the windows or off the roof.

SECTION 6

YOUR WORK SPACE

Due to several recent decapitations in the workplace the following guidelines should be adhered to.

⚠ Your work space should be as *clean* and as *clutter-free* as possible, with only the minimum amount of knives, swords and equipment necessary for ritual sacrifice.

⚠ Blood should be *stored* in the office kitchens or in an appropriate hygienic container.

⚠ All *ritual sacrifices* should be carried out according to guidelines set forth in the company handbook.

SECTION 7

EXTERNAL ATTACKS

If the building comes under attack, *security protocols* will come into play. These may vary depending on the nature of the attack, but some or all of the following may take place.

⚠ *Metal shutters* will come down over all the doors and windows, blocking anyone going in or out of the building.

⚠ If you do die in an attack, your corpse may be *re-animated* and used as a zombie in accordance with company policy. This should have been explained to you in your orientation pack, and in the accompanying literature '*Wolfram & Hart and Your Soul*'.

⚠ Please *do not try to use the lifts*. They will be shut down and cannot be over-ridden.

SECTION 8

AN APOCALYPSE

There are many nasty creatures trying to end the world as we know it, and several of them are our clients! This is what to do if the world ends.

IN CASE OF ARMAGEDDON

⚠ In the event of an Apocalypse an *alarm* will sound and there may be an announcement.

⚠ *Leave* your bags/personal belongings/kidnap victims behind.

⚠ Staff should make their way to the nearest dimensional gateway and rendezvous in the nearest safe dimension. A roll-call will be held there.

⚠ In the event of an Apocalypse *do not use the lift*.

Remember, being on the lookout for Armageddon is everyone's responsibility. If you do spot an Apocalypse please *let your Line Manager know*. 🕊

Thank you for reading these guidelines, hopefully we can work together to make this a SAFER BUILDING!

DARK ANG

She came, she Slayed, she chopped Spike's hands off – mad Slayer Dana certainly made a memorable debut in Season Five! Actress Navi Rawat discusses her shocking role in "Damage"!

BY TARA DILU

When Buffy shared her Slayer powers with the Potential Slayers of the world in the *Buffy* season finale, the audience was given a glimpse of the lasting, positive images of the changed women on the receiving end of that remarkable decision. It might have been easy to just leave us imagining a world only benefitting from the good of that choice, but *Angel* recently explored the bleaker ramifications. In this season's "Damage" former *Buffy* writers Steven S. DeKnight and Drew Goddard presented the polar opposite of a Potential prepared to use and control the powers foisted upon her – and she came in the form of the deeply troubled young woman known as Dana. A victim of intense mental and physical abuse as a small child, Dana was eventually found and institutionalized for years. Having gained her full Slayer powers, Dana breaks free from the hospital on a murderous rampage, crossing paths with Angel and Spike...

The real woman behind the bloody face-paint and limb-hacking is, thankfully, nothing like her psychotic counterpart. Actress Navi Rawat is perfectly stable and successfully forging a career in Hollywood, but she was more than happy to delve into the dark side for her gig on *Angel*. "Honestly, Dana was difficult because the character was so angry," Navi shares. "A lot of the people I've played before were the victims, fighting back, but Dana was lashing out and it emotionally came from a different place than I've played previously."

A Malibu, California native, Navi went to the Tisch School of the Arts at NYU to hone her acting craft. "I liked the school and the idea of being in the city. I got a partial scholarship to go there and I graduated in three years with a double major in British and American Literature." After graduation, she made the tough decision whether to stay in New York or

return to the West Coast. "I was trained classically, but I was concerned that because of my ethnicity, I may have had a harder time getting cast in theater in New York and I also knew television and film were a lot more profitable," she laughs.

So she returned to Los Angeles and immediately got involved in the auditioning cycle. "I think mainly it was a matter of finding the right representation and once I got that lined up, after a year of being here, things started to move along rapidly. My first job was an episode of *Roswell*."

About a year later she was cast as a character called Melanie on *24*. "It was the only show I watched before I was cast in it. I was really excited when I got it. I learned a lot and it was great to be with that cast during their first year. *24* was the first big thing that I got. I had a recurring arc

and I think people started to notice me. I've done a lot of action-thriller type stuff and I like the physical aspects of those kinds of jobs. They are really challenging, but really fun. It's not something everyone can do and it makes acting easier when you don't have to think about it, you just do it."

Navi's experience would end up serving her well when she decided to take the role of Dana on *Angel*. "The casting directors at *Angel* had cast me before on *Fastlane*. They had this part for Dana and they called me in and I met the director [Jefferson Kibbee] and I got the part." While the darkness of the part may have been a deterrent for some actors, Navi was actually well prepared to take on the role. "When my agent presented this part to me, they said it was similar to what I did for a U.S.A. movie-of-the-week called *Thought Crimes*. I played another character that was institutionalized so I was able to draw on that.

"I've actually played quite a few characters that were pretty

troubled," she continues. "I can connect with that part of myself fairly easily at this point, because I've done some roles where I've had to stay like that over a couple of months. I never really worry about connecting to that kind of stuff and when I'm working, I remain focused and try not to get distracted by being on the set. In order to do the people justice, you need to stay within yourself as much as possible."

But that's not to say she didn't have a great time with the *Angel* cast. "Everyone was great," she enthuses. "I had one scene with David [Boreanaz] and he was very funny and charming, making me laugh a lot. James [Marsters] was so supportive and I worked with him the most. He was great and I was really excited when I heard I was going to be working with him because I think he is a really talented actor." She also confesses that she turned to James for help in catching up on her Slayer history. "The show has been going on for so long and I'm not really familiar with it, so I actually did the Cliff Notes and just consulted James. I was like, 'James, help me!' and he filled me in," she chuckles.

On the more serious side, they also

shared a number of brutally intense scenes with Dana imagining Spike as her childhood torturer, which, in turn, spurs her into hacking his arms off. Navi reveals the duo took time to rehearse and prepare for those scenes as best they could. "We ran through lines a lot and talked a lot to get into it as easily as we could. We have a similar style of working so I felt like our technique was compatible."

Navi adds that the dramatic look they gave her as Dana helped complete her transformation. "Joss Whedon had a very distinct look that he wanted. I was concerned about how it would look with all the blood and how it would come off, but I'm not fussy. I'd rather look like that than be dressed up. It was fun and I'm not squeamish. I love horror films. As long as they were happy with it, I was fine. Plus I try not to think about what I want and more about what the producers want."

As Slayer-powered Dana, Navi also got to kick some butt with weapons and super human strength. "I have to be honest, *Angel* was more physical than [anything] I've ever done before. They do a lot on the show and I was fighting two people at the same time, which was tough especially

because the guys were so big, but I was good with it. The fight choreographer is one of the best I've ever worked with and he was great. He just led me into it and I did some stuff and my stunt double did some stuff."

At the end of the episode, Dana is taken into the fold by Andrew [Tom Lenk], and Navi reveals Dana might have made another appearance if *Angel* had continued into Season Six. "One of the writers mentioned that to me when we were on the set. He said this is someone with a lot of back story in the show and we hope to see her again." If *Angel* ever gets another life and she is asked back, Navi is on board. "I would absolutely come back because I had such a great time."

As for her own critical review of her performance on the show, Navi can't really comment – yet. "I haven't seen the whole thing as I was working on *The O.C.* when it aired," she sighs. "I've only seen parts of it. I liked the stuff where I am fighting Spike in the dungeon. When I was reading it those were the moments that stuck in my mind, too."

Right now, Navi's gig as Theresa on *The O.C.* is turning into a longer job than she initially expected. "I had done one episode of *The O.C.* and they kept asking

me back for more episodes. I had no idea it was going to turn into what it has turned into. It's fun and I like the cast. I just finished my fourth episode and we are negotiating how many more I'm going to do so we'll see what happens."

Navi has recently been cast in *North Shore*, an upcoming series from Fox, and she is still considering scripts for more film work. Last December, she appeared as Sir Ben Kingsley's daughter in *The House of Sand and Fog*, of which she says, "I feel really proud to have been a small part of such an amazing movie." She continues, "I think ultimately, I'd like to do more film. I like the idea of working on something for a few months and then moving onto something else, which is what film offers more than television. Everything moves a little slower and it gives me more time to connect with the character, but I like working and the more I work, the happier I am." ❦

{ "JOSS WHEDON HAD A VERY DISTINCT LOOK THAT HE WANTED [FOR DANA]. I WAS CONCERNED ABOUT HOW IT WOULD LOOK WITH ALL THE BLOOD AND HOW IT WOULD COME OFF, BUT I'M NOT FUSSY. IT WAS FUN AND I'M NOT SQUEAMISH." }

THE PUPPE SUMM

By Matt Pai

WRITTEN BY AND DIRECTED BY BEN EDLUND, FROM A STORY IDEA BY JOSS WHEDON, SEASON FIVE'S 14TH EPISODE, "SMILE TIME" PROVED TO BE A BIG HIT WITH *ANGEL* FANS EVERYWHERE. *ANGEL MAGAZINE* CHATS TO THE CREATORS OF THIS EPISODE, INCLUDING JOSS, BEN AND DREW MASSEY (WHO DESIGNED, BUILT AND CO-ORDINATED ALL OF THE PUPPETEERS), TO DISCOVER BEHIND-THE-SCENES SECRETS OF THIS INSTANT-CLASSIC EPISODE.

ANGEL MAGAZINE (TO BEN EDLUND): PUPPET ANGEL… WAS THAT A JOSS IDEA THAT WAS WRITTEN BY YOU? HOW DID IT DEVELOP?

BEN EDLUND: Joss had the idea of Angel turning into a puppet. I think that's how it started. Joss' childhood was peopled by puppets because of the work of his father.

JOSS WHEDON: I was puppet peopled, yes. My dad ran *The Electric Company*… the show from [Children's Television Workshop] back when they were doing *Sesame Street*. He actually worked on *Captain Kangaroo* before that. So a lot of our family friends were Muppet people. We were part of a whole Muppety circle. You know, it was always a big thing in my life when I was a kid, because I thought Muppets were cool. Now, I'm not talking about the ones that had their own show, I'm talking the *Sesame Street* ones. I was one of the people that felt that Kermit was a sell-out when he started his own show. I was never really into it. Fozzie Bear is just a wannabe Grover. I always thought there should have been war between the East Coast and West Coast Muppets. That's just me. I always liked puppets. They make me laugh, but they were a serious part of what I remember from my youth, so I just have a little obsession. Not so much an obsession. It's not like I'm collecting dolls or anything. Does my son have a Grover? Yes he does. Because Grover is the finest of all of them.

WAS A PUPPET EPISODE ALWAYS A GIVEN INEVITABILITY ON *ANGEL*?

JOSS: No, one day it just occurred to me. We talked about doing an all marionette *Buffy* one time, but we never really followed through on that. I don't remember how I thought of it this time. It just occurred to me that if Angel were a Muppet, it would make me very happy and that in my universe that's something that could happen. It probably couldn't have happened last year, but the bounds of reality got a little funkier on *Angel* this year.

BEN: Basically, you know, he brought this idea to the table. I always like when something odd happens. I was intrigued

by it. Initially, I thought, well, Joss loves this idea and he'll write it, but scheduling didn't allow for him to do that. I am very thankful he asked me to write it. It was based off a story that we broke. And he was very involved in that.

SO YOU GAVE YOUR PUPPET PROJECT OVER TO BEN?

JOSS: You know, I wanted to do it, but then I got all caught up in Illyria and the death of Fred. I realized that was something I couldn't turn my back on. I had planned, in fact, to write and direct ["Smile Time"] or at least write it. So I had the basic idea and outline and then I turned it over to Ben who turned it back to me whole cloth, which pretty much never

happens. There's a huge back-and-forth in terms of the plot, the ideas of the script and story. Not only did he really come up with so much of that stuff himself and completely see it through, he wrote the songs overnight. I literally picked the right man for the job.

BEN, WAS THERE ANY TREPIDATION ON YOUR PART, THIS BEING THE FIRST EPISODE THAT YOU'VE DIRECTED?

BEN: Yes! Well, the puppets were secondary to the "first episode ever directed" part to me. I didn't know what kind of trouble I was going to get into with puppets. I was worried enough with actors and sets. So, yeah, the puppets did constitute a hell of an

engineering issue. It's like every move that you take for granted on the part of an actor becomes the reinvention of the wheel when it comes to these puppets because our sets aren't designed to be shot with puppets.

JOSS: You know, "*Angel crosses room and says line*" is one person. "*Puppet crosses room and says line*" is one person for hands, one person for mouth, one person for dolly track. They're all lying down. The puppeteers are being pulled on something. It's insanely difficult.

BEN: Normally those sets are elevated five feet to allow the puppeteers to move around and station the puppets at the proper height in relation to the sets, which we were able to do in the case of the "Smile Time" set itself, but [when] we shot on the standing sets of *Angel*, we were really in a position of having to cramp puppeteers under desks and hide them as low as possible in order to get the right size relationship between the Angel Puppet and the rest of the cast. So that was a drag. And that really slowed things down. It made a normal dialog scene with some staging and blocking a whole day affair of working out angles, hiding

puppeteers' elbows and heads and just try-ing to replicate life with felt.

IN AN ESTABLISHED SET LIKE ANGEL'S OFFICE, HOW DID PUPPET ANGEL MOVE ABOUT WITHOUT PUPPETEERS BEING SEEN?

DREW MASSEY: Well it was always a challenge. I wrote Ben an email and said, basically, if you have moveable props in the background, it's a good idea to cheat those as high as possible. You can't move things like doorknobs, but if, for instance, you have a picture on a wall and a desk in the foreground, you can easily raise the desk and the picture in the background. You get a heck of a better performance out of your puppeteer. And that was done a lot in Angel's office.

WAS THERE MUCH DISCUSSION ABOUT TAKING ANGEL TO THAT NEXT LEVEL OF... PUPPETNESS?
BEN: Wow... What's that mean?

WHAT I MEAN IS, WAS THERE MUCH DISCUSSION REGARDING HOW MUCH TO PLAY UP THE SILLINESS OF THE PUPPET

INSTEAD OF IT BEING, "ANGEL IS STILL ANGEL, BUT NOW HE'S FELT"?

BEN: Oh, yes. From the beginning there were valid tonal concerns about how crazy we could make this show and make Angel a puppet, and still maintain the seat of character creditability that people look for in the show. It seems like we succeeded. I am all for yelling and frenetic comedy, so I wanted Angel to be in a certain mode where he felt very much like his normal character with these spikes of "puppet excitability". We also threw some really lame lines in about how he's excitable now and how he has "the proportionate excitability of a puppet his size." That makes no sense. It's basically a steal from the Spider-Man formula: "He's got the proportionate strength of a spider his size."

JOSS: You know, if you're going to go there, live there. My basic tenant was I wanted to see every scene we might see on an episode of *Angel*, but with a puppet in it. I want to see the "let's go get the bad guys" scene. I want to see the heartfelt scene with the girl. And we got to do all of that. If we're going to be silly, let's be serious about it!

Sesame Street and other *Muppet* projects to be able to even write this script.

HOW LONG HAVE YOU BEEN PUPPETEERING, DREW? WHAT OTHER WORK OF YOURS MIGHT WE RECOGNIZE?
DREW: I've been puppeteering for about 15 years, now. I started doing it in college. I've done *Foster Farms Chicken* commercials. I'm the driving chicken. I did one of the skinny aliens in *Men in Black*. I was also Greg the Bunny on the short-lived Fox show of the same name **(starring Seth Green, *Buffy*'s Oz – Ed)**.

IT TOOK TWO OF YOU TO OPERATE THE ANGEL PUPPET. ALICE DINNEAN VERNON OPERATED ANGEL'S HANDS. WHAT'S IT LIKE TO WORK SO CLOSELY WITH ANOTHER PUPPETEER?
DREW: She and I worked for a good two-and-a-half seasons on *My Cousin Skeeter*, so after doing that many episodes – I think we did around 50 or 60 of them – you pretty much share the same brain by the end of it. I love assisting. Personally, I think it's one of the great pleasures of puppeteering. Alice is one of the best puppeteers around. She is an amazing assist.

PUPPETS BEING NEW GROUND TO THE *ANGEL* CREW, DID YOU FIND YOURSELF WORKING ESPECIALLY CLOSE WITH THE DIRECTOR AND THE DIRECTOR OF PHOTOGRAPHY?
DREW: Yeah, there's always a good amount of that, especially with crews that haven't shot puppets before. The production team on *Angel* made it really easy for us. Usually, it's a situation where we go in and say, it's really great if we don't have floors because for puppeteers the best position to be is standing up with your arms over your head. And most production teams say, "yeah? Do you really need that?" But everyone on *Angel* was really receptive to that, as much as could be. The whole "Smile Time" set was built to our

---

BEN, YOU UTILIZED SOME TRADITIONAL PUPPET GAGS. IT HAD TO BE FUN TO FLING PUPPET ANGEL ACROSS THE ROOM—
BEN: And have it work! Yeah, stuff like that is really fun. The low-tech stuff. The western switches... where you could throw a dummy puppet past camera and have that actual puppet appear as if he's landed and turned around and popped back into frame really quickly.
DREW: People like to throw puppets through walls and across rooms. We actually had a stunt Angel puppet which was not quite as detailed and just like a big stuffed doll. Practical effects are a big part of puppetry. In fact, puppets, by their very nature, are special effects.

SPEAKING OF FLYING PUPPETS, THE SPIKE/PUPPET ANGEL FIGHT HAD TO BE THE HIGHLIGHT OF THE EPISODE.
BEN: Oh that was cool. I think that's like the nitrous oxide boost in the episode. I think it goes fine up to that point, it works, but we don't really harvest the full-on energy of this joke until Puppet Angel starts kicking Spike's ass.
[James Marsters] was rolling around on the floor. That was a big rug-burn day, I'm just assuming, for Mr. Marsters. He threw himself into it. Y'know he was puppetting

the puppet for a large part of that fight.
DREW: I have to say I was really impressed the way James Marsters wrestled with the stunt Angel puppet. I gotta give him props. Usually when you give a rag doll to an actor you think, "Oh this is going to look horrible." He totally sold that thing.
BEN: For me, the most successful shot in the show is the one where Spike throws Puppet Angel up and he lands on his feet in the foreground, because that's puppet magic, baby! That was one gag I made up and the rest is [*Angel* stunt coordinator] Mike Massa. Like all that cool fight stuff at the end wouldn't be anywhere near what it is without Massa.

DREW, HOW WAS WORKING WITH FIRST-TIME DIRECTOR, BEN EDLUND?
DREW: I really like his energy. Very laid-back, very cool guy. Like all good directors, he knows enough to pay attention to what he doesn't know. I think he learned a lot doing it and he learned it quickly. The thing I really liked about doing this episode is that Ben wrote the script, so he pretty much knew what he wanted from the puppet and the script that he wrote was very puppet-friendly. It had very doable, really great puppet gags in it. Obviously he was a fan of

RIGHT: PUPPET CONCEPT
SKETCHES

specifications and I think that really made for a much smoother shoot.

BEHIND THE SCENES, EVEN WHEN THE CAMERA WASN'T ROLLING, IT SEEMED LIKE YOU WERE STILL IN CHARACTER, PLAYING THE PUPPET. DID YOU FIND THAT CREWMEMBERS WERE INTER-ACTING WITH THE PUPPET ANGEL INSTEAD OF YOU?

DREW: That's what I aim for! I aim to make the puppet as real a character as possible, so that when I bring him down and take him off my arm that should be the point at which you look at it and think it odd to talk to. I like the whole idea that you can put something on your hand and make it come alive and that puppet could be anything.

BEN: Well, I don't have a lot of Christmas spirit. (*Laughs*) A lot of people get brought into that. In my case, I understood fully that the puppet was simply an extension of a person. I don't know what other people's problems are. Try and make me sound hostile, if you can. I think it's good for my mystique.

HOW WERE THE STAND-ALONE OR WIDE SHOTS OF PUPPET ANGEL WALKING UNASSISTED ACHIEVED?

BEN: We used Voodoo. It turned out to be twice as expensive [as visual effects]. I'm still paying that one off... (*Laughs*) No, that was Drew Massey behind the puppet slightly reversing the mode in which he was operating the puppet. The shoes of the puppet were attached to Drew's shoes and he was in some silly looking blue suit and just kinda shuffling across the floor and we digitally removed him.

DREW: [Puppet Angel] had to travel across the entire Wolfram & Hart lobby. That's no short amount of traveling for a puppet. It's a challenge to get the puppet's feet to always reach the floor. We had some shots where the puppet's shoe would catch on the carpet and his leg would be torn off. It just looked so goofy sometimes. It took a couple takes... okay 10 or 20.

BEN: [The visual effects] are pretty wild because it takes a long time for them to fully etch [Drew] out of the frame. All we wanted was Drew gone. Get rid of Drew! It was amazing to see fully polished, when Puppet Angel is standing or walking all on his own.

YOU HAD TO EMULATE ANGEL, A CHARACTER THAT DAVID BOREANAZ HAS WORKED ON FOR EIGHT YEARS NOW. WHAT WAS YOUR RELATIONSHIP WITH DAVID LIKE?

DREW: I was actually kind of afraid of approaching him initially, because I was wondering how he would take to someone else assuming the role he had origi-nated and played for so many years. But he was extremely receptive to it and I think he got a big kick out of seeing himself in puppet form. We worked pretty closely. He'd come in at the start of the day and go through the script with me and just generally go through the beats of the scene and the emotions.

IN THE CONCEPTUAL STAGES, WAS THERE ONE TRAIT IN PARTICULAR YOU WERE LOOKING FOR?

JOSS: What I was looking for was believability and charm. In my vision it could be just "people" puppets and Ben was the one who came up with making one a dog [Groofus] and, more importantly, with Ratio Hornblower. He was obsessed with Ratio Hornblower and definitely gave [the puppets] way more texture and more life than just a bunch of little "person" puppets, which is where I had been. I look at

this show and the way he shot it, and believe that this is their own show and not some new *Sesame Street*. And I'm still singing that damn "Self Esteem" song at home!

WAS THERE A NOD TO *SESAME STREET*'S "THE COUNT" WITH THE VAMPED ANGEL PUPPET?

JOSS: No, Angel's a vampire and I said one of the things he must do when he is a puppet is morph. He must

RIGHT: THE PUZZLE PLACE — "EVIL"!!

have our traditional "Angel morphs to vamp" face. I don't think the Count is going to be ripping people's heads off. He's a little more into, I think... Count-ing.

AND WHAT WERE YOUR INITIAL REACTIONS TO THE ANGEL PUPPET?

JOSS: Oh, I flipped from the moment I saw the first [conceptual] drawing. When I went on set, the first day, and really saw the puppet working and the puppeteers, I lost it. The first scene shot was the one where everyone dis-covers that he's a puppet. We couldn't get through rehearsal without laugh-ing when David was doing it, before we even brought the puppet in. It just made us laugh. And then the puppet came and it was hard to shoot. It was like making the musical [on *Buffy*].

Everyone was just so happy to work because there was a puppet.

ALONG THOSE LINES, DREW, IT MUST'VE BEEN FUN WORKING ON A MORE "ADULT" SHOW AS OPPOSED TO A KIDS' PUPPET SHOW...

DREW: Absolutely. I have been on a couple of different kids' shows that sometimes the scripts are so prickly sweet that the puppeteers, in between shots, will just do the filthiest things. You kind of have to in order to balance out your day. So it was really nice doing an adult, darker, more dramatic role with a puppet and I think that most puppeteers crave that type of role. It's always nice when you get something like that.

HAVE YOU EVER WORKED ON A CHIL-DREN'S PUPPET SHOW THAT YOU THOUGHT MIGHT BE EVIL?

DREW: They're all evil! (*Laughs and then says, without missing a beat*) *Puzzle Place*. I thought that was truly evil, at its very core.

ANGEL PUPPET EPISODE: EASIER OR HARDER THAN YOUR TYPICAL, RUN-OF-THE-MILL "HUMAN" EPISODE?

BEN: Technically speaking I think it was harder. I think we anticipated a level of difficulty, but the ease comes once you get the puppet set up and you do a shot. Because of the expertise of the puppeteers and their abilities and dedication you just inherit a tremendous amount of positive response just because there are puppets. Where the thing may have lagged and a certain directorial inexperience may have prevailed, I had puppets covering my ass, which was good. So ultimately I think that this episode has been extremely well-responded to and the puppets are a large part of that. ❦

ANGEL™
MAGAZINE

WHILE HE MAY BE BEST KNOWN FOR HIS ROLE AS DOCTOR PHLOX IN *STAR TREK: ENTERPRISE*, ACTOR JOHN BILLINGSLEY ALSO MADE A MEMORABLE APPEARANCE IN *ANGEL* AS A DOCTOR OF A DIFFERENT SORT — A WEREWOLF EXPERT! WE CAUGHT UP WITH THE ACTOR TO DISCUSS HIS TIME AS THE CREEPY CRYPTO-ZOOLOGIST, DR ROYCE...

Although John Billingsley hadn't watched much *Angel* before playing werewolf expert Dr. Royce in Season Five's "Unleashed," the show wasn't exactly unknown to him. First, his real-life wife, Bonnie Friedericy, had played Jasmine's assistant Patience in several episodes of Season Four (she also appeared as Cordelia's dress shop boss on *Buffy*); second, in his series regular role as Dr. Phlox on *Star Trek: Enterprise*, John spent most of his work days filming in soundstages literally next door to *Angel's* permanent stages on the Paramount lot.

"We [the *Enterprise* company] were very aware of [*Angel*] as our next-door neighbors," John says, "in large part because they had [high-end] catering, and we didn't. Every day, at lunch [on *Angel*], there'd be a barbecue, and there'd be bar-becued steaks and barbecued chicken and every amazing thing you could imagine. You would salivate."

This is one of John's favorite *Angel* memories. "For one precious week, I was actually able to partake of their catering services, and

I would stroll over to the [*Enterprise*] set with my steak on a plate and say," he employs a gloating voice, "'Hey, look what they're serving at *Angel* today. Anybody want a bite of my prime rib?' The caterer very nicely said, 'Oh, you can stop by any time,' after my gig was over, but I didn't push my luck," he laughs.

It's still unclear to John whether *Angel's* producers knew of his work on *Enterprise* or just liked his audition. "They may have known who I was, but they certainly didn't know me from having bumped into me on the lot," he says.

Although John was an *Enterprise* regular, many episodes only called for Phlox to appear in a few scenes, which enabled him to take other roles during the filming season. However, "I didn't literally go from one [show] to the other on the same day," he reveals, "it's too much of a gamble. You never know whether or not there's going to be some kind of problem on the set that's going to [cause] you to run late – you can't risk that. I

did, however, have a day or two on *Enterprise* during the week – plus I was filming *Angel*, and they let me use my own [*Enterprise*] trailer, which was very nice."

Something that John found initially puzzling on *Angel* was his character's musical turn for Lorne. "I don't watch a lot of television, so I didn't know that the gag was that one of the charac-ters could find out if you were a phony-baloney by listening to you sing. So when I read for it, I was scratching my head [and thinking], 'Why is he singing "Jesse's Girl?"' I mean, you can kind of infer from the scene what it's about, but... I just downloaded 'Jesse's Girl' and listened to it a bunch until I got the tune in my head, and then I went in and sang it the way somebody who isn't normally asked to sing, and doesn't think they have a very good voice, would sing it. For some reason, that seems to be the moment that actually had some resonance for people," he laughs.

As *Angel* fans may remember, Royce gets chomped by Nina the were-wolf at one point, and John

By Abbie Bernstein

obviously had a much greater effect on John than *Angel*'s abrupt end, he says he found the latter to be more startling. "I don't think [the cancellation] really affected the mood on the [*Enterprise*] set, because I think for the most part, everybody knew it was going to be our last year. During the time I was on *Angel*, I don't think people were expecting it to be canceled. There is a different mood on a set where you know that you've got a show that's continuing on for a while. There's a certain kind of relaxation and conviviality. It certainly seemed as if the folks on *Angel* were like, 'Yeah, baby! We're in the saddle.' It [the cancellation] didn't make much sense, I have to say. When *Angel* got canceled, even as a casual bystander, it was like," John recalls his amazed reaction, "'Get the **** out!'" ✝

extremely convincing, I have to say. He looked very creepy. They had a piece in his mouth to give the illusion of fangs. He couldn't really manipulate it terribly well, so it was more a question of him just placing his incisors on my ankle and they filmed that and made it look like a bite."

While the cancellation of *Enterprise* after four seasons

recalls, "They had a tall guy who was on some kind of platform shoes/stilt arrangement who was dressed as a werewolf, and it was

EYAL PODELL
DISCUSSES HIS
MEMORABLE STINT
AS ENSIGN SAM
LAWSON — THE
VAMPIRE SEEKING
REVENGE ON ANGEL

BY TARA DILULLO

What do you get when you mix vampires, a submarine, some past moral quandaries and some present-day retribution? It's called "Why We Fight" and was one of Season Five's most unique episodic offerings. In it, we learn what Angel was up to during 1943 when a secret U.S. government division "drafted" the reluctant vampire into helping seize a German U-boat prototype. Once on board, Angel crossed paths with young Ensign Sam Lawson. With the sub damaged and the crew threatened, Angel sired Lawson in order to save the boat. Damned as a demon yet retaining pieces of his humanity, Lawson wandered for 60 years until he violently sought Angel for the answer to his existence. Pretty heady stuff even for *Angel*, but Lawson was a role that actor Eyal Podell was more than a little intrigued to explore.

A Dartmouth graduate and theater actor, Eyal transferred to Hollywood five years ago and has worked in film (*Deep Blue Sea, Behind Enemy Lines*) and

television. The role of Lawson came to him as a standard audition last fall. "I knew about the show and I had a friend who was in an episode or two," Eyal explains. "I was really excited about playing the role and trying to make something of it beyond just playing a guy on *Angel*."

Eyal admits he was immediately struck by the themes in the episode. "The way the story was structured was that the present day stuff was the commentary on the past experience. I also thought the dichotomy between the present day and the past was a lot of fun as an actor because you get to play the naïve, unchanged character in the past that is slowly evolving and then the present day version. My only question for the producers was how arch to play him and they didn't want me to play him arch at all. They wanted the audience to empathize with me in a way that Angel must have gone through in that period – when he was sired and killing and didn't know what his purpose was. They wanted me to save any anger or enmity towards

Angel towards the end of the episode when I am threatening his friends. The two scenes of me punching out Alexis and tying up Amy showed that I was villainous, in a way."

"I had also never worked with prosthetics before," he continues. "It was great to get the opportunity to transform yourself in a mirror. I got to see James [Marsters] in his vamp make-up and some of the other characters, so I was excited about it. It makes you look mean and gives you a certain snarl."

Cooped up in that sub with David Boreanaz and James Marsters, Eyal reveals he had a great time picking their brains about the show. "Mostly, I talked to them about the mythology. All the questions I had about the script, like how do you vamp or can vampires breathe under water? I wanted to have a full understanding of what the episode was about, so if I saw any place I could play something up then I had the knowledge to do it." He continues, "They were both a blast. They were very professional at first

DAS VAMP

EVERYTHING YOU EVER NEEDED TO KNOW ABOUT THE PRINCE OF LIES (BUT WERE OBVIOUSLY TOO AFRAID TO ASK!)… BY MATT PARTNEY

When *Angel* executive producer Jeff Bell and "Why We Fight" writer Drew Goddard were searching for an actor to play The Prince of Lies, they lucked out with the casting of Camden Toy. Having made several appearances on *Buffy* as an Ubervamp, Gnarl ("Same Time, Same Place") and a Gentleman from "Hush," Camden was very experienced in acting under extensive make-up.

Having landed the part (he reportedly had the casting directors and producers laughing by the end of the audition), Camden started researching Nosferatu and what other actors had done with the role in the past. "I got the heads-up that he was supposed to be comic relief, so I used that knowledge and really focused on that aspect," Camden recalls. "He's a little flamboyant, [while] being very crotchety… and confused," he continues. "He's a fish out of water."

Completing the character was the eccentric costume designed by Shawna Trpcic. After looking at photos of depictions of Nosferatu, Shawna suggested a drab, high collar frock coat with a military front to it. The highlight of the costume was the pair of shoes that were a real find. Buried in a box at a Hollywood costume house, assistant costume designer, Carrie Grace discovered an old pair of blood-red and patent leather shoes. "When Camden put these shoes on he just became this wretched, old vampire," says Shawna.

And just where did the character's name come from? Does The Prince of Lies have any specific significance? "The Prince of Lies was my brainchild!" Drew Goddard exclaims. "The origin of the name goes back to a *Buffy* episode I wrote [called "Lies My Parents Told Me"]. Drusilla is suggesting nicknames for a newly sired Spike, [one of them being] Lucien, Prince of Lies. But David Fury, who directed the episode, cut it out. He cut out my Prince of Lies joke! It was all Fury's fault!" It is quite clear how proud Drew is of this character, its namesake and the fact that he finally got it in an episode, albeit *Angel*.

but once we had been working together for a while there was a good camaraderie and a great sense of humor and pranking. Watching James singing 'God Save the Queen' with a British accent or hearing David saying his German line, which always cracked us up for some reason. They do their jobs well but like to have fun, which helped in those close quarters."

Eyal has his own theories about Lawson's motivations. "I thought they basically said that my character does have part of a soul. When Angel says, 'I don't think it works that way, kid,' I felt like that line had a double meaning. Rather than it being an emphatic 'No,' I felt like Angel was saying, 'I don't know if it works that way.' Otherwise, why else would Lawson be so tortured unless a part of his own soul was still there? The guy that wanted to do good is all of a sudden doing evil and obviously some good is still there to have it taste so bad. He hated being a vampire and was so angry with Angel. I think he came back knowing he was going to get killed." ❧

MEX AND THE CITY

ANGEL EXECUTIVE PRODUCER, JEFFREY BELL, DISCUSSES THE IDEAS BEHIND AN EPISODE WHICH HE WROTE AND DIRECTED – "THE CAUTIONARY TALE OF NUMERO CINCO"

JEFF BELL: "When I [joined *Angel*] in Season Three, the first thing I pitched was Mexican wrestling, and three years later I finally got to do it and direct it. I had tried [to do a Mexican wrestling episode] on *The X-Files* and when I first came [to *Angel*], it was the first thing I pitched to Joss [Whedon]. And so it finally fit in. He was predisposed to like it. He had tried to do a Mexican wrestling movie just before that. I said, 'I'd like to see more of L.A. in *Angel*, more cultures.' And so they were very into that. It just took a while for it to fit.

"I [was] ridiculously excited by this episode. It's set in the present and back in 1953. That whole world is so rich and colorful and it's one of the things we've talked about doing but it's hard to do on a budget. L.A. has so many interesting areas and cultures. I've been here a while now and I love Mexican culture: the food, the people and the music are fantastic. There are these great old Mexican wrestling movies where these guys would fight vampires and Martians. They wear the masks [all day] – they wear them to dinner, they wear them to work and I just love the idea of a guy walking through W&H in a Mexican wrestling mask!

"What was difficult was that I would have loved to tell the whole story set back in the 1950s with these brothers. Once we found a way to tie Angel into it, it made sense for us. It was a hugely expensive episode so there was a lot we wanted to do with flashbacks. There was a reference to the Devil's Robot, and we wanted to cut back and have this giant metal hand fall into frame with all the brothers yelling 'Andale!' but we couldn't afford to do stuff like that!

"The day, we shot the flashback Mexican wrestling and the contemporary with the little people, was one of the great days of my life. I had so much fun. It was just one of my best days ever, with the period extras and the smoke. You felt very transported. Danny Mora, who played Cinco, really captured the heart of the character with a quiet dignity and humor.

"This [episode] was much harder to direct because we had four all-nighters that were pretty much all fights. In September and October, the nights aren't as long as you want. It was very tiring for everyone, but a lot of fun. Everybody responded well to the Latino culture.

"'The Cautionary Tale of Numero Cinco' isn't a big part of the *Angel* mythology, but at the end there was enough hope to get Angel to go back and read the Shanshu prophecy. 🦇

TRANSCRIBED BY TARA DiLULLO, EXTRA MATERIAL BY ABBIE BERNSTEIN

THE INCREDIBLE HOST!

WRITTEN BY MATT PARTNEY

PHOTOS COURTESY OF DAYNE JOHNSON AND ALMOST HUMAN

HE MAKES THE BEAST LOOK LIKE BAMBI, HE'S
BIGGER THAN THE CRATER-FORMERLY-KNOWN-AS-
SUNNYDALE (WELL, SORT OF), AND HE'S SCARIER
THAN PAVAYNE IN A HALLOWEEN OUTFIT DOWN A
DARK ALLEY. NO, WE'RE NOT TALKING ABOUT THE
FIRST — WE'RE TALKING ABOUT MONSTER LORNE, OF

Big. Green. Angry. And a size 68, turquoise lamé suit, complete with purple dress shirt and shiny silver sequin loafers. That's Lorne's rage-filled subconscious come-to-life in Season Five's hilarious fifth episode, "Life of the Party."

In this episode, supervising producer Ben Edlund wanted to explore Lorne's supernatural abilities and what effects might come with no sleep. "Lorne has a differently wired demon brain. "His demonic subconscious has a reality-bending power [if it's] unable to find an outlet in any other way." He elaborates, "It's something that comes from an overactive subconscious…" Makes sense? Ben puts it simply: "It's a side-effect of sleeplessness for Empath Demons."

As a result of having Wolfram & Hart remove his sleep, Lorne's subconscious actively affects those around him. *Angel*'s cast of characters become susceptible to Lorne's suggestion: Spike becomes happy; Wes and Fred drunk; Gunn starts "marking

his territory." What's more, Lorne's subconscious manifests itself physically. The result is a Brobdingnagian version of himself that crashes – violently crashes – the Wolfram & Hart Annual Halloween Party.

The creators at *Angel* had little time to conceive and design the practicalities and appearance of 'The Behemoth.' The first decision to be made: would The Behemoth be real with make-up effects (like Lorne) or completely computer-generated?

In an ideal world, The Behemoth would have been CGI – a job for *Angel*'s Visual Effects studio, ZOIC. However, co-executive producer Jeff Bell, producer Kelly Manners and Ben Edlund felt secure with leaving the design of The Behemoth with monster creators Almost Human. A TV budget just wouldn't allow for an all-CGI Behemoth.

"It certainly would've been interesting to see," says Ben Edlund, "but his job was to be somewhat goofy-looking, just in that he was wearing a suit. I was pleased. It works."

As with every demon, the *Angel* writers, producers and Almost Human toiled over the design and appearance of Behemoth Lorne. "We did two or three

conceptual designs and Jeff's worry was that it was looking a little too overboard and not so much like Lorne, but that was the important thing," explains Jason Collins of Almost Human. Some original elements remained, such as over-sized Lorne-horns, menacing teeth and hands and shoulders disproportionate to the rest of the body. In fact, two-and-a-half times the mass was added to the stunt-actor's hands using specially made gloves from sculpted forms. Essentially, Almost Human looked to the proportions of the Hulk for inspiration. If the Hulk is what happens to a human being, The Behemoth is what might happen to a Pylean. "We built everything out, just like the Hulk," adds Jason.

Since it was clad in a giant replica of the suit Lorne was wearing, designers needed only to build a simple foam body that would give the stunt-actor the mass of

MONSTER LORNE GETS READY FOR HIS SCARY CLOSE-UP!

LORNE VS LORNE – DON'T MAKE THEM ANGRY. OOPS, TOO LATE!

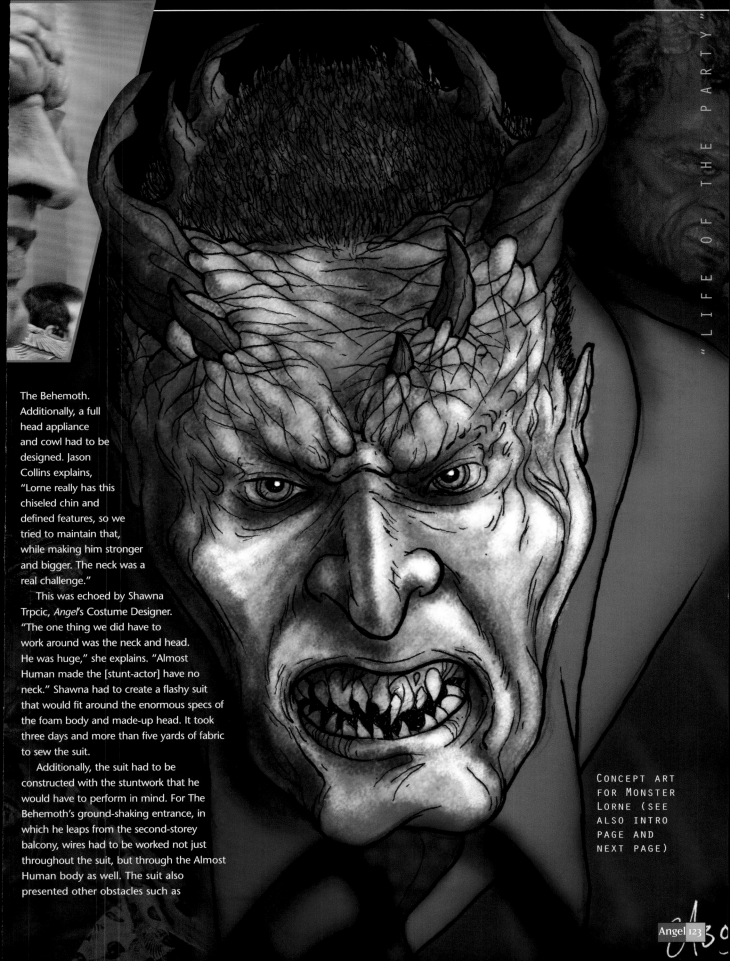

The Behemoth. Additionally, a full head appliance and cowl had to be designed. Jason Collins explains, "Lorne really has this chiseled chin and defined features, so we tried to maintain that, while making him stronger and bigger. The neck was a real challenge."

This was echoed by Shawna Trpcic, *Angel*'s Costume Designer. "The one thing we did have to work around was the neck and head. He was huge," she explains. "Almost Human made the [stunt-actor] have no neck." Shawna had to create a flashy suit that would fit around the enormous specs of the foam body and made-up head. It took three days and more than five yards of fabric to sew the suit.

Additionally, the suit had to be constructed with the stuntwork that he would have to perform in mind. For The Behemoth's ground-shaking entrance, in which he leaps from the second-storey balcony, wires had to be worked not just throughout the suit, but through the Almost Human body as well. The suit also presented other obstacles such as

CONCEPT ART
FOR MONSTER
LORNE (SEE
ALSO INTRO
PAGE AND
NEXT PAGE)

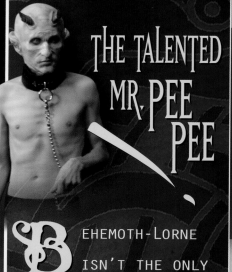

THE TALENTED MR. PEE PEE

BEHEMOTH-LORNE ISN'T THE ONLY THING THAT STICKS IN THE MEMORY AFTER VIEWING "LIFE OF THE PARTY" — THERE'S ALSO THAT TINY, GIMPY SLAVE-DEMON...

'Pee pee.' With these two simple words, a new star was born in Episode Five of *Angel*. Though his role was as minute as the character was in size, Archduke Sebassis' Demon Slave became one of the highlights of an already hilarious episode. Affectionately known as 'Mr. Pee Pee' by cast, crew and fans alike, the Demon Slave was played with comic brilliance by actor Ryan Alvarez.

The role, which consisted of only two lines of dialog ("pee pee" and "ick"), called for a rather skinny actor who was also slight in stature, and Ryan knew he was the right guy for the part. "I know I'm a pretty skinny guy so I went to the audition wearing the tightest T-shirt I could find and... well, I acted like a slave," says the 5'5", 110-pound actor.

Ryan took the character and, with an act that ranged from lifeless resolve to elated excitement, made it markedly memorable with his delivery of two words. "When I said ['pee pee'], everybody on set was just cracking up," Ryan shares. "So I knew I had made some sort of impact."

With only two lines of dialog, the least of Ryan's worries would have been his

(continues opposite...)

"ANGEL'S DONE WHAT??!"

restrictiveness and overheating. Shawna shares, "The Almost Human body was one thing, but the costume is just that. It's like wearing a normal man's suit."

All the hard work that went into producing a gigantic suit paid off. "In addition to making The Behemoth more practical, it was a creature of Lorne's imagination and it helped make it its own creature in our minds," says Ben Edlund. Besides, "If he didn't have a perfectly tailored giant monster suit, then The Behemoth would've most likely been the TV equivalent of naked." A big angry Lorne is one thing. A *naked*, big angry, Lorne – that would have been a whole other monster!

And what was Andy Hallett's reaction to seeing a giant version of his Lorne self? "I was reminded of the episodes in Season Two, when we all went to Pylea [Lorne's home dimension]," says the Host actor. "I was surrounded by 100 other actors in demon make-up that looked just like me. It was great that the writers were spending time on Lorne, his history and his family."

Andy was also flattered by all the attention being paid to Lorne. "When I heard they were doing this, I was just excited, head-over-tea-kettle," quips Andy. "And when I got my first look at him standing up on the balcony over the entire cast and crew, I was hysterical. He was just such a ridiculous sight. He was also absolutely massive. Just massive!"

Unfortunately, stunt-actor Dave Mattey, who played The Behemoth, had a negative reaction to the make-up. "He was a trooper," praises Andy. "I always feel for actors in extensive make-up and he was in a lot of discomfort. If I had to go through just a bit of what he was experiencing, I'd

have been unable to handle it." Dave not only endured hours of make-up application and costume, but performed his own stunts and acting throughout the entirety of the scenes.

Ben Edlund quickly noticed Andy's empathy for Dave trapped under the mass of rubber, foam and contact lenses. "Andy does [make-up] day in and day out, so there was a kind of kinship there." Smiling, Ben adds, "It was the veteran helping the newbie. It was kinda sweet actually."

"The whole experience was just surreal, really," concludes Andy. "Looking at Behemoth Lorne, I thought to myself, 'just look at all that green paint!'" ❦

WHAT AN ENTRANCE!

HUMAN 2003

ALMOST HUMAN

MR PEE PEE PAYS A
WEE VISIT TO W&H

lines. "It didn't take that many 'takes' to get it right. I had a couple chances to get the subtle nuances of the 'pee pee' just right," he jokes.

Ryan endured two-and-a-half hours of make-up that covered his entire body and head. Unlike the six other pasty-white demons who were fully clothed, Ryan had to be painted head-to-toe. Dayne Johnson, *Angel*'s head make-up artist explains, "We started with a water-based 'pancake' make-up, which we applied with a sponge. Then we sprayed a sealant on top of that. Ryan was so patient and had a lot of fun, all things considered."

Ryan spent five days on set in the make-up in nothing but a pair of black Speedos and a leash. "It was a little cold," he explains, "but they gave me a warm brown robe to wear. I just got used to the long stares and the cold."

And that brown robe actually caused a near disaster one day on set. Having not yet been sprayed with the protective sealer, Ryan went to set clad in his warm robe, not aware that every step he took was rubbing the paint off his body. "By the time Ryan reached the set, much of his white body paint had been [removed]," explains Dayne. The make-up department hurriedly re-applied the make-up on set without delay. "It was just a little stressful!" adds Dayne.

On the odd popularity of his character, Ryan has experienced the fanatic following unique to *Angel*. Ryan's brother attended a Halloween Party where a gentleman was dressed just like 'Mr. Pee Pee,' down to the horns, white make-up and Speedos. "I didn't realize that he'd garnered such a cult following!" says Ryan.

"Life of the Party" didn't mark Ryan's last appearnce on *Angel* – "I didn't die in Episode Five, I just ran away," he says. Mr. Pee Pee appeared briefly in "You're Welcome" ("I thought it was a great explanation of where he had been all this time") and then died tragically in the series finale.

But there's one question on everybody's lips: can we expect a Mr. Pee Pee TV movie in the future? "We don't really know his whole story," says Ryan, "so we may still see him again..."

YOU'RE SO PAVAYNE

He came, he haunted, he scared the life out of us. Pavayne is set to be one of the most memorable Season Five villains — let's just hope he stays in that sub-basement prison! Actor Simon Templeman talks us through "Hell Bound"

The Reaper comes calling for Spike in Season Five's ghoulish episode, "Hell Bound," and it ain't pretty. An 18th Century doctor with a penchant for performing unnecessary surgery on his patients, Matthias Pavayne is evil incarnate and a creepy cellar dweller at Wolfram & Hart. Luckily for the actor behind Pavayne, Simon Templeman is nothing like his alter ego. The delightfully funny British actor loves donning the guise of villains on the job, but the scariest thing he encounters in real life may be the frequent nappy changes of his baby girl.

A graduate of London's Central School of Speech and Drama, Simon has been acting for 25 years. "I did a bunch of theater with the RSC and the National Theatre." A resident of Los Angeles for some years now, Simon has done a range of work in television, video game voiceovers and theater work. He's also married to actress Rosalind Chao, who played Keiko O'Brien on *Star Trek: The Next Generation* and *Deep Space Nine*. Simon got the call to audition for *Angel* late last summer out of the blue. "These things tend to happen very fast. It's nice because you never know what is around the corner but it's horrible because you never know what is around the corner," he laughs.

"It keeps you fresh. But I knew the show and this was a particularly fun job."

Pavayne immediately came across to Simon as a rather distinct villain. "The way Steven [DeKnight] had written it was rather poetic on the page, which was a little unusual. Normally, television is rather behavioral and rather thrown away and he wrote something more heightened. Plus, they wanted to steer away from the 'Mwa-ha-ha' vibe. I thought it was interesting."

Simon adds with a chuckle that Pavayne's nationality came by default. "Originally, they weren't even thinking English, but I'm such a one-trick pony – that's all I do! So Pavayne ended up English anyway."

Once cast, Simon got the full make-up and costume treatment to bring Pavayne to life. "It was good fun. It didn't take too long. We got it down to about an hour and Dayne [Johnson] is just fantastic. I loved all that airbrush stuff. You look in the mirror and you are completely different. I think most actors love to completely change, with all that hair and the teeth and the make-up. I liked the costumes, too. The big old riding boots and the strange coat felt really good. But the thing I loved most was the teeth. I did have fun driving home one night because I didn't take the make-up off and I remember pulling up at a traffic light and smiling at somebody and I realized what I had done. I beat them at the green light. I remember that!"

Pavayne spends just about the entire episode torturing Spike, so obviously Simon got to work closely with James Marsters for the shoot duration. "I had seen James before and I'd just thought, 'Oh, it's another Brit in town.' It was only when I met him that it turned out he's from California! I was so

impressed. I was imagining he was from the north of London and I couldn't figure out why I hadn't come across him in the casting corridor," he shares. "Maybe my ear is going but if somebody is doing an English accent, often it's quite easy to spot it. It's something about the manner so I guess James is just very English."

The intensity of "Hell Bound" was so strong that the episode ran with parental disclaimers before it aired in the States – a first for the series. Many scenes centered on the disturbing images and ghosts brought forth by Pavayne to torture Spike, making for some powerful moments for the actors. "I hadn't worked with [James] before so it was nice to watch him work and see how he prepares. It was harder for James because there were so many changes. It was all broken up but it's played as one scene. His togs would come off and then he would be called to do something else, back and forth to his trailer. But James comes ready. He doesn't warm up slowly and get into it – he's just ready to go."

Pavayne not only got to mess with Spike mentally – the two also squared off for quite the battle in the last act. "The thing that was most challenging was the fight. I thought I took a terrible licking," Simon laughs. "I had to get up to speed on the action, which was a bit alarming. The stunt guys are so fast and so good at their stuff. You get the moves just before you shoot and it's high intensity. It's good because it gives you a great energy.

"Unfortunately, most of it felt like I was being knocked around, which was all that was happening really. I've done a lot of stage fighting in Shakespeare roles like *Hamlet* and *Romeo and Juliet* but you don't get to do a lot of it on TV. I got beat up by Superman once

Interview by Tara

on *Lois and Clark* and that was fun," Simon chuckles.

"James is very good too," he contin-ues. "It took me by sur-prise because he is really sharp on that stuff. You can tell he has done a lot of it. He is very proficient and very safe too. He got me through it, actually. I screwed my back up the week before [the shoot] and I thought, 'This is all I need' but didn't get hurt, thankfully."

Believe it or not, four months after his part was shot and the episode has aired, Simon still has no idea how his villainous appearance ranked. "I haven't seen the episode yet because I was on another set," he laughs. "But, I'm going to have to get a tape and watch soon." Simon, just make sure you keep the lights on!

illusso

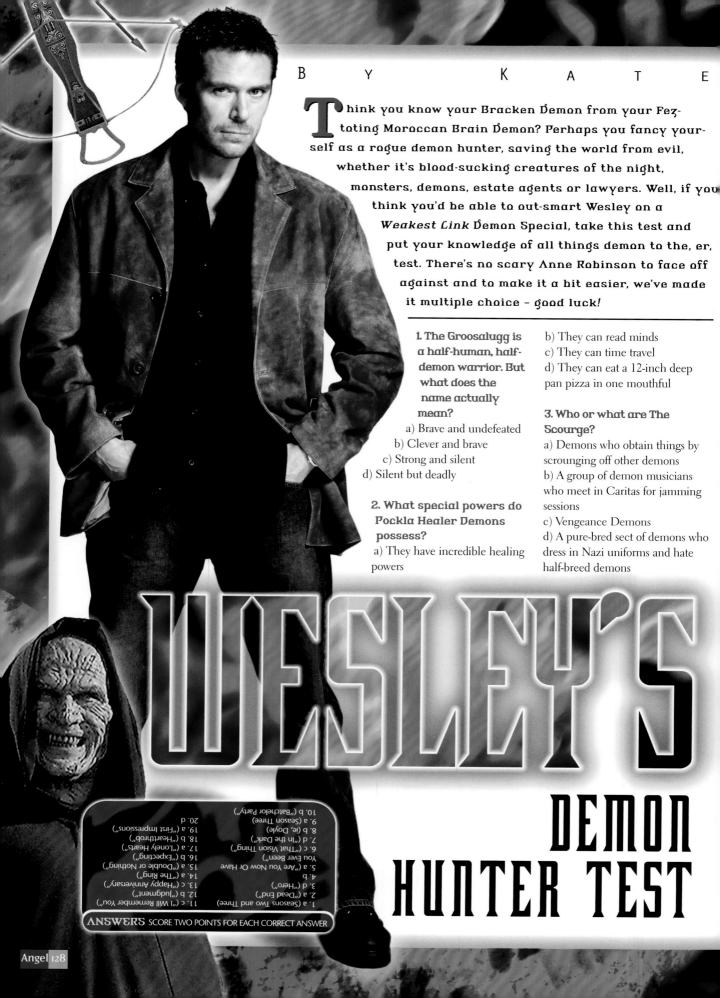

B Y   K A T E

Think you know your Bracken Demon from your Fez-toting Moroccan Brain Demon? Perhaps you fancy yourself as a rogue demon hunter, saving the world from evil, whether it's blood-sucking creatures of the night, monsters, demons, estate agents or lawyers. Well, if you think you'd be able to out-smart Wesley on a *Weakest Link* Demon Special, take this test and put your knowledge of all things demon to the, er, test. There's no scary Anne Robinson to face off against and to make it a bit easier, we've made it multiple choice – good luck!

1. The Groosalugg is a half-human, half-demon warrior. But what does the name actually mean?
a) Brave and undefeated
b) Clever and brave
c) Strong and silent
d) Silent but deadly

2. What special powers do Pockla Healer Demons possess?
a) They have incredible healing powers

b) They can read minds
c) They can time travel
d) They can eat a 12-inch deep pan pizza in one mouthful

3. Who or what are The Scourge?
a) Demons who obtain things by scrounging off other demons
b) A group of demon musicians who meet in Caritas for jamming sessions
c) Vengeance Demons
d) A pure-bred sect of demons who dress in Nazi uniforms and hate half-breed demons

WESLEY'S
DEMON HUNTER TEST

ANSWERS SCORE TWO POINTS FOR EACH CORRECT ANSWER

1. a (Seasons *Two* and *Three*)
2. a ("Dead End")
3. d ("Hero")
4. b
5. a ("Are You Now Or Have You Ever Been")
6. c ("That Vision Thing")
7. d ("In the Dark")
8. b (ie, Doyle)
9. a (*Season Three*)
10. b ("Bachelor Party")
11. c ("I Will Remember You")
12. b ("Judgment")
13. c ("Happy Anniversary")
14. a ("The Ring")
15. a ("Double or Nothing")
16. b ("Expecting")
17. a ("Lonely Hearts")
18. b ("Heartthrob")
19. a ("First Impressions")
20. d

4. What type of demon is The Host?
a) A Karaoke Demon
b) An Anagogic Demon
c) A Flamboyant Demon
d) A Hospitable Demon

5. Thesulac Demons feed on a person's insecurities. But what exactly happens to their victims?
a) They go mad or can commit murder
b) They burst into song at the drop of a hat
c) They go into a deep sleep from which they never wake up
d) They have a laughing fit

6. The Fez-toting Moroccan Brain Demon has the ability to...
a) Turn invisible
b) Bend metallic objects by thought alone
c) Levitate
d) Become invincible

7. What's the name of the ring that can make vampires invincible if they wear it?
a) The Gem of Tamara
b) The Gem of Invincibility
c) The Gem of Andorra
d) The Gem of Amarra

8. These peace-loving demons have crimson eyes and blue-green skin adorned with spikes...
a) Serenity Demons
b) Bracken Demons
c) Bramble Demons
d) Hedgehog Demons

9. What was the name of the time-traveling demon whom Holtz made a deal with to turn him into stone for over 200 years so he could get revenge in the future?
a) SahJhan   b) Sacerdotal
c) Saurian   d) Satyr

10. Doyle's ex-wife Harry was set to marry a guy called Richard. But he was a demon and his family had a rather bizarre tradition... What was it?
a) To have the ex-husband be best man at the wedding
b) To eat the ex-husband's brain
c) To kill the ex-husband on the eve of the wedding
d) They didn't have one

11. How do you permanently kill Mohra Demons, the Soldiers of Darkness whose sole purpose is to kill warriors serving The Powers That Be?
a) Chop off their heads
b) Chop off their hands, arms and legs
c) Smash the jewel in their forehead
d) They can't be killed

12. Prio Motu Demons are bred to...
a) Spread peace and happiness
b) Massacre and maim
c) Breed and then die
d) Eat each other

13. Lubber Demons are known for having an amazing knowledge of...
a) Mathematics   b) Languages
c) Physics   d) Soap operas

14. Which type of lizard demon is known for eating its young upon hatching?
a) Cribb Demon b) Drokken Demon
c) Snake Demon d) Kaliff Demon

15. Jenoff the Soul-Sucker has the power to suck a person's soul by...
a) Jamming his fingers into their eyes
b) Thought alone
c) Magic
d) Touch

16. How does the Haxil Beast, a giant monster with sharp teeth and horns, continue the survival of its species?
a) By mating with one of its own kind
b) It impregnates human women via human men carrying its seed
c) It transforms itself into a human male and impregnates unsuspecting human women
d) By rubbing horns with female Haxil Beasts

17. Burrower Demons are parasites that live in the bodies of humans. How can this type of demon be destroyed?
a) By fire
b) By destroying its host
c) By exposing them to extreme cold
d) They are invincible and can't be killed

18. To get revenge on Angel for killing his sweetheart Elizabeth, vampire James had which organ removed to make him temporarily invincible?
a) His lungs
b) His heart
c) His kidney
d) His liver

19. This tall, disfigured demon with long arms and clawed hands, which can transform itself into a human male, is called...
a) Deevak   b) Davric
c) Durslar   d) Davros

20. We know The Host has a heart the size of Los Angeles, but do you know whereabouts it's located?
a) He doesn't physically have a heart
b) In his big toe
c) In his head
d) In his left buttock

RESULTS

Less than 10 points
CRIKEY, WHAT A DISASTER!
Oh dear, you don't know your demons from your dormice, do you? Must try harder!

Between 11 and 20 points
COMMISERATIONS, OLD CHAP!
Not bad, but could have been a lot better!

Between 21 and 30 points
JOLLY GOOD SHOW!
Not bad at all, old bean!

Between 31 and 40 points
BLOODY MARVELLOUS!
Are you sure you're not already a demon hunter?

TWO OF A KIN

An interview with Julie Benz and Juliet Landau

Buffy and *Angel* may have graced our screens for eight years, but the show's mythology spans a much longer time period — over 250 years — and Darla and Drusilla played an important part of that. *Angel Magazine* managed to catch up with the two extremely busy actresses behind these vamps to talk about their time on *Buffy* and *Angel*.

D

JULIET LANDAU'S
ANGEL/BUFFY CREDITS

ANGEL MAGAZINE: YOU BOTH WORKED ON BUFFY, BUT NEVER ACTUALLY WORKED TOGETHER UNTIL ANGEL SEASON TWO'S "DEAR BOY." HAD YOU MET BEFORE THEN AND DID YOU KNOW THAT YOUR CHARACTERS WOULD EVENTUALLY MEET SOMEDAY?

JULIE BENZ: I met Juliet at an audition and I introduced myself because we both worked on *Buffy*. I don't think nearly as creatively as the writing staff, so when I read that [Darla] was dead, I figured, "I'm dead." And since I cooked, which is my technical term for being dusted, I really thought there was no way to be put back together. So I was surprised every time I got called!

JULIET LANDAU: When I got [the role of] Dru, right afterwards, we had a creative meeting where Joss filled me in on the whole vampire lore of the *Buffy* universe, and my character's history with Angelus, so I was aware it would happen, but I wasn't sure when we would get to it.

IN "DEAR BOY," DRU IS TERRORIZED BY ANGELUS AND THEN SHE WATCHES HIM AND DARLA MAKE OUT WITH ONE ANOTHER ON TOP OF HER. QUITE THE INTRODUCTION...!

JULIET: [*Laughs*] It was a bizarre sequence. I'm profusely weeping and they are having a sexual encounter on top of me! Can it get any stranger than that? But it was perfect in terms of Dru's madness and showing the inception of those elements and why she became what she became.

JULIE: Oh, I felt so bad for Juliet when we were doing that scene! The funny thing is that I was in a corset and they wanted David and I to passionately kiss and fall to the ground, and roll around on top of Juliet as we are enjoying ourselves. I couldn't bend at the waist so I would literally fall over like a ton of bricks onto David and we just kept laughing every time. Poor Juliet is crying and we are there laughing at my sack-of-potatoes fall.

JULIET: Yeah, Julie was all glammed up in the corset and I'm in a potato sack with my hair all kinked and having a nervous breakdown. It was perfect! [*Laughing*]

THE CHEMISTRY CREATED BY THE FANGED FOUR WAS SUCH A NEW AND FRESH DYNAMIC IN THE SHOW'S VAMPIRE MYTHOLOGY. WERE YOU SURPRISED HOW WELL THE FOUR OF YOU WORKED TOGETHER?

JULIET: We all felt the chemistry and I'm glad it translated to the screen. It was palpable between us and felt like a great doubles tennis match.

JULIE: It is rare for that to happen, but I think when you have four actors on set who take the work seriously and are trying to be true to the characters and what they are revealing, the chemistry comes out of that naturally. There were no egos and we were all there for the work – not for the fame. There was always something magical when we were in period costume, too. Each and every flashback we did, there was something in the air and it was exciting with the horses and hay and corsets and lots of hair. We *all* had *lots* of hair. [*Laughs*]

YOU EVENTUALLY GOT TO JUST WORK TOGETHER AND EXPLORE THE FEMININE SIDE OF YOUR CHARACTERS' CHEMISTRY DURING ANGEL SEASON TWO. WAS IT NICE TO GET SOME ALONE-TIME?

JULIE: I absolutely loved working with David, but it was wonderful to explore this other side to Darla and her relationship with women through another female

> "I TEND TO THINK SOMEWHERE IN THE UNIVERSE THAT DRU AND SPIKE WERE RECONCILED. I DEFINITELY THINK THEY KEPT A FLAME FOR EACH OTHER DESPITE ALL OF THAT BUFFY STUFF. EVIL SPIKE IS LOTS OF FUN." JULIET LANDAU

"i was pleasantly surprised when they called and asked if i would [play darla one last time]. David is one of my most favorite people to work with, and to be able to work with James and Juliet again was amazing."

Julie Benz

vampire. We had some of that in Season Two and it was really wonderful to work with Juliet. We come from the same training background so we speak the same language as actors. She takes it just as seriously as I do and she is just extraordinary. Some of the stuff she does as Drusilla just tickles me, and I find it hard not to laugh.

JULIET: Julie is great and right from the get-go, there was a creative spark that we were able to just bounce off each other. Our characters shared so much and are so very different. Having that commonality of history and yet the disparate natures gave us a lot of room to play.

WERE THERE ANY MOMENTS YOU CREATED ON THE SPOT THAT CAME OUT OF YOUR EASE AND RAPPORT WITH ONE ANOTHER?

JULIE: In "Fool for Love," in the scene where Drusilla is crying about wanting her own play-thing, she calls me "Grand-mamma." David started laughing at that and I hit him with my purse and that was all improv. I always feel it was charming to see the relationship between the three of us.

JULIET: I would come up with all kinds of things and a lot was kept and used. I do remember in "Reunion," we were shooting

a sequence where I'm rubbing up and down a pole. Then Julie strung together all the things that I had done that day into a charades-like move, and then the crew was running around doing it too. Looking at it from the outside was really funny. [*Laughs*]

SPEAKING OF THOSE DRU/DARLA ANGEL EPISODES, DID YOU HAVE A FAVORITE MOMENT IN THEM?

JULIE: For me personally, the scene I loved the most was when we got set on fire in "Redefinition."

JULIET: Yes!

JULIE: I love that scene because we were dealing with an element, which we hadn't faced before – being doused with water. We didn't get to rehearse and it was a freezing cold night, it was below 30 degrees.

JULIET: And I don't know if Julie remembers, but she had the flu and we were working so closely, of course I came down with it too.

JULIE: We were flying by the seat of our pants and we didn't know what to expect and they yell, "Action" and the water starts and it was a *ton* of water! Juliet had a lot of emotional work to do, and she is looking at me and the water is drowning me! I'm trying to protect her from some of it by

JULIE BENZ'S ANGEL/BUFFY CREDITS

covering her, but at the same time keeping her open for the camera.

JULIET: And I was closer to the water source! During one of the takes, there was so much water I couldn't speak. [*Laughs*]

JULIET: When they yelled, "Cut." I just remember us laughing! They didn't tell us it would be that much water! I don't think I would have made it through the scene with anyone else but her.

AFTER THOSE EPISODES, YOU DIDN'T WORK TOGETHER AGAIN UNTIL "THE GIRL IN QUESTION." THE CANCELATION WAS KNOWN, SO HOW DID YOU GET CALLED TO COME BACK ONE LAST TIME?

JULIE: I was hoping to be able to return to play Darla for one last time, but I was pleasantly surprised when they called and asked if I would. I was very excited when I got the call. Juliet and I talk on the phone once a week, and she mentioned that she got a call too and we wondered if it would be for the same episode. I was hoping it would work out and it did. I was hoping to go back and play one last time with everybody, especially David, because he is one of my most favorite people to work with, and to be able to work with James and Juliet again was amazing.

JULIET: It was great that it was the four of us together, getting to be there with David and Julie and James. You couldn't have asked for a better end. Plus, David Greenwalt was directing the episode and he was fantastic. I never read for Dru originally, but I had a meeting right at the beginning with Joss and David where we threw around ideas, and then he was doing my last episode!

THAT LAST EPISODE WAS PLAYED FOR THE COMEDY AND IT HYSTERICALLY ADDRESSED ALL THE SEXUAL SUBTEXT ALLUDED TO OVER THE YEARS. WERE YOU SHOCKED?

JULIE: When they sent me the script and I read that I would be naked and all this other stuff, I was like, "Whoa!" We thought it was

funny that they did something with The Immortal that they never let the guys do. The guys were really upset about it!

JULIET: It was so fun! We were laughing at the boys and their responses and we'd have to hold our laughter until they said cut because they were cracking us up. When we walk off and are giggling, we really are giggling because there was that sense of mischief and fun.

JULIE: I'm very klutzy on-set. My sheet got stuck on the camera dolly and I fell off the bed. I was a mess! But it was nice to play the comedy side of Darla.

IN ALL THE YEARS YOU PLAYED THESE WOMEN, WAS THERE A SCENE THAT WAS HARDEST FOR YOU TO DO?

JULIE: For me it was this one, because I had to change into a robe on set and David Greenwalt wanted a bareback shot, so obviously I was bare-fronted… in front of David and James. I was nervous, but everyone was really kind and respectful and I knew that Juliet was right behind the curtain, so that was good. The first time I did it, I was supposed to be talking while I

dropped the robe, but I forgot all my lines!

JULIET: She was really brave, and it was tastefully done. I didn't even know she was shy because she did it so comfortably!

WAS THERE ANOTHER TIME PERIOD YOU WANTED TO EXPLORE?

JULIE: I always wanted to do the '70s because I believe that Darla hung out with Andy Warhol and the Studio 54 crowd. Maybe she was a roller disco queen. I imagine her with a big blonde 'fro!

JULIET: I think the flapper era '20s or '30s would have been a fun Dru era. Can't you see Dru in a little bob?

WHAT DO YOU THINK WAS JULIET'S FINEST MOMENT ON THE SHOW?

JULIET: Oh, there are a lot of them! In "Dear Boy," there is a whole sequence where she confronts Angel in the pillars, and she was incredible.

JULIE: I have to go back to that first scene in "Dear Boy," where we are rolling around on top of her when she is sobbing. She had such focus and wasn't distracted and really worked off it, that just blew me away from the start!

DRU IS STILL AROUND - WHERE DO YOU THINK SHE IS TODAY?

JULIE: I think Darla would have been very smart to stick with her. Dru is probably off raising hell somewhere. [*Giggles*]

JULIET: I tend to think that Dru and Spike are reconciled somewhere. I would bring him back to evil. Evil Spike is lots of fun.

LASTLY, IF YOU COULD DESCRIBE ONE ANOTHER IN THREE WORDS - WHAT WOULD THEY BE?

JULIE: Juliet is elegant, focused and quirky, which is a weird dichotomy but so her!

JULIET: Oh Julie is playful, intelligent and talented.

LADIES, THANK YOU VERY MUCH!

THE GOOD

Almost a year after *Angel*'s cancellation, *Angel Magazine* thought it was about time we caught up with actress Amy Acker, who portrayed Fred for just over three seasons. Amy shares some special anecdotes and provides her thoughts on the best *Angel* kisser...

INTERVIEW BY

Bye GIRL

So imagine how you would feel. You've just flown over to the U.K., spent an exhausting weekend making on-stage appearances at a special *Angel* convention, answered all manner of probing questions from inquisitive fans, and posed and smiled for about 1000 official convention photos. Oh, and you're heavily pregnant. Well that's just what Amy Acker has been through, as *Angel Magazine* sits down to talk to her after a long convention weekend, and yet she is still friendly, smiley and lively – exactly as you imagine the Fred actress would be in real life.

Somehow, this comes as no surprise, considering the fun atmosphere the *Angel* set must have had. It's obvious that Amy has many fond memories of her three years working on the show, and she spends most of the interview smiling and chuckling. Her biggest laugh is saved for her memories of her first day working on the show – where she fell off a horse – an out-take (pictured overleaf, top right)

MARTIN EDEN

J.L. AMY

AMY CHATS ABOUT HER GUEST STINT AS THE HUNTRESS ON THE JUSTICE LEAGUE ANIMATED SERIES

"I DID THREE OR FOUR EPISODES OF THAT. I THINK THE PEOPLE WHO RUN THE SHOW ARE VERY BIG JOSS WHEDON FANS AND THERE'S A BUNCH OF *BUFFY* AND *ANGEL* AND *FIREFLY* PEOPLE INVOLVED WITH IT. I HAD NEVER DONE ANY ANIMATION WORK BEFORE AND I WAS TERRIFIED, BUT I THINK THEY WANTED AN ILLYRIA TYPE OF CHARACTER SO IT WAS COOL. "WHAT DID THE HUNTRESS GET UP TO? WELL, KIND OF A LOT WITH THE QUESTION. IT'S A BIZARRE SORT OF LOVE STORY. IT'S BEEN INTERESTING, ESPECIALLY COS THE GUY WHO PLAYS 'THE QUESTION' HAS TWO KIDS WHO ARE IN HIGH SCHOOL, SO IT'S AN INTERESTING MATCH!"

which is featured on the Season Five DVD. "Oh yes, that was really me," she chuckles. "I was on the horse with David [Boreanaz, Angel], whose girl-friend used to work on a Rodeo, and he was say-ing that he thought it would be more believ-able if the horse was running, and I was like, 'yeah, great!' And so he runs up the hill, and I was afraid to hang on to him too tightly because I didn't want him to think 'this girl's weird!' So I went fly-ing off and David tried to grab me and save me, but he just fell on top of me. I had a little bit of a bump on my head and my neck was really tight, but one of the stunt-guys offered to massage my neck. He turned out to be a chiropractor, and he snapped my neck back into place! I didn't like that at all!"

Indeed, there were plenty of humorous incidents on the *Angel* set. "There was something funny going on pretty much every day," Amy shares. "Pretty much any time Andy [Hallett,

Huntress Artwork © DC Comics

Lorne] was on set we had great fun! We would always make fun of him because he had certain things he would do – like he would do the double takes that Lorne does, then we would have this thing where we would see if we could get him to do a quadruple take! So we would always do little things, and he would always say little things that we would make fun of." Poor Andy!

Another fun experience was Season Five's "Life of the Party" episode, where Fred and Wes became inebriated, meaning Amy Acker and Alexis Denisof had to pretend to be totally drunk. Just how does one rehearse for something like that? "That was the funniest thing, because I was talking to Alexis and I was saying, 'now, are you going to be really drunk or just a little drunk?', and he was like, 'well I'm not going to do anything crazy…', and we went to rehearse the first scene and he was all 'hwuuuuurrrgh' (*makes drunk sound*). I was like, 'oh… so you've developed this whole character thing, so I should probably have done something other than pretend that I'm sleepy!' So we sort of just played with that all day, and it just got progressively crazier as the day went on."

There was just as much fun behind the cameras as in front – mainly in the form of practical jokes. "I think I was the victim of most of the practical jokes, although I would sometimes participate with the other guys. We did steal Andy's video camera one day and went around and got all the cast and crew to talk about how horrible he was to work with and what a diva he was. He was looking all day for his camera and he went home and found all these people just saying 'Andy's such a bitch!'" Poor Andy, again!

Of course, things became a little more serious for Amy when she took over the very different role of Illyria. "I'm not sure if I had a preference between playing Fred or Illyria," Amy says, after being asked to choose between the two. "Really, the combination of both of them made me like parts of each of them more. So when I was getting to play Illyria, it made me realize how nice it was to come to work and not have to put two hours' worth of make-up on!

"With Fred," Amy contines, "I got to experience a lot of emotion, especially with the scenes with Wesley towards the end. They were just two totally different things and it was nice to get to play both of them."

But which character would she prefer to be in real life? "I think it would be a little tiring to be Illyria for the rest of my life," Amy laughs. "She has a lot of issues that she has to work out!"

Playing Fred – and Illyria – have had their effects on Amy's own life, too. "I feel like before I started playing Fred, I was a little shy – and not as weird (*laughs*). I guess being around these guys every day, who were always cracking jokes, and playing such a character for so long starts to take an effect… Like now I just ramble on forever about nothing (*laughs*)."

Of course, it wasn't always light, comedy scenes with Fred – Amy had to deliver a lot of scientific lines too. "For some reason it was easier for me to do that," she says. "I feel like when I had to say a long paragraph of just stuff that didn't make sense, that's easier for me because I was like, 'Okay, I have to memorize all of this'. Then, every time I had a scene where I had just one word I would miss my line! If I had to do a whole thing of science talk, I could usually do it."

Amy didn't share all of Fred's traits, however. Prepare yourselves for a shock, readers – she's not a massive Dixie Chicks fan! "I probably wouldn't recognize much of their stuff. I think I would maybe recognize one of their songs. Music-wise, I pretty much like everything. My husband has gotten me into music that I never would have thought I'd listen to. I was always like an indie-rock kind of person – I always liked Pavement and things like that."

Picking out favorite *Angel* moments isn't a problem for Amy. "The Pylea stuff was really fun because it was my first time on the show and it was my first job in L.A. And I really liked the episode that Joss directed where we went to the ballet ['Waiting in the Wings']. That episode actually came about because Joss was saying, 'oh you did ballet', and I was like, 'yeah I did it for 14 years'. Of course, he didn't ask me which years of my life that was. I hadn't danced for seven years! But me and Alexis got to do a lovely ballet number. It's probably better that it wasn't in the show! **(It's on the Season Three DVD extras – Ed)** Alexis was quite the natural ballet dancer. He was wearing a red g-string under his costume, and it turned into rather a comedy experience. It was fun!

KISS AND TELL

WHO'S THE BEST KISSER IN THE ANGEL CAST? AMY REVEALS ALL – SORT OF…

"I GOT TO KISS ALL OF THEM. IT WAS ALL SO SPREAD OUT. I DON'T KNOW THAT I REMEMBER WHO WAS THE BEST. (*LAUGHS*) I SEEM TO REMEMBER BEING NERVOUS HAVING TO KISS ALL OF THE GUYS. I GUESS THEY WERE ALL GOOD!"

{ "I THINK IT WOULD BE A LITTLE TIRING TO BE ILLYRIA FOR THE REST OF MY LIFE. SHE HAS A LOT OF ISSUES THAT SHE HAS TO WORK OUT!" }

"As for favorite Illyria moments," continues Amy, "I liked beating up Spike so much. That was a lot of fun. That was the first time I ever got to really beat up one of the boys. I loved the Illyria stuff in the last episode with Wesley, switching back between Fred and Illyria."

Speaking of that particular scene, *Angel Magazine* asks Amy which was the most difficult to perform – Fred's death scene or Wes'? "Fred's death scene was pretty much a day from 8am until 9pm with Joss, me and Alexis being locked in a room, pretty much starting crying at 8 o'clock until the end, so it was just a hard day. We were all like, 'let's go for a drink after work', but we were just so exhausted and had to go home. It was just a hard day. I didn't think saying goodbye to Fred would be as difficult as it ended up being.

"We were lucky that Joss was directing that episode. We did the scene four or five times and the first take is good but Joss is really pushing you to the next level, so I think having him there was good. Luckily, there was a lot of waterproof make-up. Joss had been thinking of the times Buffy died and that she looked so beautiful and he wanted Fred to look sickly and pale, and for the blue to be coming through and for Fred to look unflattering. It seemed to work!

"With Wesley's death scene," Amy continues, "that was his final day of working on *Angel* so everyone was kind of in shock that we were canceled and it was my last time to work with Alexis. So it was hard, but I guess that one lasted about two hours and the other one was 14 hours…"

Amy has only seen the final *Angel* episode once so far. "I think, eventually, I want to watch it again. I've just been

WHAT HAPPENED NEXT!

DID AMY GET ANY HINTS FROM THE ANGEL WRITERS ABOUT THE DIRECTION SEASON SIX WOULD HAVE TAKEN?

"I THINK IT WAS GONNA BE A CONTINUATION OF THE FINALE, WITH US FIGHTING ALL OF THESE PEOPLE ON OUR OWN AND GOING OUT AGAINST THESE EVIL *SOPRANO* MAFIA THINGS – WE'RE TRYING TO KILL THESE PEOPLE. I THINK IT WOULD HAVE BEEN REALLY INTERESTING. ACCORDING TO JOSS, ILLYRIA SURVIVED THE FINALE."

really sad that we didn't go back, even now. You just think about things from the first year and you think, 'oh isn't it sweet, we were doing this…'

Amy did, however, get to see her big episode – "A Hole in the World" – quite a few times, and one occasion in particular stands out. "Joss and Alexis and I went to do the commentary for the DVD and we sat there for 20 minutes, and everyone was so sad that we didn't even say anything! The guy in the booth was like, 'erm shall I rewind it, because someone needs to talk on this thing…?' We had to start over and do it again."

Angel fans may have heard some Amy Acker rumors over the last few months, so *Angel Magazine* decides to put the record straight. One rumor had Amy

linked with the sequel to the *Texas Chainsaw Massacre* remake. "I don't know where that came from," she laughs. And there's also been a Lois Lane rumor flying around. "Yeah, someone asked me about that the other day. They're auditioning people right now, but I haven't even got an audition. I would like to."

And then there are some rumors that *completely* baffle the actress. "When I'd first gotten married," Amy reveals, "I showed up at Paramount and my husband, James, drove me there. The guard was a big *Angel* fan and he said to me, 'I thought you got married to Skip the Demon and you're already cheating on him?' So I guess there was some rumor that Skip the Demon and I got married, and I was like, 'Okay…' I never even met him out of make-up – I don't know what he looks like!"

After an hour of reminiscing, it's time to draw the interview to a close. *Angel Magazine* asks Amy if she has any special message for the readers and *Angel* fans. "I just thought it was amazing that everyone tried so hard to keep the show going, and that people were still watching it. We all wanted it to continue. It was such a fun thing for all of us," she concludes, "and I'm glad that other people enjoyed it as much as we did."

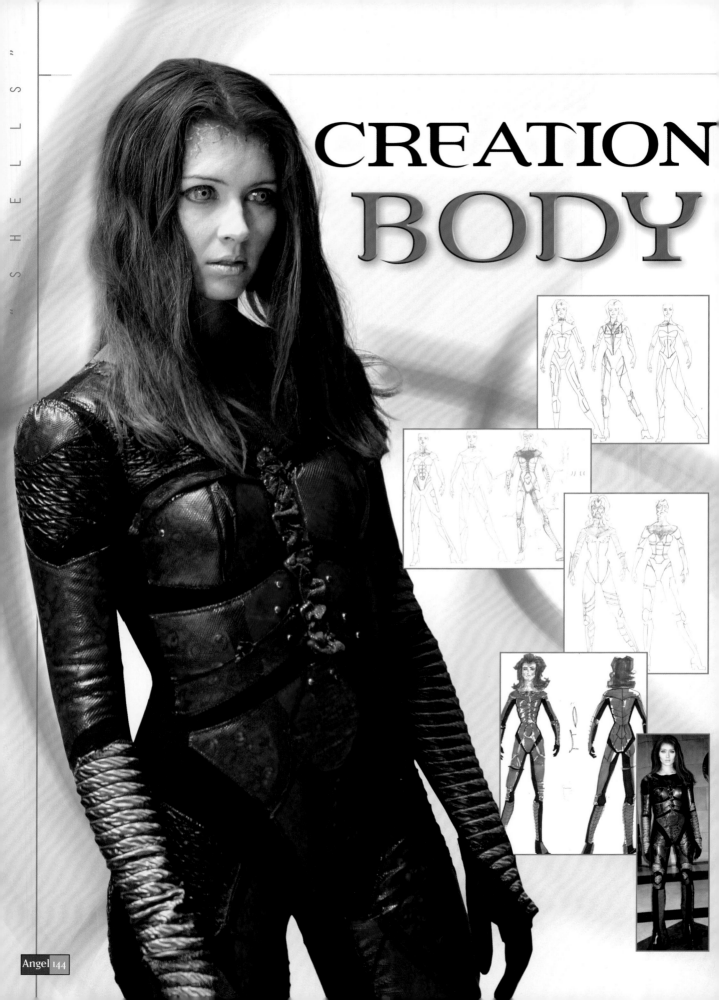

CREATION
BODY

OF THE SNATCHER

BY COREY EVETT

ANGEL MAGAZINE TAKES A LOOK AT THE DEVELOPMENT OF ILLYRIA — FROM SCRIPT TO SCREEN!

Fred's shocking transformation into demon goddess Illyria provided the various production departments of *Angel* with a difficult task: creating an entirely new character being portrayed by a familiar actress.

In the script detailing Illyria's dramatic first appearance, she is described in just a few short lines: "Her eyes are blue… A similar color has crept in at the edges of her face in a striking mottle that has even bled streaks of blue into her face."

It was from this basic description that Dayne Johnson, head of the Make-up Department, drew his inspiration. "[Joss Whedon] didn't want her to be completely blue like [Mystique] on *X-Men*, or look like a Smurf," laughs Dayne. So Dayne came up with the concept of fading various shades of blue together instead of using just one stock color. During a typical application, a dark blue is applied near Amy Acker's forehead, followed by an aqua-marine, then a lighter shade of blue. These are subtly faded together, which is then covered in an alabaster shade, which lends a deathly pallor to her skin.

After completing an initial make-up test, Dayne decided to make a few adjustments. "I ran the original photo through Photoshop," he notes, adding a little bit of texturing to the skin. This formed the basis for the writhing veins on Amy's scalp that appear to creep into her hair.

"Initially, I airbrushed blue streaks into her hair, because they said it was sort of bleeding from her scalp into her hair," Diana Acrey, head of the Hair Department, explains, "but they didn't like how it photographed." Amy's hair couldn't be dyed because of potential continuity problems, so the decision was made to use a wig. Working closely with Dayne, Diana extended the faded blue motif into the wig. "I didn't want it to be uniformly blue," she notes. "I felt it would be more unusual to have more blue in the front, and have a little less streaking through." By doing this, Diana was able to further illustrate the idea that Illyria has infected every fibre of Fred's being.

Meanwhile, Illyria's skin-tight costume was a huge departure from what Fred usually wore. When Amy Acker told costume designer Shawna Trpcic that the new character would be some sort of demon, Shawna immediately pictured something "skin-tight and sexy," and Amy happily agreed.

With that heads-up Shawna began researching a new costume. "Joss wanted her costume to be either green or red, so I went for a forest green and blood red. The visuals he gave me were H.R. Giger and Catwoman," Shawna reveals. Utilizing ideas from Michelle Pfeiffer's skin-tight Catwoman outfit and H.R. Giger's biomechanical *Alien* look, Shawna worked on the idea that the suit was a living extension of Illyria. This sectional, exo-skeletal look became a driving force for the final costume. After bringing Joss photos from the original fitting, Shawna says, "he literally drew on it to break it up because he was picturing something a little more asymmetrical."

With these modifications in hand, Shawna used liquid latex, usually used in body-painting, and painted directly onto the costume, breaking it up exactly as Joss had illustrated. She then went a step further. "I went back in with different acrylic paints to separate it even more to bring out different shapes," Shawna adds.

The patchwork costume has a cotton Lycra bodysuit as its base, with vinyl, taffeta, various brocades and rat-tail (a special detailing fabric) thrown into the mix. The finishing touch is a pair of black thick-soled boots. Shawna says, "we sewed the mic [into the costume] and we plugged it into her boot, which is where the radio pack was located."

The final result is spectacular, with the uber-talented Amy Acker breathing life into the new character. Joss had told Amy that the character was going to be blue, but hadn't yet worked out all the details. So at her behest, he wrote her a few scenes to help her feel out the character. "[Joss] had written two scenes," Amy explains, "and had me and Alexis [Denisof, Wesley] come over to his house one weekend, [to work on] the character." From these rehearsals, Amy was able to create Illyria's signature insect-like movements.

Bringing a new character to life, especially one as design-intensive as Illyria, is a daunting task for any production company, but it's safe to say that the experienced crew and Amy all stepped up to the challenge. As Dayne Johnson puts it, "The contacts, the wardrobe, her hair and her voice… that's what puts it all together. Creating Illyria involves Hair, Make-up, Wardrobe and Amy." Or, as Amy says, "Everyone just put a little bit into it." ❧

Friend or foe? Goodie or baddie? The jury was out on Fred's mysterious employee, Knox, for quite some time – and the ultimate revelations proved to be devastating! Actor Jonathan Woodward discusses his *Angel* role

With Angel's takeover of Wolfram & Hart in Season Five, the gang found themselves dealing with a building full of evil employees, all potentially ready and willing to turn on their new bosses at any time. Team Angel weeded out many of the worst and put fear into the rest, but there were a few that defied categorization – one being Fred's right-hand man, Knox. The white-coated lab geek was seemingly Fred's perfect match – a sweet-faced brainiac always ready to help when the situation was at its worst. Yet for all his good deeds, something just had to be wrong with Mr. Perfect. Jonathan M. Woodward, who played the scientist, admits, "I [didn't] get told and I liked it that way. I think it was just really clear that he was supposed to be the nicest guy in the universe, which was a tip-off that he was probably going to be awful later, so [I was] having fun making him nice [at the start]!"

The Auburn, Maine native developed a love for acting at the young age of six, when he first performed in local productions, but it wasn't a career aspiration until later in life. "If I had known the ramifications of the decision to become an actor, I might have been too freaked out to make it," he laughs. He eventually attended N.Y.U. for Experimental Theater. "It was entirely based on performance and performance theory. It was very non-traditional. It was great and I still work with them today." Out of school, he pursued New York theater, never intending to jump to television. "It was the East Coast mentality to shun TV. I ended up with an agent coming out of school and so I began auditioning. It was slow. It was probably three straight years of auditioning and I really didn't know what I was doing. I did a commercial or two, but I was mostly doing plays with friends and working on a dance piece that we took on a tour to France and Italy. Eventually, I got booked for a film and that changed everything. It was such a gift." That role was in Emma Thompson's drama, *Wit*.

A few years later he moved to Los Angeles, and television came calling. Astute viewers will recognize Jonathan as Holden Webster, the psych-student vamp in the Season Seven *Buffy* episode, "Conversations with Dead People." His impressive stint in that episode then led to his casting as Tracey in the unaired *Firefly* episode, "The Message." "They wrote Tracey in *Firefly* with me in mind and they wrote Knox for me on *Angel*." In that episode ['Home'], Knox gave Fred the tour of the Wolfram & Hart Science Division in hopes of tempting her to jump onboard. "When they called me up for the end of [Season Four], it was hinted that I might come back in the next season," Jonathan comments. "I was on set with Amy Acker and we were talking and she said, 'If we come back, we may see you in September.'"

As Jonathan hoped, Knox did come back.

"When the season got kicked off, they booked me for three [episodes] and I always operated off the assumption that if I wasn't dead by the end of the episode, I would probably come back for one more so they could kill me," he smiles.

Jonathan says working on *Angel* was great. "Everyone had his or her rhythm and I got comfortable enough, finally, and I [didn't] get nervous." Due to his work on *Buffy* and *Firefly*, Jonathan also got to work with some familiar faces on the crew. "Shawna Trpcic, the costume designer worked on *Firefly* and then came over to *Angel* and so did Diana [Acrey-Doyle] from Hair, so when I showed up on *Angel* I knew both of those guys and that was very exciting. It was a nice feeling."

The steady work is always a plus, too. "I like being recurring. I've never been a

series regular. I was drawn to acting because it was always a different project and that's important, but I'm rethinking that now because that's not how the world works and I find TV fun. It's nice to go to work every day and hone a character."

Knox's presence started off low-key in Season Five, with his appearances consisting mostly of science talk and a little bit of flirting between him and Fred, a storyline he was enjoying, too. "I dig Amy. She is the sweetest thing in the universe. [Knox] was completely in love with the girl. Otherwise, it was mostly fun, quiet, lab stuff. It's always lab coats for me," he chuckles.

But as we all now know, the evil Knox was eventually revealed – much to Team Angel's devastation. Jonathan liked the twist, and was happy that he only found out at a late stage. "I [would just] come in and say, 'Hi, I'm Knox' and look cute, so something interesting eventually had to happen. I [was] much happier getting surprised like everyone else. Plus, if I [had known], I wouldn't [have wanted] to unconsciously tip my hat. Yes," he concludes, "there [were] some really interesting episodes for Knox…!"

"I THINK IT WAS REALLY CLEAR THAT [Knox] WAS SUPPOSED TO BE THE NICEST GUY IN THE UNIVERSE, WHICH WAS A TIP-OFF THAT HE WAS PROBABLY GOING TO BE AWFUL LATER!"

She's the werewolf that stole, or at least put a down-payment on, Angel's heart in Season Five — and this issue, we catch up with actress Jenny Mollen to discuss her time with Team Angel, her latest projects, and her passion for painting!

Although she only made three appearances during *Angel*'s final season as the werewolf Nina Ash, Jenny Mollen made a lasting impression on Angel and his friends, as well as with the audience. A fan of the show before she joined, Jenny loved working with David Boreanaz and the gang, as she explained to us at the Starfury: Fusion event last year…

HOW DID YOU GET CAST AS NINA?
It was just through auditioning. Actually, I met Joss Whedon because of mutual friends. I had done a Shakespeare reading at his house so he had seen me 'quasi-act.' He had requested that I come in and read for the role of Nina. He probably didn't know that I had read two weeks before for the role of Eve for the casting people – or I assume he didn't know. Maybe he did! All of a sudden, the casting people called and said that Joss Whedon wanted to see me. It was all a little overwhelming, one of the most nerve-wracking auditions of my life. I went in with seven other girls for a producer session,

MOON STRUC

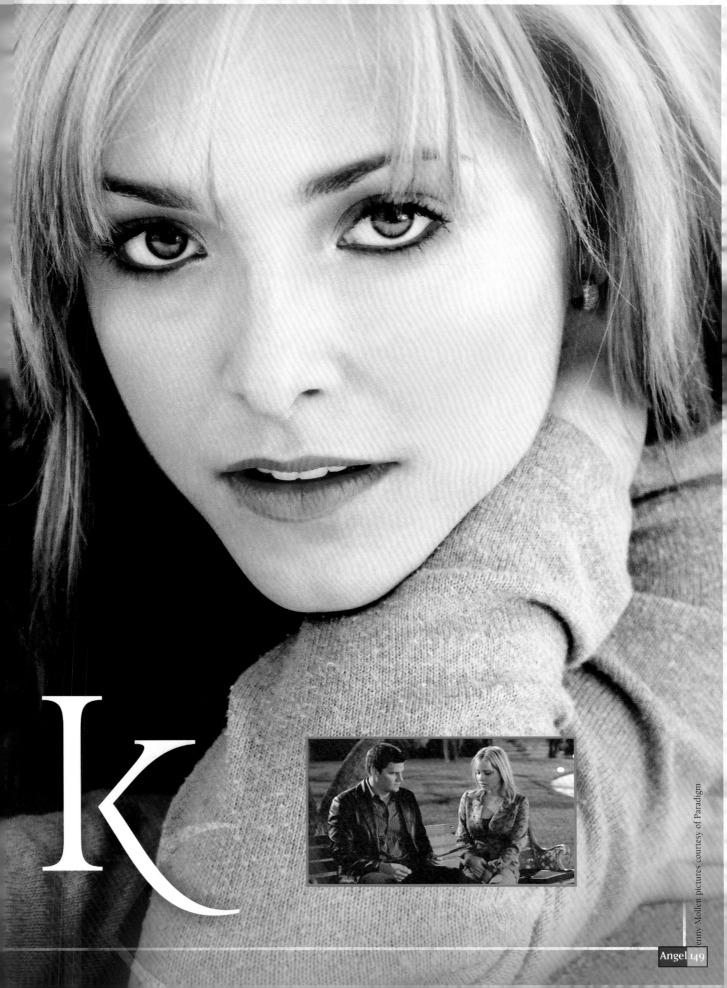

K

Jenny Mollen pictures courtesy of Paradigm

and then had to wait to find out if I was going to do it or not.

WHAT DID THEY TELL YOU ABOUT THE CHARACTER?

I knew that she was a werewolf. I also knew that she had to be strong enough to stand up to David. I think they had found that oftentimes, casting opposite David can be hard, because he is such a presence. They needed somebody to walk in there and take control of the scene and go toe-to-toe with this guy who is such a force. That's all I knew. It was really instinct. At that point I knew that all I could bring to it was who I am and what I do, so I took a risk.

WHAT DO YOU THINK YOU DID THAT WAS DIFFERENT FROM THE OTHERS?

I don't know! I wish I could have sat in on the other auditions. I heard a lot of other people screaming the lines. It's always weird when you're outside and you hear from an audition room these girls with these off-the-wall inter-pretations of lines that you've practised. You're certain that they've got to be just the way you see it in your head, then you hear them going crazy and thrash-ing about the room. I went in there and kept my anger more con-tained, and was a little teary-eyed.

ANGEL'S RAGE IS MOSTLY KEPT INTERNAL, BUT

OCCASIONALLY HE LETS IT LOOSE, AND A WERE-WOLF OPERATES IN MUCH THE SAME WAY...

Exactly – and you do have to look to him. The reason that Nina worked so well on the show was that she was Angel and his issues in woman form. You were able to add the vulnerability of a woman. I always saw it as; you're addicted to drugs, you're addicted to alcohol, you're addicted to sex, you're addicted to food, whatever it is, you're living with it. It's something

that you wake up every morning and you make a choice – how am I going to play it today? What kind of day is it going to be? I feel like with Nina that I took David's lead. He's been playing this character long enough – how is he doing it? What is he doing with the charac-ter of Angel, and how would a woman deal with it, how would an

art student? You break it down that way.

DID YOU EXPECT HER TO BE A RECURRING CHARACTER?

I just remember when I read the script for "Unleashed," and it said, "See you next month!" I went "Yes!! Maybe there'll be a next month! Maybe I'll come back." But I don't think I knew. I hoped. I had my fingers crossed.

HOW DID IT FEEL, COM-ING INTO THE FIFTH SEASON OF THE SHOW?

I realized right off the bat that when a show's been on the air [that long] that people are so pro-fessional. There's no question. It functions. It's like a well-oiled machine. Kelly Manners kept that ship moving. I couldn't believe it: it felt like a normal job. Sometimes on film sets, as I've experienced in the recent past, you can get into bad situations where you've got to be able to protect yourself because nobody is look-ing out for you. There's no SAG rep around. Things can really get out of hand, and you can get really screwed. On *Angel*, I was so pro-tected by everybody. There was no question about anything. It was all handled. I was spoiled, and all I kept saying when I was in Romania on *Return of the Living Dead*, standing on a scaffold I saw built that day with just a couple of nails and a piece of wood, "I wish I was still working in TV"!

IT SEEMED LIKE A LONG GAP BETWEEN YOUR APPEARANCES – HAD THEY TRIED TO BRING YOU BACK EARLIER?

I was working on something else in-between, but they also had to wrap the story with Cordelia up.

> The reason that Nina worked so well on the show was that she was Angel and his issues in woman form.

They did not want to take away from that relationship, which I agreed with.

THEY DIDN'T WANT ANGEL TO BE PERCEIVED TO BE TWO-TIMING HER...

Or let him move on too fast, because that was a serious relationship that spanned a very long time. They needed to split that up a little bit. The submarine episode was in-between as sort of a gap.

IT WAS A RARE STAND-ALONE EPISODE IN THAT SEASON...

I think they wanted more stand-alones, and I think that was a problem as far as the network was concerned: "How do we pitch this to an audience?" My mom, who hadn't seen *Angel* before, was wondering, "Who's the green guy? Why is he green?" When they got into things like the puppet episode, the producers were giving the fans exactly what they want. As a fan, I hate stand-alone episodes. Tell me about the relationships. I don't care about the monsters! Tell me what's happening between these two people.

WHEN YOU RETURNED, WAS IT STILL UPBEAT?

Yes, for "Smile Time," but for "Power Play," it was really sad. It was Jim Contner's last episode. My shot on the park bench, I think, was the last thing he ever shot on *Angel*. It was bittersweet, certainly. Everyone there knew that fans were protesting over at The WB. We heard about all these crazy things happening. People were looking for new jobs and trying to figure out what they were doing next year. They knew it was over, but it was almost like graduating high school. You know you have to move forward, but you don't want to let go.

DID YOU FEEL NINA REMAINED TRUE TO HERSELF?

The show was called *Angel*, so it was always about what purpose did she serve? Why was she there? I always felt that she got a little too clingy, but I think she was just scared. You saw her go from, "Who are you? What the hell do you want with me?" to, "God, make this stop" to, "I kind of like you" to, "I need to be with you because that's the only way I know myself any more." She definitely had an arc, but I would have liked the show to have continued, just to experiment and play that out a bit more.

WHAT HAVE YOU BEEN DOING SINCE *Angel*?

I was in *Return of the Living Dead*, which I starred in with Peter Coyote, and then I just finished a movie with Tom Sizemore and Gina Phillips called *Fear Itself*. Both of those features took up most of my time. *Fear Itself* finished right before I went to Houston where I did my only U.S. appearance for *Angel*. I'm not going to go back to theater until I've got more money – I can't afford to live in L.A. and do theater. I need to do my time in L.A., and keep building the resume before I can be in a position to go to New York and do something great.

WHAT ABOUT DIRECTING?

I've no interest in going behind the camera. I have no patience. I look at directors and

think that their job sucks. They have to be there all day and all night. Writing is where I feel more in my element. Directing any sort of crew? I'm taking a course in lighting because I'm really interested. I'd like to know how to take the camera apart and put it back together. I want to be able to help them do their job. If you know what they're looking for, it makes a huge difference, and if you can tell how you're coming across, it really changes.

IF YOU WERE ASKED TO REPRISE NINA, WOULD YOU WANT TO?

I'd be thrilled, definitely. ✛

JENNY MOLLEN, ARTIST

In real life, Jenny Mollen has something in common with her *Angel* character Nina Ash: they're both... artists. (What did you think – they're both were-wolves?) Jenny does uncommonly layered paintings, often provocative depictions of women, with oil, applied to surfaces like kimono silk rather than ordinary canvas, then covered with boat lacquer.

Speaking at the *Angel* Booster Bash, where two of her works have just sold for $600 each at a charity auction, Jenny says with a laugh, "I think the painting came out of my frustration with the consistency of acting. The painting has been really cathartic. You're not working for three to four months, and then you have a job and you're working 16-hour days and then nothing, except for trying to find another job. So for me, it was something tangible that I could put my emotion and my anger and longing into, that I could actually hold and it wasn't as ephemeral as, say, shooting a scene and then never seeing it again."

There is a connection between the multiple layers of her artwork and the types of roles she chooses, Jenny explains. "I don't really see myself playing [ditzy] or bitchy cheerleaders. Because of my background and where I've come from, I definitely have an aversion to the typical 'I'm blonde and I'm just completely vapid' or 'I have no life experience.' So that's just not what I want to do and I think it comes out a lot in the paintings. I don't want to do anything straightforward, I want there to be different levels and different aspects of ways of interpreting. I also love the lacquer because it's closure and you seal it and it won't be touched, it can't be touched. I love that."

Jenny has had several exhibitions of her art, including one in Los Angeles in November 2004 (where all of the pieces sold) and one in New York in August 2005. For the Los Angeles show, Jenny says, "I had an installation piece in a warehouse loft. It had these amazing brass rails around the room, so there were two or three layers of racks all around the room. I went in and made it look like a man's closet that had been disheveled and torn apart – I wanted it to look like a break-up in a way, and I had a giant suitcase tipped over with all sorts of things coming out of it and a lamp tipped over, and there was a giant mirror on the ground standing up and it said the name of the show in lipstick across it. And then I had an enormous bed frame that I brought in. The room was its own experience. I was at the Biannale in Venice several years back, and I was so inspired by the fact that art isn't just what's hanging on the walls – you could actually turn the entire room into your piece and it's an entire experience. And I love that – that really excites me."

BY ABBIE BERNSTEIN

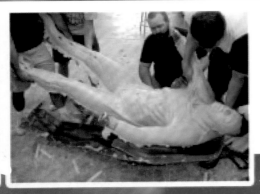

SEASON FIVE'S FIFTH EPISODE, "UNLEASHED", BRINGS A FAMILIAR AND FRIGHTENING CONCEPT TO THE *ANGEL* UNIVERSE – WEREWOLVES! BUT THE *ANGEL* CREATORS WERE DETERMINED TO DO THINGS DIFFERENTLY. MATT PARTNEY INVESTIGATES.

Something new is lurking in sunny Los Angeles, but only for three nights a month. Werewolves have made their way to *Angel*, but they may not be what fans expect. Towering at 6'3", on two legs, *Lycanthropus Exterus* isn't your typical *Buffy* werewolf...

Described by a Wolfram & Hart cryptozoologist as a rare breed of werewolf not previously found in North America, this particular beast is a mishmash of classic werewolf lore with some interesting twists. In the same way that *Angel* (and *Buffy* before it) reinterprets vampire lore, choosing some existing elements while invent-

ing others, the producers and make-up effects team took characteristics from classic werewolf movies and folklore and hybridized them with some new concepts.

"Silver still affects them," co-executive producer Jeff Bell reveals. "They still transform with the full moon: the night before, the night of, and the night after, as established in *Buffy*." However, the look of this new species is meaner, scarier and wholly unlike what was presented on *Buffy* in previous seasons.

And Jeff Bell doesn't mince words about it. The werewolf of *Buffy* has

AN AMERICAN
WEREW
IN ANGEL

OLF

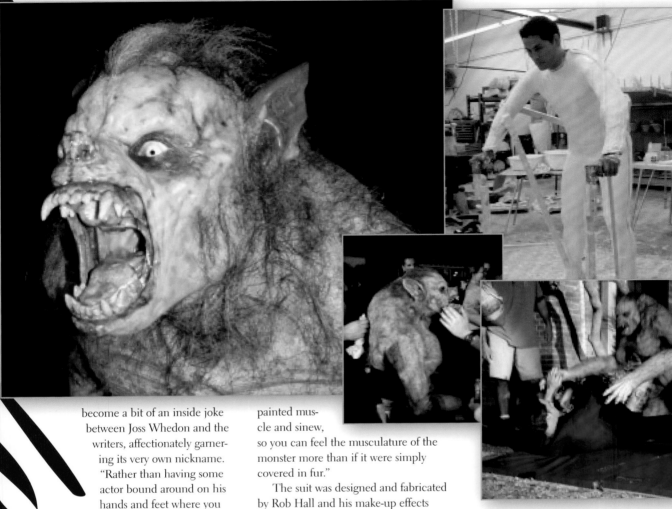

become a bit of an inside joke between Joss Whedon and the writers, affectionately garnering its very own nickname. "Rather than having some actor bound around on his hands and feet where you go, 'Oh, Big Gay Possum' – not that there's anything wrong with a Big Gay Possum – we wanted to at least buy the movement. We thought that we could [improve] upon that by it being upright, like in The Howling and Dog Soldiers."

The next characteristic to be changed was the overall furriness of the werewolf. "The Big Gay Possum was just a big fur suit," Jeff points out. "So this werewolf is intentionally less hairy. There will be plenty of hair, but underneath it will be painted muscle and sinew, so you can feel the musculature of the monster more than if it were simply covered in fur."

The suit was designed and fabricated by Rob Hall and his make-up effects shop, Almost Human, which does all of the make-up effects for Angel. Rob worked closely with Jeff in creating a werewolf that was completely unlike the one last seen on Buffy, if not unlike any werewolf depicted on-screen to date. "I purposefully tried not to look at the Buffy werewolf because we were trying to stay away from that," says Rob.

The suit is a creation on a par with, if not exceeding, the specs of The Beast from last season. "We applied a lot from what we learned with The Beast," Rob explains. "We found [an advantage in] making the suit soft, but also dense enough that it could take a fall and hit the ground in a fight." And it does. The werewolf suit was put to the test in two knock-down, drag-out fights. 'Dummy' arms were fabricated to replace the mechanical ones in fight sequences to protect the fragile arms from damage. This allowed the stunt performer to move with greater stealth and speed.

Rob credits the hair as the "trickiest" of the suit's features. "Any time you do

anything with lots of hair it always adds time, cost and difficulty." Rob had two fabricators sewing hair into every crevice of the suit. The suit itself is very lightweight to accentuate the stunt performer's musculature and incorporate that into the overall appearance of the werewolf.

With only two weeks to build the suit, Rob enlisted the help of his entire shop (14 employees in all) from mechanics and sculptors to mold-makers, fabricators and painters. In fact, Almost Human put all it had into creating this one costume in a phenomenally short amount of time. "I wanted a werewolf with demon-like qualities," explains Rob. "Not just a man, not just a wolf, but something with really vicious-looking demon qualities."

The new werewolf is also much larger and imposing than species previously seen on *Buffy*. "He has these really long, cool arms," says Rob. A 'backwards' canine ankle, achieved by small stilts, will add height to the stunt/performer inside. "His feet will basically be in a really 'high heel shoe' position." Adding to the werewolf's inhuman and almost demonic look is a bulbous backbone that runs up to the base of the neck, an idea Rob had from the start.

The design of the werewolf's head and face was the one element that was most toiled over and proved to be the most challenging. Some original conceptual designs included a traditional wolf snout, while others were more flat and demonic-looking. "There were some visual things we did in order to keep it in the 'Angel-verse,'" says Jeff. These included the incorporation of a vampire-like brow. "You'll notice on our show our vampires have a bumpy brow and some of our

demons have it as well," explains Jeff. "The werewolf has the same kind of brow."

To avoid costly animatronics, the face was designed to be fairly close to the stunt performer's face. Jeff wanted something the actor could manipulate with his own face, rather than by someone else via remote control. "What you'll see will be the actor's actual eyes and expressions," notes Jeff. "The actor is actually opening and closing the mouth, as opposed to a really long wolf snout." "We tried to keep some of the human elements in there," says Rob. "If you'll notice in the design, there's actually a human nose that's been squished up."

"It's not so much about the transformation," says Jeff Bell of the onscreen imagery and visual effects of the werewolf. Instead, it's left to our imagination. The combination of sound effects and the stretched and taught shape of the werewolf body creates a clear idea of the trauma caused to the human body during the transformation from human to werewolf.

Almost Human spent a lot of time with the stunt performer, Steve Upton. "It's been a pretty involved process," Rob admits. With a normal demon, the team at Almost Human meets with a performer just once

before arriving on set. Steve had no less than five sessions, starting with molding of teeth, feet and hands and face mask sculpting, to a full body cast. Then Steve had to spend time learning how to walk in the special feet and operating the mechanical hand extensions that were created.

"We needed someone who could do stunt work but also do some acting and emote, all the while having the ability to walk on small stilts," explains Rob. Having spent three months in a cumbersome 'Morlock' suit in the 2002 feature film, *The Time Machine*, Steve knew how to handle himself.

As with all his monstrous creations, Rob is proud of the finished werewolf and optimistic about its reception by fans. "My ultimate goal is to have fans watch the show and say, 'Okay, that's different. I haven't seen that a million-and-a-half times.'"

Jeff Bell is equally as excited about the new concept on a classic creature. "With a TV budget, we can't [afford to] reinvent the werewolf," Jeff explains. "All we can do is create something that's really cool, really scary and not… a Big Gay Possum." ❦

Written by Sheriff Matt Partney

WANTED, UNDEAD, OR ALIVE: THE BLACK THORN

IF YOU SEE ANY OF THE FOLLOWING PEOPLE, DO NOT APPROACH THEM! INSTEAD, READ THEIR PROFILES...

1 ARCHDUKE SEBASSIS

"THE CROWN JEWEL OF THE UNDERWORLD JET SET" - LORNE

The Archduke is the key player in The Circle. All other members take cues from him. Demons and humans alike respect and fear him. Like all members of The Circle, he is a client of Wolfram & Hart. With over 40 legions under his power, he is the living-end of a pure bloodline of demonic royalty. Interestingly, he possesses telekinetic powers and prefers to drink the blue blood from the wrist artery of his demon slave (a.k.a., the talented Mr. Pee Pee).

2 IZZERIAL THE DEVIL (A.K.A., "IZZY")

"YOU'RE REALLY COMING THROUGH BIG GUY. THERE'S A REAL BUZZ ABOUT YOU." - IZZY (TO ANGEL)

Izzy is a demon who looks every bit like the classic depiction of Satan… He exudes the attitude of a smarmy, business weasel, and guides Angel's entry into The Circle of the Black Thorn. He's also frequently Angel's racquetball partner.

SENATOR HELEN BRUCKER

"I DIDN'T CLAW MY WAY UP FROM HELL AND GET INSTALLED IN A HUMAN BODY, JUST TO HAVE SOME PAEDOPHILE STEAL MY SENATE SEAT." -SENATOR BRUCKER

The California state senator is a high-powered client who is as well-connected in Washington D.C. as she is in the demon world. Senator Brucker intends on becoming President in 2008 by any means necessary. She may look like a charming human woman, but she is anything but that. Down to her green blood, the senator is pure Hellspawn.

4 THE FELL BRETHREN

"The Fell are everywhere! We are a force of nature!" - Fell Brother

Vaguely described by Marcus Hamilton as "very big players," the Fell Brethren are a religious sect of demons who are obsessed with a human baby they believe to be some kind of prophesied "Holy One". Angry, ugly and scaly, they are surprisingly gentle in doting over the mother and child. However, their deceit remains as they fully intend on ritually sacrificing the child on his 13th birthday. The robed Fell simply call the baby Gordobach.

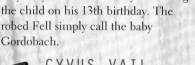

WANTED

ARTIST'S IMPRESSION
THE FELL BRETHREN

5 CYVUS VAIL

"I crap better magic than you." - Cyvus Vail (to Wesley)

Possibly the most mystically powerful of the players of The Circle, Vail is a potent sorcerer and head of a large demon empire of his own. He specializes in memory reconstruction, mind control, and temporal and reality shifts. The red and wrinkled one is Wolfram & Hart's go-to warlock for magical tampering. He built Connor's memories and the new reality that supported them the day Team Angel took over Wolfram & Hart. The ancient Vail appears physically weak and reliant on his mobile body fluid I.V., but he does possess a considerable amount of physical strength. He is also protected by violent Kith-harn demons. It is worth noting that he has a blood feud with SahJhan. The only one who can kill SahJhan is Connor.

WANTED

CYVUS

6 THE SAHRVIN

"Did you know they think poodles are wicked bad luck?" -Harmony

A vicious desert-dwelling demon clan who are, among other things, finicky about manners. Wolfram & Hart mediated a feud between them and the all-female Vinji demon clan that had lasted five generations. Unlike the attractive Vinji, the Sahrvin appear to be plagued by illness, with mottled skin, bulging goiters, oozing sores and facial quills. They only improve their image by robing themselves in tattered, drab, open-weave cloth and turbans. As researched by Harmony, we know that the Sahrvin treat Camel meat as a delicacy, usually tearing one apart with their bare hands. That's of course, only after its hump has been cut off and its heart stabbed by a red-hot poker...

WANTED

THE SAHRVIN

7 MARCUS HAMILTON

"I'm part of them. The Wolf, Ram and Hart. Their strength flows through my veins. My blood is filled with their ancient power." - Marcus Hamilton

Hamilton is Eve's replacement as Angel's liaison to the Senior Partners. Not only does he possess immortality and a close connection with the Senior Partners, he has strength greater than that of Angel and even Illyria. Though he's never seen with The Circle, the mere fact that he physically represents Wolfram & Hart likely makes him a power player.

WANTED

HAMILTON

THE VICIOUS CIRCLE

Interviews with The Circle of the Black Thorn

A t first, as *Angel* demons go, they don't seem all that bad. After all, Archduke Sebassis attends the Wolfram & Hart Halloween party and doesn't wind up killing anybody (although he almost shoots Lorne and Angel); Izzy the Devil is Angel's racquetball partner; Cyvus Vail wants SahJhan dead (don't we all?) and gave Connor happy childhood memories (even if he blackmails Angel with them); Fell Brethren leader Ed is helping a pregnant lady with her medical bills (even if he plans to sacrifice the kid in 13 years); Senator Brucker is a beautiful politician (okay, that's a sign of real evil). But who could have guessed they are all really members of the Circle of the Black Thorn, representatives of the Senior Partners' Earthly power?

Six months after *Angel* wrapped, we caught up with the five key Circle members – Leland Crooke, Dennis Christopher, Marc Colson, Jeff Yagher, and Stacey Travis. The actors have only seen each other's real faces in passing in the make-up trailer at 4am, so there's a sense of curiosity as they re-introduce themselves and propose various looks for our special photo shoot (Stacey Travis couldn't make it, so we chatted to her separately). Leland remembers the chant in the boardroom scene: "Didn't we sit with our hands like this?" He strikes the pose and the others follow, all happy to recall their shared demonic past...

Written by Abbie Bernstein

Actor photography by Albert L. Ortega, assisted by Lisa Berube.
Actor photo location: Wireimage Studio, Hollywood.

"POWER PLA"

THE DEVIL YOU KNOW

Mark Colson as Izzy the Devil

Over the years, demons have persuaded Angel to do many unlikely things, from fighting for the Slayer (Whistler) to singing "Mandy" (Lorne), but only one has ever induced the vampire to… play racquetball!

Mark Colson, who portrays Iziriel the Devil – Izzy for short – recalls that in "Power Play," he and David Boreanaz had a real game: "We never decided [who should win], we were just shooting. I want to say that I had the upper hand, but David would probably disagree with me," Mark laughs. "I hadn't played racquetball in years, but I'm a tennis player. I actually got out to a racquetball court beforehand, just so I wouldn't completely embarrass myself. I don't think that racquetball was really [David Boreanaz'] first sport either, so we were pretty much on the same playing level, so that was helpful.

"[The Angel production team] spared no expense – it was a full-on usable racquetball court. They put me in these really short shorts." This led to a slight mishap: "We put the [red] make-up [on Izzy's legs] on in the trailer and then when we went on the soundstage and I squatted down, my white skin started showing. I had to go back in the back and pull my pants down and get the make-up up with my underwear line," Mark laughs.

Izzy's personality came from the writing, Mark says. "There seemed to be sort of a New York/Brooklyn thing to it. I didn't want to overplay that, but that was an element that was fun to incorporate in the piece. He was almost like a goodfella, sort of, 'Hail fellow, well met, hey, I got your back.' Angel has a fine line between this elevated language and [being] completely contemporary and colloquial,

down to earth at the same time. You have to run in both of those worlds."

As for Mark's favorite bit: "It was a small, honest moment between David and myself [in "Power Play"] when we're talking about what a great turnout it is. He'd just killed [Drogyn]."

Illyria kills Izzy offscreen in the finale, though we do see the devil's reaction to her appearance. "I think more than anything, [it] was just the shock of, 'Oh, my God, who is this?!'

"Everybody was so nice and professional on that show," Mark observes, noting he's especially grateful he got along well with his make-up artist, Gabriel DeCunto: "You've got to be with this person for four hours. He's a great guy and very artistic. My biggest regret is that the show isn't coming back, so I can't do it again, because it was a blast." ❦

> " [Izzy] was almost like a goodfella, sort of, 'Hail fellow, well met, hey, I got your back. "

NEVER TRUST A POLITICIAN

Stacey Travis as Senator Helen Brucker

Brucker Senate

S enator Helen Brucker is the only demon in the Circle of the Black Thorn who appears as a human. Actress Stacey Travis – whose credits include *Hardware*, *Dracula Rising* and a recurring role on *Desperate Housewives* – shares her theory: "My take on it was that she was such a new demon that [the Senior Partners think], 'We could send this person to do our dirty work on Earth. The rest have just done this for too long and have no interest in changing shape.' So I felt like I might have been young enough that that was still not only something that I could do, but probably something I wanted to do."

When Stacey read for the role, "I asked the producers if I was good or bad. [They] said, 'You are all about power.' It wasn't until I got the script that I realized, 'Oh, I'm actually a demon.' The first day I shot was the Circle of the Black Thorn induction meeting with Angel. I'm surrounded by the [other Circle members] and they're in make-up, looking like fantastic creatures, and I felt like the odd woman out. Angel and I are the only ones dressed normal. It was a funny, surreal introduction to the show."

There are subtle hints that Stacey employed to indicate Brucker's true nature: "I did something different with my eyes – I didn't blink as much. Acting-wise, I just tried to take any softness out, any vulnerability."

There's a pecking order within the Circle, Stacey believes. "I think [the actors discussed it] at lunch one day.

[Sebassis'] title is the Archduke and there's a regalness with which he carries himself. It felt very much like he was our leader. I think Cyvus Vail was [second], because of his age. I felt the fact that I was talking to Angel about the Shanshu Prophecy [meant] that I was probably third in command – in my own head, anyway!" Stacey laughs.

Did the Senator underestimate Gunn? "One, she's a demon, two, she's

> " I was probably third in command [of the Black Thorn] – in my own head, anyway!"

got all these vampires around her, and three, she's a member of the Black Thorn. So however effective [Gunn] is at killing people, I think her immediate thought was, 'Oh, I'm busy doing what I've got to do to get re-elected and I've got to do to get re-elected and I

don't have time for this,' and she just waves her hand at her vampires, like, 'Take care of this, it's a nuisance.' I don't think she had any inkling that he was about to hurl an axe at her."

To show the effects of that axe toss, Stacey finally joined her Circle comrades in wearing some heavy make-up: "[The make-up artists] put the prosthetic on, then they dripped the blood the way they wanted it, then I leaned my head back and they came over and they literally took a screwdriver and screwed [the axe handle] in. I walked outside for some air and people were walking around the Paramount lot, and I've got an axe screwed into my head," she laughs.

What did Stacey find unique about working on *Angel*? "I'd never been on a set where they knew they were doing a show the fans love. Everybody still loved coming to work. I had a great time and I was really lucky that I got to be a part of the show before it came to an end."

RED MENACE

Dennis Christopher as Cyvus Vail

Although Dennis Christopher is well-known for his starring turn in 1979's mainstream coming-of-age hit film *Breaking Away*, a hippie in Federico Fellini's *Roma* and a persecuted Suliban on *Star Trek: Enterprise*, he's portrayed his share of baddies, from the crazed film fan in *Fade to Black* to diabolical serial killer Jack of All Trades in several seasons of *Profiler*. However, Dennis says he was instructed *not* to act evil when he auditioned for Cyvus Vail: "I said, 'Is there anything you want to tell me about the character?' They said, 'Just don't play it villainous.' Which I wasn't really going to anyway. I think the reason I got the part was because I used a really funny voice and just kept it up for the whole audition and made the horrible wheezing sounds that were written in the sidelines."

The intricate make-up for Cyvus helped Dennis create the performance. "There are so many hours of [getting the make-up applied], your imagination runs wild. At least mine did, the first day. It was all the subtext I needed, from the script and then watching your face be put on, piece by piece. It's kind of a surrealistic experience. It's how I figured out what he was going to be like. You've got all that stuff on you. You can't stand up straight and just walk into a room. You start to naturally shuffle and bend over, like an old guy. Suddenly, you're snorting and you start channeling every old person you've ever known," he laughs. "I really felt like that character by the time he was done in make-up. It's one of the easiest jobs I've ever had as far as finding who this guy was. And you think it would be hard, because there's no rules – what the hell was he?

"The make-up on *Angel* is so incredibly brilliant," Dennis continues. "When you go in and you see the almighty members of the Circle of the Black Thorn, it feels a little bit like this evil United Nations. The make-up was just so distinctive and distinguished that it really made you feel like one of the most horrible creatures in the universe, because we were all there to outdo each other and to share our power. When I saw some of them, I was very jealous. I thought Leland's make-up [as Sebassis] was fantastic. I had monster envy!"

No one in the Circle griped about the long hours or uncomfortable make-up: "We felt we were in very rarified air and nobody was going to be complaining, because we were all glad to come back and kvetching is just not something that gets you into character as a super-villain," Dennis laughs.

As the killer of Wesley Wyndam-Pryce, Cyvus is arguably the most heinous member of the Circle. He also gets the most spectacular on-screen comeuppance, as Illyria punches straight through his head. "I thought she over-reacted, just a tiny bit," Dennis

> "I thought Illyria over-reacted, just a tiny bit."

laughs. "You and I both loved [Wesley] very much, but how often do you get to kill a beloved series regular?"

Had *Angel* continued, Dennis sees possibilities for the Cyvus/Angel/Connor storyline: "Angel was [Connor's] father, but he didn't know that it was his father – and I assumed I was going to really rub [Angel's] nose in it, that [Connor] was *my* son, because I created what he is like now. I wanted there to be a fatherly rivalry between me and Angel for the allegiance and possession of this boy, with maybe the [adoptive] father getting in on it and getting murdered."

Angel was a great show to work on, Dennis says: "Sometimes you guest-star on a show and it's such a tight group that there's no way to get in. But there's something about that three or four hours of make-up, sitting in that chair, that makes you feel like you deserve to be there. There's none of that insecurity we feel sometimes – 'Well, maybe I'll screw up and maybe they'll find out now that I'm really a fraud.' After about the third hour in the make-up chair, you just think, 'I own this. Nobody can do this as good as I'm going to be able to do this.' And you have a different kind of confidence that makes people respond to you. From the casting women to the make-up people – Greg Funk, Jamie Kelman and Gabe DeCunto [at various times applied Cyvus' make-up] – they were all so nice and so accommodating. I love to work and to be on a set that is a good experience for everybody involved."

THE FELL GUY

Jeff Yagher as Ed, Leader of the Fell Brethren

Of all the actors playing members of the Circle of the Black Thorn, Jeff Yagher – who fought aliens on the series *V* and just wrapped a guest arc on *Six Feet Under* – probably has the most experience with heavy-duty prosthetics make-up, and not just because his guise as the Fell Brethren leader Ed encased his entire head. Jeff's brother is special effects make-up maestro Kevin Yagher, of Freddy Krueger and *Child's Play* fame. "I've grown up with this stuff," Jeff notes. Previous experiences being submerged in latex include a *Star Trek: Voyager* alien and the Crypt Keeper's literally two-faced father on the "Lower Berth" episode of *Tales From the Crypt*, directed by brother Kevin.

On *Angel*, Jeff observes, "They've got [prosthetics make-up] down to a science – they do it pretty fast. I think it took about an hour and a half. It's a full prosthesis. I had contact lenses and the only thing I think that was mine was my tongue," he laughs. "*Tales From the Crypt* was the same thing – full head make-up – but that one took seven hours."

As leader of the Fell Brethren, Jeff really did get to lead. "It was the director's [Vern Gillum's] idea that [the other Fell] do everything I do. So whatever body movement I assumed, they assumed, as a gesture of reverence."

> "[The make-up was] a full prosthesis. The only thing I think that was mine was my tongue."

Jeff and his fellow Fell also had to invent their own dialect. "When we were talking to the human characters, we spoke English, but when we spoke amongst ourselves, we had to come up with a language that was demonic. We were having a great time because everybody would start talking over each other and I'd have to make these clicking sounds to get everybody to shut up. You know when you play a [vinyl] record backwards? We decided to make those sounds, [like] when people were listening to Black Sabbath records backwards... So you'll have to play us backwards in order to really hear something," he laughs.

Jeff is not in *Angel*'s finale and consequently is not one of the Fell demons killed by Spike. Even if he had been, Jeff observes, that might not keep him down: "Dying doesn't mean much to a demon."

THE HORN SUPREMACY

Leland Crooke as Sebassis

After auditioning for the roles of Holtz and Pavayne, the third *Angel* audition for Archduke Sebassis proved the charm for Leland Crooke. "I'm glad I saved it all for the Archduke – I really enjoyed playing that part."

From reading the first meeting between Sebassis and Angel in "Life of the Party," Leland says, "I got that he was probably pretty aloof and above it all and arrogant. [At] the audition, I sat back in the chair and did this," he makes a bored gesture, "with my fingernail the whole way through.

"I'm of the mind that Sebassis really doesn't have that much [magical] power," Leland continues. "On the other hand, he's extremely shrewd. He's got all kinds of contingencies as far as protecting himself – except for his one weakness, which is the Pee-Pee demon. I developed some real camaraderie with Ryan [Alvarez]. He was my fountain, essentially, I think it would hurt the Duke to lose his little Pee-Pee demon."

Leland had prior experience with heavy prosthetic make-up, playing aliens on *Star Trek: Deep Space Nine* and *Enterprise*. He's also the only Circle actor to have appeared (out of make-up) on *Buffy*, as the poetry professor in "Tough Love." "On *Angel*, they did the whole thing where they cover your face in alginate and [take facial] moulds, so I was expecting a lot more [make-up]. It was very thin on my face. I could move my eyebrows [and] nuance the performance – I didn't feel like I was trying to act through a foam rubber pillow," he laughs. "They actually screwed the horns into the top of the [bald] cap, so

you'd see them putting a screwdriver to my head."

Sebassis was likewise physically connected to his slave. "I kept forgetting that Ryan was attached to me. They'd call 'Cut!' and I'd take off and Ryan was, 'Arrggh!'" Leland mimes being choked by a collar. "Finally, we switched the thing so he could snap himself loose when he saw himself starting to [get dragged]."

The first day of filming "Life of the Party" had some unexpected moments: "The very first scene we shot of the Duke was me bursting through the doors and discovering Angel making out with [Eve], and I knew that. Fortunately, they shot me first, because when we did the turnaround, I didn't know that David Boreanaz was going to be stark-assed naked. I didn't break **(drop out of character – Ed)** thank goodness – I didn't ruin any of the takes or anything – but perhaps they should have told me that!" Leland laughs.

Otherwise, Leland says, "It's been a wonderful experience. I wish the series had continued. Ryan and I were talking and we decided that the Duke and the Pee-Pee

> " My minions would have revived me at the last second!"

demon could give concerts, where the Pee-Pee demon would play [piano], and I'd play the theremin, and we'd play this eerie music with demons applauding us," he laughs.

In fact, Leland points out, "I was very happy that they didn't show the reveal of me dead, so if it ever becomes a movie, I could have had an antidote. My minions would have revived us at the last second!"

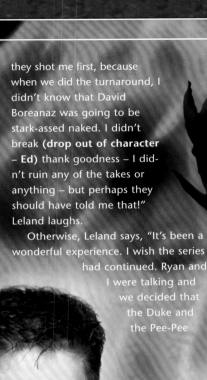

Father FIGURE

WE'VE MET A LOT OF TEAM ANGEL'S FAMILY MEMBERS, BUT DIDN'T GET TO MEET ONE OF WESLEY'S UNTIL THE SEVENTH EPISODE OF SEASON FIVE… BUT IT WAS WORTH THE WAIT! ACTOR ROY DOTRICE TALKS TO TARA DILULLO ABOUT HIS *ANGEL* EXPERIENCE.

As a former rogue demon hunter and leader of Angel Investigations, Wesley Wyndam-Pryce has had to face some pretty terrifying foes. Yet with years of apocalypse and demon-vanquishing under his belt, even he was unprepared when confronted with his worst nightmare in Season Five – a visit from his father. While Wesley's father had been alluded to in previous episodes and their less-than-amicable relationship was well documented, Roger Wyndam-Pryce hadn't actually made an appearance in the first four seasons of *Angel*. "Lineage" saw Mr Wyndam-Pryce Sr, show up at Wolfram & Hart looking to possibly reinstate his disappointment-of-a-son back into the rebuilding Council of Watchers.

When casting, the *Angel* producers knew precisely where to go to find the man imposing enough to make even Wesley buckle under his glare – the

venerable actor Roy Dotrice. His face is one that is instantly recognizable to fans of sci-fi genre television considering his many appearances in shows like *Babylon 5*, *Hercules*, *Sliders* and his most famous role of "Father" in *Beauty and the Beast*.

An actor for more than half a century, Roy's path to his profession itself sounds like something out of a movie. "It was destiny," he explains. "My home was in the Channel Islands just off the coast of France. I was there for the German occupation and on the third night of the occupation, a group of us got on a fishing boat and escaped and we arrived three days later in England. I tried to get into the Royal Airforce and they told me to come back when I was older. But I was able to put my age on and get in. I flew with them for two-and-a-half years and got shot down and became a prisoner of war. We had a lot of actors in our camp and the only entertainment was what we made for ourselves. We

did small productions and because I was so young, I was roped into playing the female parts. Eventually, I did graduate to male parts for which my wife has never ceased to be grateful," he laughs. Upon release from the camp, Roy returned to England where he did 13 years of repertory theater in over 500 different parts and directed over 300 plays at the Manchester Rep Company. His esteemed career has only grown since then, earning him critical praise in hundreds of other roles in stage, films and television.

When the part of Roger Wyndam-Pryce came across his desk, Roy was intrigued. "I don't read a lot of science fiction or fantasy and I hadn't seen the show before, but I thought it was a very interesting role," he shares. He accepted the part and showed up on set ready to dive into the complicated father/son relationship. "It was fairly easy because, obviously, Wesley's relationship with his

father was a strained one. His father was never lovey-dovey and quite stern with him. His attitude was one of criticism. I was never very nice to him on the phone and I certainly wasn't nice to him when I met him. I just had to stand back and be analytical and critical of him, which was easy to play."

Roy was also pleased by the fact the writers made Roger more than just a one-note role. "I did like the way they inserted that softer side. It made the character more convincing. He was very human like when he says, 'Have you told the girl you love her?' That was the best scene for me because it showed an attraction and sympathy towards the son. It was the most real part if it."

Having never worked on the show before, Roy was delighted with his experience. "The nice thing about working on *Angel* is that a lot of the people on the show have a theater background, which is fascinating. Amy [Acker] was sweet and the other actors were quite wonderful too. I thought the director, Jefferson Kibbee, was awfully good. He was an actor's director in that he trusted the actors. I thought he was great and I liked working with him. It was an easy job to do because everybody knew what they were doing, which made it easy for me to fit in."

Roy holds particular praise for his co-star, Alexis Denisof. "I had nearly all my scenes with Alexis. He is a theater actor, trained in England and he was very English. We sat for hours just talking about English theater and telling stories from the past. He was also great because whenever I had a question, he would explain the backstory to me. He was a delightful man, I really enjoyed his company."

For the climactic face-off in the last act, Roy was excited to participate in a full-out action scene. "I love working on location because it inspires you to another level of performance. We were on a rooftop and it was quite wonderful, actually. It was late at night and we were on top of a skyscraper and there were skyscrapers all around us. It was magical. They had something like a hot air balloon that went about 50 feet in the air and lit the whole set. It was like a vast moon hanging over the skyscraper. It was a neat idea. I hadn't seen it before but it worked awfully well because it gave a natural moonlight look."

Roy will next be seen in the miniseries, *La Femme Musketeer* with Gerard Depardieu and Michael York in 2004. But considering the twist in the final act of "Lineage," the door is certainly open for Roger to make a comeback in Wesley's life, if any *Angel* TV movies were to happen. "I'd love to explore the relationship," Roy enthuses. "I'd love to see if they will ever get together with empathy." With a twinkle in his eye, he adds, "I just hope that he does appear in the flesh someday."

{ "I HAD NEARLY ALL MY SCENES WITH ALEXIS [DENISOF, WESLEY]. HE WAS A DELIGHTFUL MAN, I REALLY ENJOYED HIS COMPANY." }

As the first lady of the Circle of the Black thorn, Stacey Travis made some memorable appearances during *Angel* Season Five. We caught up with the actress to recall her time on the show as Senator Helen Brucker...

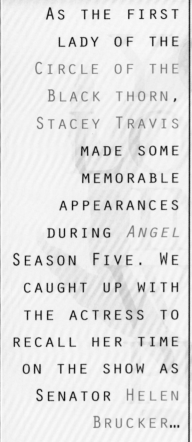

Stacey Travis made a strong impression as Senator Helen Brucker, the only human-appearing member of the Circle of the Black Thorn, during *Angel*'s final season. The evil politician was just one of many strong roles that the actress has played over the years, and we sat down with the *Angel* fan at the Starfury Q'uor Toth convention to revisit her time on the show...

How did you get involved in *Angel* in the first place?

I had read for [the role] a couple of times – I think it was my third time that I read that I got the Senator. A friend of mine, Christine Eastabrook, was in the waiting room, and she was saying. 'This is my favorite show, and my kids' favorite show, I've got to get this job.' I thought, if she doesn't get it and I do get it, she's going to be really bummed out with me. Sure enough, when I got it, a day or two later I ran into her and she was, like, 'You got that *Angel*!' She was laughing about it – not at all seriously upset. We're friends: she was quite happy for me to get it, and if it wasn't her it should have been me, and vice versa for me.

What did they tell you about the part?

They just said she was a Senator. Because I know the show a little bit, when I was in the audition I asked the producer if she was a demon, and he said, 'Don't worry about that, all you need to know is that she's all about power.' I said, 'Okay.' That's all I played, and I got the job. Then when I got the script, I was like, 'She *is* a demon.' It was interesting that he chose not to tell me that in the room, because maybe he felt like he didn't want

By Paul Simpson

Politically INCOR

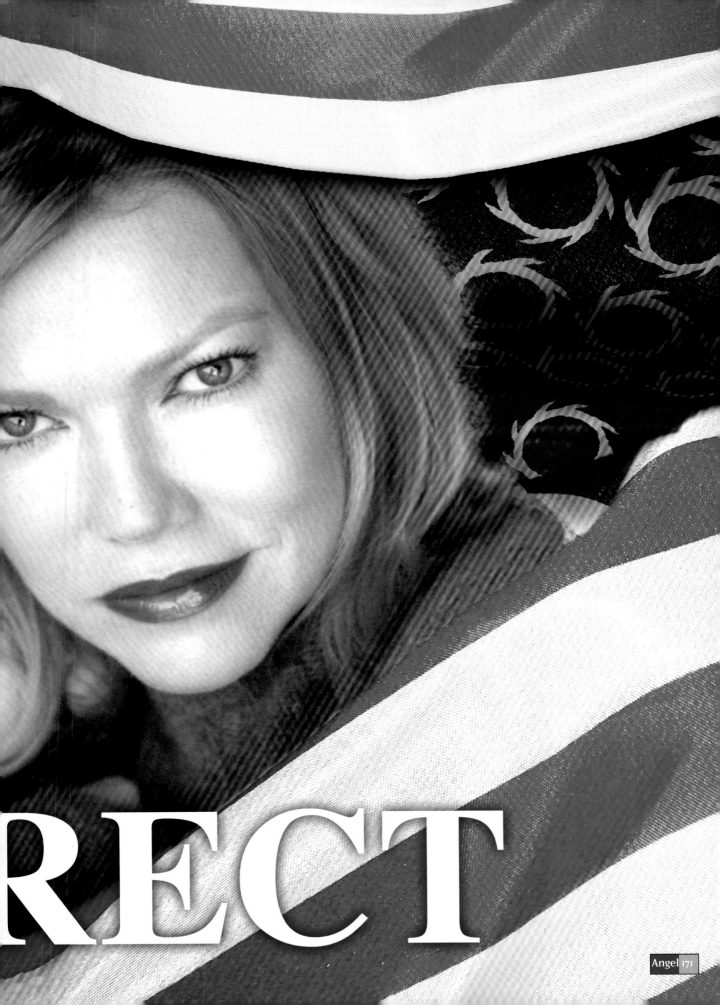

RECT

me to play some weird demon acting, just to make this character real. My character in the Circle of the Black Thorn was the only one in human form, and so for whatever reason, she needed to be passable as a human and as a senator, so I don't think they wanted me playing any sort of strange demon acting. Whether I could be believable as a senator was more important.

YOUR FIRST EPISODE WAS SHOT AROUND THE TIME THAT THE NEWS OF THE SHOW'S CANCELATION CAME THROUGH...

It was close. When I was on set during "Power Play," it had not come through, but it was not looking good. The fans had rallied, and I was told that they were doing a blood drive and everything. The mood on the set was really, really hoping, from all the crew members and nearly all the cast, that they really didn't want it to be over, and they hoped it wasn't going to be.

But when I did "Not Fade Away," it was a very different vibe: a lot of sadness, bittersweet feelings, and people having really understood that no matter what the fans did, and no matter how much money they'd raised, it was basically done. At that point, we were wondering what they were going to do with all the money the fans had raised – it was so frustrating. The fans for this show are so phenomenal and they'd really gone out of their way to raise all this money, and for the network just to ignore it... But it's not as simple as 'we

want a show on the air, we like it, therefore they'll keep it.' There's so much politics and conglomerates and corporations involved that it's not that simple. It's sad.

And you never know how long a show will last – ever! The network heads who love shows – and greenlight them – they change, and two years into a show, someone new is there. Four or five years into the show, someone else new is there. The passion from the person who originally green-lit it is not there to protect it any more. It happens on so many shows. I get really frustrated – there was one show I got into and it was just gone. I understand the fans of this, they're so loyal to Joss. Coming from *Buffy* they had *Angel* at least, and then they took that.

ON THE FINAL EPISODE, DID YOU GET THE FULL SCRIPT, OR JUST THE SIDES FOR YOUR SCENES?

No, I got the full script. I know some very die-hard *Angel* fans that were asking if I had the script. I said, 'I do, but I'm not going to ruin it for you. It's the end of the series and if I tell you it'll ruin it.' I was very protective of the storyline – even though no-one told me to be. I didn't want anyone to know. I've been around enough to know that those kind of shows, you tell one friend and they tell someone and all of a sudden it's on the internet and you're in trouble. Maybe they don't find out who did it, but it diminishes the excitement for the fans.

WHAT WAS THE EXPERIENCE OF PLAYING THE SENATOR LIKE?

It was fun. My first scene was late at night – it was a Circle of the Black Thorn scene. Not the one where we make Angel sign the prophecy, but the one where we initiate him into the Circle. We shot it out of sequence. It was late at night, I walk in and the set is dark and smoky and David's [Boreanaz] been there all day. I'm standing there, and I'm the only person there besides David who is dressed as a human. I looked around and thought, 'Where am I? What's happening? It's midnight and I'm chanting this strange Circle of Thorn chant' – it was surreal! It was a good introduction into what my next two weeks were going to be like: odd! But I got into it.

YOU HAD TO DO A BRIEF AMOUNT OF PROSTHETIC WORK FOR THE EPISODE: HAD YOU DONE MUCH PREVIOUSLY?

I did a movie where I was burned at the stake, and I had a skullcap on, and had some effects make-up at the end. But I've never been in full outfit. For *Angel*, just to do my prosthetic face, they did a face mask and a head mask

YOU'RE LOOKING IN THE WRONG PLACE.

up to my shoulders. Later they said they thought the guys were having fun because they only needed my forehead! Getting immersed and putting the straw in was so freaky – it was really a trip. It was very claustrophobic. I was quite happy when it came off.

WHAT HAVE YOU BEEN UP TO SINCE?

I've done about four films; *Fun with Dick and Jane*, with Jim Carrey; a horror film, which was called *Backwater* and is now *The Reaper* [and was released as *Venom*] that stars Agnes Bruckner and Bijou Phillips and quite a few young stars. I did an independent film with Melissa Joan Hart and Robert Guillaume called *Jack Satin*, and I have a small part, as a favor, in *Art School Confidential*. I did a *CSI: New York* and a couple of episodes of *Desperate Housewives* where I got one of the Housewives hooked on ADD medication. That was a lot of fun.

WHAT DO YOU THINK THE APPEAL OF *ANGEL* IS?

I think it means something different to each fan. I'd be interested to see what each fan's take on it is. If they're coming from *Buffy* and they miss that show and

they want Joss' writing, they'd come for that reason – but *Angel* was much darker. I think that you tap into people who love vampire movies and the vampire genre, from Anne Rice up. It's also good versus evil – our world is so chaotic and it's nice to have a show that acknowledged that the world was complicated and bad. There's no way to get rid of all the evil, but you could slowly take it down one person at a time and do your best. The demons are probably a metaphor for corruption and greed and everything that's going down.

Then you have the appeal of lots of cute guys, and cute girls. There are fun characters, like Lorne, and even if they die, you know they can come back, like Fred and Illyria. And there's pathos in there – you start to care for Angel, and worry about his son and the son being banished, all the different women in his life. And you've got the appeal of going back in history: history buffs can watch episodes where Juliet Landau's in the 18th Century.

WHY DID YOU WATCH *ANGEL*?

I like Joss' writing. I think it's clever and funny, with the throwaway digs he does at contemporary society. I sometimes watched it because I thought the plots were really fun. I didn't catch every episode of every season, but I'd tune in for six or seven every season. It's hard because I just got TIVO – I'd be much more up on it if I had had it earlier! ✤

> My first scene was late at night – it was a Circle of Black Thorn scene. I looked around and thought, 'Where am I? What's happening? It's midnight and I'm chanting this strange Circle of Thorn chant.'

ANGEL

OTHER GREAT TV TIE-IN COMPANIONS FROM TITAN
ON SALE NOW!

**The X-Files
- The Agents**
ISBN 9781782763710

**The X-Files
- Little Green Men**
ISBN 9781782763727

**The X-Files
- Conspiracy Theory**
ISBN 9781782763734

**Angel - Heroes &
Guardian Angels**
ISBN 9781782763680

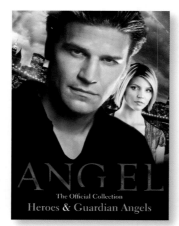

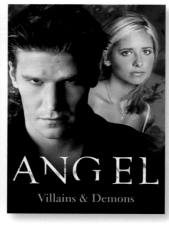

**Angel - Villains
& Demons**
ISBN 9781782763697

COMING SOON

**Buffy - Welcome To The
Hellmouth**
ISBN 9781782763642

**Buffy
- Fear, Itself**
ISBN 9781782763659

**Buffy - Bewitched,
Bothered & Bewildered**
ISBN 9781782763666

For more information visit www.titan-comics.com